Promising, intending, and moral autonomy

CAMBRIDGE STUDIES IN PHILOSOPHY

General editor SYDNEY SHOEMAKER

Advisory editors J. E. J. ALTHAM, SIMON BLACKBURN,
GILBERT HARMAN, MARTIN HOLLIS, FRANK JACKSON,
JONATHAN LEAR, JOHN PERRY, T. J. SMILEY, BARRY STROUD

Promising, intending, and moral autonomy

Michael H. Robins

Bowling Green State University, Ohio

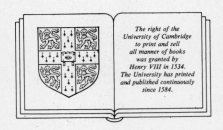

The right of the
University of Cambridge
to print and sell
all manner of books
was granted by
Henry VIII in 1534.
The University has printed
and published continuously
since 1584.

Cambridge University Press

Cambridge

London   New York   New Rochelle
Melbourne   Sydney

Published by the Press Syndicate of the University of Cambridge
The Pitt Building, Trumpington Street, Cambridge CB2 1RP
32 East 57th Street, New York, NY 10022, USA
296 Beaconsfield Parade, Middle Park, Melbourne 3206, Australia

© Cambridge University Press 1984

First published 1984

Printed in Great Britain by
REDWOOD BURN LIMITED
Trowbridge, Wiltshire

Library of Congress catalogue card number: 83–26271

British Library Cataloguing in Publication Data
Robins, Michael H.
Promising, intending, and moral autonomy.
– (Cambridge studies in philosophy)
1. Duty   2. Responsibility   3. Ethics
I. Title
170   BJ151
ISBN 0 521 26076 0

For Andy and Brent

Contents

vii

Preface

Although much has been written on action theory in the last twenty years, almost all of its orientation has been metaphysical. This no doubt has borne much fruit, but at the cost of neglecting its usefulness for normative studies, despite the lip service to such that is paid on publishers' book jackets of many works on the subject. This book is one of the first, if not fledgling, attempts to fill this void, for its credo is that there is much in the theory of action, particularly the fertile concept of intending, that is distinctly normative and can accordingly provide a good part of the foundations of ethics. Hence the first part of the book (roughly Chapters 2–4) is on action theory, the second part (Chapters 5–6) on ethics.

The two areas are linked through the concept of promising, or, more broadly, the notion of voluntary obligation, which is involved in such diverse undertakings as vows, promises, agreements, and some conventions. The concept of voluntary obligation plays such a pivotal role for two reasons: first, a careful investigation of these specimens qua *obligations* cannot go very far without a systematic understanding of such psychological acts as willing and intending. The force of this is that even though promising is a social act, it is constructed out of *normative* elements which are non-social and psychological. Second, the concept of voluntary obligation is intimately tied to 'commitment,' and this, I hold, is fundamental to the justification of *non-voluntary* obligations. In fact, as I attempt to show in the last chapter, the whole conception of moral objectivity is fashioned out of moral autonomy.

The theory developed here was first presented inchoately in my doctoral dissertation at Northwestern University in 1970 under the direction of Henry Veatch, to whom I am much indebted in more ways than he will ever know. I say 'inchoately,' not only for the usual reasons with respect to dissertations, but because my exposure to contemporary action theory, then in its infancy, was negligible. Indeed, some of the most important work – at least for my purposes

– had yet to be published. In the years since then, particularly after 1975, I was drawn to this area again and again in my search for a viable concept of the will, even though, paradoxically, that notion was the universal bane of contemporary action theorists prior to 1975. Nevertheless, they had much to teach me about it in spite of themselves.

Some of the main ideas in this book were presented in less systematic form in some of my previously published papers or will be presented in a forthcoming paper. Parts of Chapter 5 are to be found in 'The primacy of promising,' *Mind* **85** (July 1976), 321–40, and in 'Promissory obligations and Rawls's contractarianism,' *Analysis* **36** (June 1976), 190–8; parts of Chapters 2 and 6 are in 'Practical reasoning, commitment, and rational action,' *American Philosophical Quarterly* **21** (April 1984), and, finally, the theory in Chapter 3 will be extended in 'Deviant causal chains and non-basic action,' *Australasian Journal of Philosophy* (forthcoming). I wish to thank the editors of these journals for permitting me to draw upon this material again.

The research for this book was supported primarily by a Fellowship-in-Residence from the National Endowment for the Humanities in 1978–9 at the University of Michigan (in connection with Richard Brandt's academic year seminar) and in small part by National Endowment for the Humanities Summer Seminars at the University of Michigan in 1975 (for Richard Brandt's seminar) and at Princeton University in 1982 (for Gilbert Harman's seminar). During the summer of 1978 and for the following academic year I was also funded respectively by a small research grant and supplemental faculty research leave awarded by the Faculty Research Committee of Bowling Green State University. I gratefully acknowledge the generous support from these sources.

I am very indebted to many people over the years who read the manuscript in whole or part or who discussed the ideas in it presented in some of my earlier papers. The whole manuscript was read meticulously by Gilbert Harman, Henry Veatch, Andrew Altman, and Páll S. Árdal. Andrew Altman, my former colleague, saved me from some grievous errors in Chapter 5, a critical chapter, and raised scintillating objections that forced me to clarify many claims in Chapters 2 and 6. In addition he spent many hours with me going through the whole first draft of the manuscript, which was an exercise so valuable that my gratitude to him cannot be adequately expressed here. Gilbert Harman made many penetrating criticisms, but particularly noteworthy is his critique of my foundational theory of *akrasia* in Chapter 2, which critique would have been devastating if left unanswered or unnoticed. I am particularly fortunate to have had this pointed out before my omissions got etched in stone. I also acknowledge his keen insights on the concept of decisions and in his theory of 'full' vs. 'tentative' acceptance developed in his Summer Seminar, and which are particularly germane to Chapter 4. Henry Veatch helped to clarify a number of issues in Chapters 1 and 2, particularly some implications of my normative theory of commitment and some paradoxes of 'creating obligations.' But more generally – and I should add, as always – he made sure that my purview did not miss the forest for the trees. Páll S. Árdal, an expert on the subject of promising, made innumerable painstaking suggestions and insights, both philosophical and stylistic. Most prominent among them are his suggestions about deathbed promises, promises vs. threats discussed in Chapter 5 and his views on promises as statements vs. performatives germane to Chapter 2.

Others generously gave their time to discuss parts of the manuscript. Myles Brand, Alvin Goldman, Richard Brandt, Barry Loewer, William Richards, Michael Bradie, William Shaw, and Michael Corrado helped with various aspects of the theory of intention set out in Chapter 2. I also acknowledge the fine commentary that Myles Brand delivered to the American Philosophical Association (Boston, 1980) on a paper of mine based in part on Chapter 3. That chapter also benefitted from the careful suggestions of Nancy Cunningham-Butler, a former graduate student in my seminar on philosophical psychology. The last section of Chapter 5 on insincere promises was largely the result of the objections of Baruch Brody and Patrick Atiyah, and, finally, still other points in Chapter 6 are the results of the shared insights of Robert Audi, William Shaw, and Michael Corrado.

These acknowledgments would contain a glaring omission if they did not also cite the adroit comments of the readers of Cambridge University Press, which helped me to close a few glaring gaps in the theory. Without the generous help of all those people, this work would have been of a quality considerably inferior to that of its present form, however defective that still is. Needless to say, all of the errors remaining are mine alone.

Finally, I owe a debt of gratitude to the expert and intelligent typing of Deborah Magrum on the first draft, Tamara Sharp on the second draft, and to Susan Frost and Laura Bell for their accurate and cheerful typing of all my tedious revisions. And last, but not in importance, I wish to thank my wife, Denise, for help of a different kind.

Introduction

Promising seems to be an act of intentionally creating an obligation where none existed before, but how is such a thing accomplished? In this we are reminded of the near-universal deprecation, inspired by Hume, of the idea that real, binding obligations can somehow be 'willed' into existence, as one can will into existence the movement of one's arm. On the other hand, there is almost as widespread a stricture against a rival conception that obligations come from the facts of 'nature.' Now the juxtaposition of these positions should be of concern to anybody who is not a moral nihilist. Together they tell us that obligations are products neither of nature nor of the will! (The dilemma is intended to be more exhaustive but not totally so, if we assume that 'convention' goes on the 'will' side, albeit indirectly, and that 'psychology' can go on either side depending upon whether there are psychological laws of a relevant kind.)

It is the thesis of this book that the second horn of this dilemma – the one about 'will' – is false. Obligations *are* creatures of the will, not nature, but in spite of this, they can be woven into an objective moral order. The reconciliation of autonomy with objectivity can be brought off by a better understanding of what promissory, voluntary obligations are. Accordingly, in Chapters 1 and 5, I show that promissory obligations are unintelligible without presupposing a more primitive concept of commitment. By calling this more primitive, I mean in part that it cannot be fashioned out of the various social relations that seem to constitute promising, as is common in virtually all of the published accounts. That is, you cannot construct promissory obligations out of 'creating expectations,' or out of a social convention, or out of a social, Rawlsian principle of fairness, etc. For I argue that these accounts foist on us the illusion of explaining promissory obligations only by smuggling in a yet unexplained, non-social sense of commitment which comes dangerously close to 'willing an obligation.'

In Chapter 2, entitled 'Commitment and basic action,' I argue that

1

this concept of commitment is primitive more precisely because it is embedded in the very possibility of *intending*, pure and simple, and that promissory commitments are possible only by building on this. It is argued right from the outset that this is a *normative* concept of commitment, which is best defended against the foil of a causal concept of it gleaned from the causal theory of action. This concept is normative because it is necessarily invoked in accounting for a man's being mistaken in his *action* in a way that cannot be traced simply to a mistaken *intention* (or belief).

Because the commitment is normative, it issues in a 'mandate' which varies in scope and strength depending upon the kind of intention in which it is nested. At the level of basic action it is the principle that one is to honor one's non-mistaken intentions, which effectively rules out changing one's intentions or not abiding by it for reasons of *akrasia*, but allowing changes for any other reason. When *akrasia* occurs, it is a genuine mistake in performance, as opposed to other changes of intention, which can be seen as correcting a mistake in intention.

Upon such a foundation an architectonic can be constructed whereby each ascending floor represents a different kind of intention or action which is governed, correspondingly, by a distinctive 'mandate' that was reconstituted out of the one governing the lower floor. Such is the plan of the rest of the book. The second floor is represented by a non-basic action (Chapter 3), the next floor by a special kind of intention associated with decisions and vows (Chapter 4), and the next by distinctive social acts, like promises, agreements, and certain forms of conventions (Chapter 5). The ascent from vows to promises is very critical because I see it as an ascent from private acts to acts that are genuinely social.

In the final chapter (6) the task is to show that, contrary to appearances, this moral autonomy actually makes possible the very idea of moral objectivity. This is possible because the apparent basic principles of morality, e.g., Ross's list of prima facie duties, can be taken as commitments derived from our ordinary promises and vows. The crucial notion of 'derived commitment' is therein elaborated at length and should not even in appearance be confounded with a tacit promise, an old blunderbuss of contractarianism.

From the perspective of this final chapter we can restate the line of argument of the whole book. It is that we live under an objective moral order because it was fashioned out of our own will. The con-

2

nection between these two is possible because both autonomy and objectivity have as their linchpin the primitive concept of commitment. The main burden of the book – or at least that of the final chapter – is to show that living under an objective moral order is something like the clothing of our own agency.

1

Promising and the primacy of intention

In much of contemporary ethics the mystery of promising has occupied center stage. This is so primarily because of the resurgence of contractarian theories and with them the more general idea that a man can be bound only by his consent, that obligations arise in part, if not ultimately, from his own volition. Indeed as David Lyons notes, commenting on John Rawls, if we concede with the skeptic that we cannot *discover* valid moral principles by any independent (i.e., naturalistic) criterion, we can still provide a rational justification by showing that such principles are literally *created* out of a procedure we agree is fair (Lyons, 1974, pp. 1073–5). This notion of creating moral principles is also to be found in the earlier theory of prescriptivism, to the effect that our basic moral principles are ultimately 'decisions of principle' (Hare, 1952, pp. 56–78).

At root here is the powerful idea of autonomy and morality lucidly expressed by Joseph Raz:

> The analysis of promising as creating an obligation indicates that to acknowledge the validity of voluntary obligations is to accept a . . . view of practical reason . . . according to which what a man ought to do depends not only on the way things happen to turn out in the world (drought in another country; war, poverty . . .). What one ought to do depends in part on oneself, and this is not only because the behavior, needs, tastes, and desires of the agent count just as much as those of any other person, but because the agent has the power intentionally to shape the form of his moral world, to obligate himself to follow certain goals, or to create bonds and alliances with certain people and not others.   (Raz, 1977, p. 228)

The power intentionally to shape the form of our moral world is a compelling idea, but no less mysterious for that. For it is just this notion that we *can* create binding obligations out of thin air, by an act of will, that is at the center of the mystery. Consider, for example, a familiar enough case of creating an obligation in which a bridegroom says (in the right circumstances): 'I hereby (promise, vow to) take this woman as my wife.' Common sense has it that he is

4

obligated to do just that, and becomes so approximately when he freely uttered those words. But that is just a statement of the problem: for what is it about what he has said or done that creates the obligation? Is it that saying 'I do (promise)' expresses his intention to become so obligated? That would attribute the obligation essentially to an act of will, the social setting being a mere trapping. However, according to philosophical lore, that just underscores the real difficulty. For how is it possible to will an obligation? Does anyone suppose, so the philosophical story goes, that the bridegroom can will into existence an obligation as he can will into existence the movement of his arm? Hume thought that such a notion is not even intelligible, comparing it to transubstantiation or holy orders.[1] But even if somehow willing an obligation were intelligible as a solitary act, Hume goes on to ask how the obligation thus willed would be binding or objectively valid rather than an obligation the agent merely thinks he is under (Hume, 1888, Book III, Sec. V, pp. 516, 518–19). The implication is that if we can create obligations as products of the will, that just makes them bogus to start with.[2]

Here, then, is a philosophical problem that ceases to go away. On the one side, creating bona fide obligations out of our own volition is a 'manifest absurdity,' writes Hume, 'to anybody who is not blinded by prejudice' (Hume, 1888, Book III, Sec. V, p. 517). On the other side, many philosophers who seem not blinded by prejudice believe that only if obligations are created by or at least involve our 'will' can we ever be bound to anything at all. As Lyons implies, to these philosophers the idea of voluntary obligations is our last bulwark against skepticism.

According to the philosophical tradition, the way out of this impasse, even for people like John Rawls and H. A. Prichard who were sympathetic to the idea of voluntary obligation, is to look for the source of promissory obligation, not in an act of will, but in something else that the promiser *does* or *brings about*. The bridegroom's marital obligations, for example, might be found in his having *said* 'I do (promise),' or in his having led the bride to expect and rely on the performance of the thing promised. The force of these maneuvers is to liken promissory obligations to those that

---

[1] Referring to the theological doctrine whereby 'a certain form of words, along with a certain intention, changes entirely the nature of an external object, and even of a human creature' (Hume, 1888, Book III, Sec. V, p. 524).

[2] I owe to Henry Veatch this way of throwing down the gauntlet as well as some of the examples and arguments appearing on the next page.

arise from such things as siring a child, buying a piece of land, or moving into a new or different community, in that what is *done* in such cases is that of voluntarily entering into new and different relations. And it is from these *relations*, rather than from any 'willing,' that new and different responsibilities are acquired. At the same time, these responsibilities are voluntary obligations because the relations or situations which give use to them are presumably brought about by our own voluntary acts; but these voluntary acts no more directly 'create' the obligations than does the voluntary act of my moving from the right of you to the left of you directly 'create' a new spatial relation.

This is all well and good, but perhaps we may be pardoned if we return to a promise as a paradigm of voluntary obligation, and ask exactly *what* (besides the mental act) the promiser does or brings about that is the source of this obligation. However, before the search can even get off the ground we must be careful to note, following Prichard, that this other thing cannot be a situation from which it merely *follows* that there is an obligation – not even if that situation is brought about intentionally (Prichard, 1928, p. 170). And this little observation might be enough to disarm some of the facile examples of voluntary obligations adduced above. For intentionally siring a child, and such structurally similar things as intentionally harming somebody or intentionally misleading someone, each apparently satisfy the specification but are unlikely paradigms for promising. For although the obligation in each case arises from an antecedent intentional act, the obligation itself was not intended. In fact, even if any of these acts is performed in such a way that the obligation is foreseeable, that would still make the obligation only a logical side-effect of the intention, not part of what was intended.[3] Hence, if promising is still to be regarded as an act of intentionally creating an obligation – albeit indirectly – then something stronger is required: one must intentionally bring about this other thing with the further intention that by doing so one will be obligating oneself. Stated loosely in the idiom of action theory, 'creating an obligation' must be the name of an intentional non-basic act (i.e., roughly some-

[3] In this respect such obligations seem to behave logically like the concept of belief in that it also appears necessarily to be a logical or evidential side-effect of our intentions. For a belief is not the kind of thing that we can intend to bring into existence, not even indirectly. We can at most only foresee that it can follow from a situation which we may intentionally bring about or intentionally put ourselves into. This is in contrast to the doxastic voluntarism of Descartes.

thing we do by doing something else), and not an intentional basic action with a foreseeable but unintended side-effect. This idiom also emphasizes that this other thing is not done *merely with* the further intention to obligate oneself, but with the further intention to do so *by means of* doing that other thing. This stricture rules out, for example, doing some other thing *while* also (directly) intending to obligate oneself. The search, then is for the other thing that satisfied this twofold requirement.

I. The social sources of promissory obligations

What all of the proposed solutions have in common is the idea that a promise (unlike, perhaps, a vow or resolve) is essentially a social act: to obligate oneself is to obligate oneself *to* a promisee; one confers a right on him to the future performance of some action. As a holder of this right, he can waive it, thus *releasing* the promiser from the obligation. Hence, it seemed natural enough to look for the extra element in some dimension of our social life.

Various candidates suggested themselves. And in Chapter 5, I will examine them all from the point of view I wish to defend. For the present, it should suffice to get a glimpse of the main contenders in order to see how their apparent weaknesses can be repaired by the position I wish to put forward.

The first contender is the utilitarian theory of promising (recognizing, of course, that there really is not one theory but a cluster of them). The main point, though, is that creating an obligation has something to do partly with the interest of the promisee and partly with his expectations, which in turn lead to reliance, etc. Promising, on this conception, is not intentionally undertaking an obligation directly (for this has been ruled out) but intentionally producing in the promisee the expectation that the promise will be kept; and then, satisfying Prichard's strictures, intentionally doing this with the further intention that *by doing so*, one will obligate oneself (see, e.g., MacCormick, 1972; Narveson, 1971; Árdal, 1976). Thus, both the expectations and the obligation are to be produced intentionally, the latter by means of the former. I will argue, however, that this order is perverse: that you cannot intentionally obligate yourself by means of intentionally inducing expectations, but rather can intentionally induce expectations (of the right kind) only by first directly, intentionally obligating yourself.

The utilitarian's difficulties begin to surface when you concen-

7

trate on the promisee's expectations and acts of reliance, and ask whether they are supposed to constitute epistemic expectations that the promise *will* be kept, or moral expectations that the promise *is* to be kept. Similar questions can be asked about any *entitlement* of the promisee that surrounds those expectations. Again, is this an epistemic entitlement to conformative behavior – a rational warrant to believe that such behavior will occur – or is it some kind of normative entitlement – the kind that makes a *claim* against the promiser and presumably is what gives rise to the obligation? Now I think that the utilitarian position is that the expectations are epistemic but that the entitlement is normative. Its exponents intend to move from the expectations to the entitlement by requiring that the promiser produce the epistemic expectations intentionally. This is to be contrasted with producing expectations incidentally, as when a man merely states an intention or behaves in certain predictable ways, in which case the addressee can at most have epistemic expectations wholly devoid of any such claim against his interlocutor.

Our question, then, is whether the promiser can generate the desired sort of moral claim against himself simply *by* producing epistemic expectations intentionally. The answer, however, seems to be no, and remains so even if it be added that the promisee knows that his expectations were induced intentionally and that the promiser intended that he know. The reason is that the act of intentionally inducing expectations is more like an act of advising rather than promising[4] (and that advising is too weak, as we shall see, to do the work required of it). As an example, consider a case in which George tells Sam that Sam can expect George to come to the office on Saturday. George says this meaning that it is far more likely that he will come than he will not, and that Sam would be well advised (in a decision-theoretic way) to consider this in his plans. At the same time George makes it clear that he is not bound to Sam to come to the office, and that he could, in fact, may, change his mind. Here George intentionally induced reliance without promising. And this is because such intentionally induced expectations in another are too weak to *entitle* the other to demand the satisfaction of those expectations.

The weakness of this advising relation is made more perspicuous

---

[4] This point is made persuasively by Joseph Raz (1972) in his criticism of Neil Mac-Cormick (1972), and in his article 'Promises and obligations' (1977).

by changing the example so that George advises Sam with respect to a third party. In intentionally inducing expectations about that party, does George give Sam any entitlement to demand that George get the party to act as predicted? Surely not. Yet why should it be any different if George gives advice about his own action? The most obvious explanation is that when George gives advice about himself we tend to think that he is *also* communicating that he intends to obligate himself. This would, of course, entitle Sam to demand that George conform to Sam's expectations, but, as indicated earlier, hardly in the way required by Prichard's constraint. For instead of generating the obligation and the entitlement *by* intentionally inducing expectations, George would be generating the expectations and the entitlement *by first* convincing Sam that he directly intended to obligate himself. (That the order cannot be reversed is shown by the fact that promissory obligations cannot be constructed out of advising.) In brief, if the central mystery is *how* we can really intentionally obligate ourselves, however indirectly, it is no less mysterious to imply (as the present view seems to) that we can do so by intentionally producing in others the (presumably true) belief that we have intentionally obligated ourselves.[5]

Deontological thinkers have taken a different line, and of them, there is a miscellany of views. Since promising is agreed to be a social act, dependent upon rules and conventions, some have sought to explain the obligation in terms of these. Thus John Searle, the most persuasive spokesman for his school, says that to ask how a promise can create an obligation is like asking how a touchdown can create six points (Searle, 1969, pp. 35ff). The solution is to be found in the promising game or institution, which has as one of its rules the requirement that it is to be kept. The obligation of a promiser to do what he said he would is, then, essentially like the obligation of a baseball batter to leave the field after he struck out (*ibid.*, pp. 185–6). Yet it is Prichard who noticed the difficulty that if an obligation seems to be the kind of thing which is impossible to create directly out of a volition (and not by means of doing something else), then it seems no more possible to create out of a convention (Prichard, 1928, p. 172). The difficulty may be immediately revealed by the suspicion that these conventions appear to be agreements them-

---

[5] As a cautionary note, however, this criticism does not even touch the rule-utilitarian version of promising, which is not assessed until Chapter 5.

selves,[6] and so if an obligation cannot be created out of our own volitions severally, it seems difficult to believe that it can be created out of our volitions collectively, by our agreement to create a convention that creates it. And this is in fact the line that critics have intimated against Searle (see below, Chapter 5, pp. 125–7). If promising is a game, then why am I obligated to its rules? Not simply by using the word 'promise.' And just as all conventions as such are not necessarily binding on me, why is the promising game? Pressed on this point, Searle seems to come close to saying, it is binding on me because I have promised to use the word 'promise' in accordance with its literal meaning (1969, pp. 189–90, 194–5). And this is remarkably like Prichard's difficulty, that saying certain words can create a situation in virtue of which I am intentionally bound, only because I made a certain general promise not to use words of that kind without obligating myself to the thing promised (1928, p. 179).

Another deontological approach, which bears surprising resemblance to Hume's solution (1888, Book III, Sec. V), is offered by Rawls (1971, Sec. 52, pp. 342–50), who is all too aware of the difficulties proposed by Prichard and Hume. His solution is the assimilation of promising to something like the gratitude that befalls one who voluntarily accepted the benefits of some scheme that requires the voluntary cooperation of others.[7] The benefits connected with promising are what make possible small schemes of cooperation, in the sense that in accepting a promise of another, I can rely on him in a way that would not be possible without the promise. If I have been able to enjoy the benefit of relying on the word of others, I am obligated to do my fair share, that is, keep my word, when my turn comes. The principle is that one cannot in good conscience accept the benefits of a cooperative scheme without being obligated to do one's part.

Like gratitude, the principle of fairness is essentially a social one. But as Rawls is all too aware, not any voluntary acceptance of a benefit, not even one that requires the cooperation of others, is enough to bind my will. I am bound only if, in accepting such benefits, it is understood that I am so obligating myself. Pursuant to

---

[6] David Lewis (1969) to the contrary notwithstanding, discussed below in Chapter 5, pp. 135–7.

[7] Although he finds this concept of fairness – as he later calls it – different from gratitude (Rawls, 1963).

my interpretation of Prichard's constraint, does this mean that I am indirectly obligating myself *by* voluntarily accepting those benefits, or only directly obligating myself *while* also accepting those benefits? To put this another way, is my voluntary act of accepting the benefits merely a signal to others that I am therein tacitly and directly obligating myself, or is the accepting of the benefits supposed to play some non-communicative role *through which* I intend indirectly to secure the obligation? On its face, it is hard to believe it is the latter option because the very notion of voluntarily accepting benefits seems open to a number of counterexamples when it is cast in this role. Among them are the following. First, I can voluntarily accept the benefits of something in the sense of giving passive acquiescence to (not actively resisting) a cooperative scheme, which hardly seems strong enough to incur a reciprocal obligation. Second, even if my 'voluntary acceptance' is whole-hearted, it may be acceptance only of the benefits without *knowing* that they were the result of a cooperative scheme, and, therefore, I can hardly be said to be obligated to do my fair share. Third, and most important, even if I accept fully the benefits with the *knowledge* that they are attached to such a scheme, i.e., with the knowledge of the *costs* of those benefits, I may still not be obligated especially if *my* acceptance of the benefits does not diminish the share of benefits of those who *are* cooperating. Consider Nozick's example of a public radio station (1974, p. 93–5), to which we should add that it can survive only by the small contributions of a minimum number of public spirited citizens. 'Voluntarily accepting the benefits' might mean simply voluntarily tuning in on that radio frequency, and 'not doing one's fair share' would mean not sending in, say, the annual contribution.

In fact the whole matter of the principle of fairness is even more complex than this, which is discussed thoroughly in Chapter 5. Suffice it to say here, it seems that only if one *accepts* fully not only the benefits of a cooperative scheme, but also the costs in return for them, is one obligated to do one's fair share; but then we are back to directly obligating oneself by some kind of tacit consent *while* also accepting the benefits.

This apparent priority of tacit consent over fairness is something of a prelude to the route that Rawls himself actually takes: the principle of fairness itself, and the institutions so governed by it, are binding only if they are the outcome of a prior and more basic agree-

11

ment – though, in his view, a hypothetical one, to be sure.[8]

The gravamen of all my complaints is a legacy of Prichard's difficulty (see pp. 9–10). If promising is a mystery as a solitary (albeit non-basic) act, it becomes no less so as a social one. To think that obligations of the kind that promising represents can be derived from some dimension of our social life is simply to shift the problem one step back, and to smuggle in the very idea that we were to explain: that the will can obligate itself. This is most transparent in Prichard's own view and in Rawls's hypothetical social contract, and almost as transparent in Searle's notion of *committing* ourselves to use the word 'promise' in accordance with its literal meaning. This is not, of course, to deny the truism that much can be created in social acts; it is only to deny that obligation is among this.

II.   *The primacy of intention and action theory*

It therefore seems that we would do better to look again at that solitary act of will which has been smuggled into the above accounts of social acts to see if the rudiments of voluntary obligation can perhaps be found there. I will argue that they can be found in the structure of intentional action. For I believe that the concept of commitment, which is so crucial for understanding promissory obligations in the ordinary, social sense, gets its first foothold there: 'commitment' seems to be primitive in the sense that it is a relation that binds together the very concept of intention with that of volition; neither is an isolated act of the soul; neither can be understood except in a commitment relation to the other. This sense of commitment is loosely the sense in which intention is a commitment to act. I will argue, against rival interpretations, that right there the commitment must be understood to be irreducibly normative (as opposed to causal). For the notion of intention makes a man stand to his own future actions (or omissions) in a special way: only in relation to a normative commitment can a man's *performance* be *mistaken*, as we have said, as opposed to this being attributed to his

[8] Some other minor deontological positions worthy of short note include, first, A. I. Melden's view (1977, pp. 32–55), according to which the obligation to keep a promise derives from a special right conferred on the promisee which arises when two lives are joined in a certain way, and where it is understood that the agency of one supports the agency of the other. Finally, there is George Warnock's veracity theory of promising, which derives the obligation from the fact that in saying, 'I said I would,' I am obligated to make my prediction true, just as my assertions in general commit me to have my words conform to the world (1971, pp. 101–17).

12

intention. In fact, this distinction is at the very core of practical reasoning.

Because the commitment is normative right from the outset, it gives rise to a 'mandate' which admits of various forms corresponding to the kind of intention from which it derives. Beginning with the intention to perform a basic action,[9] it is, as noted, the principle that one ought to honor one's non-mistaken intentions, the principle being justified by its close connection to the intelligibility of acting intentionally, really its connection to the concept of agency. This mandate also shapes both the content of the volition and at the same time allows for a glimpse of the nature of the causal connection between volition and movement.

From that foundation, the plan is to erect an architectonic, tracing the mandate up through intentional non-basic action, to vows and decisions, and finally to genuine social acts like promising and conformity to convention.[10] We shall find that each level in the architectonic transforms the elemental mandate in distinctive ways, not found in, but instead fashioned out of, the adjacent lower level. Thus at the level of non-basic action, I shall try to show how the intention to perform such acts in various strata increases the elemental mandate in scope, but not in strength. The essential idea in this is that successful intentional non-basic action depends as much upon us as it does upon the world. Commitment and its relata capture the part that depends upon us. For as we intend our basic action to achieve increasingly higher levels of non-basic action,[11] we augment the basic action mandate with new normative requirements corresponding to the various levels. The theory that the non-basic stratification of action implies the augmentation of basic action commitments is what I shall call the normative stratification of action.

The next step in the architectonic contrasts with this, because for the first time the mandate is increased in strength rather than in scope. This is the transition from intending to vowing and deciding.

[9] Although this notion has been thought to be discredited, see below, p. 46, we shall attempt to sketch a new basis for the distinction between basic and non-basic action, utilizing the findings in this section.

[10] Vows differ from promises in that they are not social but private acts, which can become public when they are communicated. But the communication of a vow to others no more makes it a *social* act than does the communication of an intention. More about this below in Chapters 4 and 5.

[11] 'Level-generation' is a more technical synonym that will be expounded in Chapter 3. The term is Alvin Goldman's (1970, pp. 20–48).

Accordingly, I take vows and decisions to exemplify a second order, exclusionary intention about one's ordinary, first order intention to act, which second order intention has the added dimension that it is an intention not to change one's mind; more technically, an intention that excludes or at least limits the changing of the first order intention.[12] The first order intention is a commitment that does allow for the changing of one's mind for any reasons except that deriving from a certain form of *akrasia*, while a vow is a commitment that not only rules that out, but much more.

These inherently private acts, I will argue, provide all that is needed to derive social acts like promising and its cousins. A promise is a social act in that it not only creates an obligation, but a *right* of another, to whom the obligation is owed. The main challenge in the transition from vows to promises is to derive a right on the part of another from an act that essentially creates no rights at all (but from one that creates an exclusionary mandate; my thesis here is that *this* mandate is the precursor to 'obligation' properly so called). This strategy is carried out by conceiving of promises as simply transferring to another the exclusionary mandate already created by a vow, the transfer being effected conditionally upon the promisee's continuing assent. When the transfer is effected, the promisee holds the exclusionary mandate over the promiser. It is suggested that 'transfer' simply means change of possession or control, that it does not presuppose 'ownership,' or a prior panoply of rights or social relations. Once we derive promises, we shall finally be in a position to make sense out of conventional behavior. Here I shall follow D. S. Shwayder and David Lewis in defining convention as a regularity of behavior motivated by a certain system of expectations (Shwayder, 1965, pp. 252–62, 300–8; Lewis, 1969, pp. 39–42, 52–82), but, unlike them, argue that these expectations are parasitic upon commitment and promising rather than self-interest.

In deriving promising from intentional action, we shall be able to remove the air of paradox of intentionally creating obligations that did not exist before – something which I believe the rival theories fail to do. For if there is any magic in this, it is a magic that must be traced, if I am right, to the primitive sense of commitment

---

[12] Readers familiar with Raz's writings will recognize the kinship between exclusionary intention and his doctrine of exclusionary reasons, to which I am much indebted. But some differences will be noted below. (See 1975a, and 1975b, pp. 35–48, 58–84.)

embedded in intention, without which intention would be unintelligible.

III. *Autonomy and objectivity*

Our analysis of social acts will thus enable us to arrive at a viable conception of intentionally creating the form of our moral world, but how is this idea of moral autonomy to be reconciled with moral objectivity? In the final chapter, we reconcile these opposites in something like the spirit of the contractarian tradition. We shall try to see if basic moral principles other than promising – the kind that are intuitively taken as *ceteris paribus* restrictions on ordinary promissory obligations – can be conceived as foundational commitments in a way analogous to contractarianism's understanding of law and morality as deriving from some foundational promise – indeed the promise that is the social compact. But unlike contractarianism, our foundational commitments are neither tacit nor hypothetical promises – in fact they are not themselves promises at all. They are rather commitments that can be *derived* from our actual promises – express or tacit. This maneuver is possible because, while promising is open under implication, commitment is not.[13] It is this distinction which allows us to see how ordinary promises commit us to certain principles in ways of which we may be completely unaware. Moral principles that are basic and that override, say, immoral promises, turn out to be exactly the derived commitments we are likely to have *if* we make any promises at all. They are principles binding upon us in the very exercise of our autonomy. In this book the derivation is carried out with respect to three such principles: respect for persons, veracity, and fair play.

IV. *Intention vs. convention*

I have indicated that I resolve the antinomy between autonomy and objectivity in the spirit of contractarianism, but it will strike the reader that this is not the only resemblance to contractarianism. There is also much in the architectonic to resemble a kind of 'state of nature theory,'[14] whereby various elements in the justification of moral and political obligation are represented in a 'history' as to how

---

[13] Roughly this means that a promise that p, when p implies q, does not imply a *promise* that q, but it *does* imply a *commitment* that q.

[14] The term and the ensuing definition is essentially Robdert Nozick's (1974, pp. 3–10).

15

such obligations arose out of the raw materials available in a state of nature. The 'state of nature' in the present work is the domain of non-social, uncoordinated, intentional action up through vows. It is a state where mandates exist without either obligations or rights. But it should be noted that the main thrust of my position reverses the flow of gravity of the contractarian and related analytic traditions. By this I mean that my position makes private acts prior normatively and conceptually to social ones; the position does not allow any social act to create a binding sense of obligation unless the possibility of obligation is embedded in non-social intentional action. In this fashion, it takes social philosophy and ethics to depend upon action theory.

Traditional and contemporary contractarian theory, with the possible exception of Locke, take the opposite view: uncoordinated action constitutes only an amoral state of nature, motivated by self-interest and prudence. From that foundation, it tries to erect an elaborate structure of political or moral obligation, where the obligation is irreducibly social, created by the social compact. The most extreme form of this, perhaps a caricature, is Rousseau's doctrine of the general will. On this, he writes:

The commitments which bind us to the social body are obligatory only because they are mutual; and their nature is such that in fulfilling them we cannot work for others without working for ourselves...
What man loses by the social contract is his natural liberty and the absolute right to anything that tempts him and that he can take; what he gains by the social contract is civil liberty and the legal right of property in what he possesses...
We might also add that man acquires with civil society moral freedom, which alone makes man the master of himself; for to be governed by appetite alone is slavery, while obedience to a law one prescribes to oneself is freedom. (1968, pp. 75 and 65)

Against this, my position is that any such structure of law, morality, or even language must totter on the brink of collapse unless founded in a sense of obligation, but obligation can hardly be constructed *ex nihilo* on the soil of a state of nature involving only the shifting sands of interest and prudence.[15]

Much of analytic philosophy – especially the ordinary language

[15] For a criticism of an attempt to derive language and convention directly out of interest, without an intervening social contract, see my critique of David Lewis's *Convention* (1969) in my article 'The Primacy of Promising' (1976b, pp. 332–6).

period – seems to share in common with the contractarian tradition the priority – this time conceptual – of social and public acts over private. This is evident enough in later Wittgenstein's and Quine's behaviorism, and incidentally was mirrored somewhat in the behavioristic tradition in psychology. The calling card of this otherwise heterogenous school of thought can well be Wittgenstein's statement: 'You learn the *concept* pain when you learn language' (Wittgenstein, 1953, Part I, Sec. 384; see also Sellars, 1963, p. 167; Quine, 1960).[16]

But perhaps the most systematic expression of this view – as well as one that transparently reveals its weaknesses – is to be found in Austin's performatives (1965). These remarkable utterances supposedly enable me, by merely *saying* some canonical *words* 'I hereby ϕ,' *to make it the case* that I ϕed! For if we look at such things as the nature of contract or at a christening, we would indeed find it as mysterious as transubstantiation to suppose that we could effect such changes by a mental act, or, more fatuously, by 'a movement of the soul.' It is not intentions, so the doctrine goes, that make such changes possible, but certain social conventions. The same goes for the more narrowly linguistic acts such as referring or communicating. To refer is not merely to intend to refer or will it, but to be able to satisfy a set of conventional conditions. And similar strictures applied against the possibility of Gricean intentions (cf. Strawson, 1964; Searle, 1969, pp. 72–94, 157–74; Schiffer, 1972).

As for performatives, it did not go unnoticed, even in their heyday, that they work only in the first person. Thus, 'I hereby promise' makes it the case that I promised, but not so with 'You hereby promise.' It is difficult to believe that the basis of this difference lies in convention. And interestingly enough in the last ten years or so the shift in the flow of gravity mentioned above has begun to take place. One of the first attempts, I believe, was Zeno Vendler's book (1972; see also Sellars, 1963), which tried to trace the basis of illocutionary acts in the structure of underlying propositional attitudes. And indeed Searle himself has contributed to this shift in his recent work by locating the source of illocutionary taxonomy in the structure of intentionality, as the mark of the

---

[16] It should be noted that many interpreters of Wittgenstein do not believe he was a behaviorist, but even so, the main point would be that his *conventionalism* emphasizes the priority of social acts over the private.

mental (1979, esp. chapter on 'A Taxonomy of Illocutionary Acts,' pp. 1–29).[17] Also to be noted here are the post-behavioristic developments in psychology, namely, neobehaviorism, cognitive psychology, as well as the new interdiscipline called 'cognitive science.'

At the same time, what I have said should not be taken to imply that the structure of intention can carry the whole burden of making fine distinctions in either meaning, illocutionary force, or in a host of other things. On this point, I agree with some of the criticism of Grice that has been leveled by Strawson (1964), Searle (1969), Schiffer (1972), and Bennett (1976) – criticisms to the effect that conventions make certain intentions possible, and for purposes of communication linguistic conventions have a function of clarifying our intentions. My point rather is that there are certain kinds of intentions that are fundamental qua intentions, e.g., commitment (and perhaps referring), that these must be presupposed in any conventions that can clarify and give them effect.

---

[17] Castaneda's work on practitions in *Thinking and Doing* (1975) as the basic unit of practical thinking likewise falls into this genre. It is a mentalist interpretation of some of the old insights of Hare on imperatives.

2

Commitment and basic action

My quarry in this chapter is that of intentional basic action. As indicated, I believe this will serve as the foundation of intentional non-basic action, and vows, which are to follow. Of course, intentional basic action is an amalgam of two controversial and somewhat intractable subjects: intentional action and basic action; and so it is with not a little trepidation that I even approach the topic. But I believe that we shall be able to get somewhere by explaining intention in terms of commitment, where we take 'commitment' to be a kind of primitive relation, instead of perhaps the more natural idea of explaining commitment in terms of intention. To say that commitment is a primitive relation is not to imply that not much can be said about it. Quite the contrary, the point is that it is a unifying relation which holds together the various elements of intentional (basic) action: intention and intending, the bodily movement executing the intention, and finally 'volition.' Sorting these various things out is what has proven so difficult. If we are moderately successful in relating all of these things through commitment, we shall see that it is normative, rather than causal, and that it forms the center of gravity for the concept of agency.[1]

The theory which I shall defend is that when an agent acts intentionally (where his action is preceded by an intending or preparatory intentional act), he successfully exercises a causal power. But the causal power does *not* run, as some have thought, from the intention to the bodily movements. Rather when he forms the intention, this

---

[1] I am not assuming that every intentional act is preceded by a separate (mental) act of intending. To take one of Lawrence Davis's counterexamples, brushing one's teeth absentmindedly probably was not preceded by an intending, but it was preceded by certain preparatory acts, e.g., getting the toothbrush out of the medicine chest, which were *done with the intention* to later brush one's teeth (see Davis, 1979, p. 59). These preparatory intentional acts will do as well as surrogates for pure intending. What does seem to be left out of the characterization above is an intentional act not preceded by either an act of intending or an intentional act, for example, 'tearing off a thread which one just noticed hanging on one's shirt' (*ibid.*). These cases I will put to one side, hoping to accommodate them on another occasion.

act – let us call it an act of intending – is non-causally related to a volition which later executes that intention. It is only from this volition that the causal power is exercised. What, then, is the relation between this volition and the earlier intending? It is that of commitment, a three-place operator ranging over an intending, a volition, and an agent. The picture that emerges is that an agent *acts* through *two* vehicles: intending and volition. When he intends at time t_i to do A, he commits *himself* to do a further *act* of his at time t_j, an act of volition. At time t_j, he exercises a causal power over his bodily movements. So conceived, intending, though psychologically real, is epi-phenomenal with regard to the causal order explaining intentional action. Its role is a normative one, linked through the normative commitment operator to other acts which are causally efficacious. I shall argue that this picture also retains the best elements out of the Cartesian and physicalist traditions – at least as they appear in action theory.

PART I

INTENTION AS COMMITMENT

Let us take as our starting point the idea that to intend to do A is to commit oneself to do A (leaving open at this point exactly what commitment means as well as the elements of 'doing' A). Some people, though not too many, have thought that this is a useful way of explicating intention.[2] Arthur Danto, for example, uses the idea to show that intending is not an 'isolated act of the soul' (1973, p. 192; cf. pp. 193, 25). That is, I cannot intend to do A without committing myself to actually doing A (when the opportunity arises).

---

[2] The reason that not too many theorists have fixed on this is that until recently the functionalist program in action theory was thought to be better served by ignoring intending altogether. All questions about intention were pre-empted by the then master locution, 'the intention with which one acts,' which, not necessarily referring to an event preceding action or to a contemporaneous quality of action, was analyzed syncategoramically as 'the reason for which one acts,' where 'the reason' referred to the appropriate desires and beliefs whose credentials in the causal order were bona fide. (See, for example, Davidson, 1963, and 1971.)

However, nagging questions remained about this mysterious mental act of intending which not only appeared to precede the action, but sometimes occurred without any action issuing. Functionalist motives, however, were still satisfied by either passing it as soft currency, or by being epi-phenomenal, or by exchanging it for the hard currency of believing or desiring. For attempts to reduce it to desiring see Audi, 1973, and 1979; Beardsley, 1978; and Davidson, 1978. For attempts to reduce it to believing, see Locke, 1974 and Harman, 1976.

From this he draws the important conclusion that we cannot form intentions frivolously, as we can, for example, entertain thoughts and wishes frivolously. Because intention does involve a kind of commitment, to form an intention frivolously is to be committed to act just for the sake of forming it. This inverts the direction of intention, for it implies that we act for the sake of forming an intention, instead of forming an intention for the sake of acting.

Bruce Aune takes a traditional line, invoking the idea of commitment to make sense of the practical syllogism. Thus he writes:

> The only kind of practical premise that, taken together with statements expressing beliefs, can imply a practical conclusion directly committing one to act is one that expresses or formulates an intention . . . Observe that the only kind of answer that directly answers the practical question 'What shall I do . . .?' has the form 'I will do A.' Statements like 'I want to do A' or 'I ought to do A' or 'Doing A is the best, most reasonable thing for me to do,' or even self-addressed imperatives like 'Do A!' do not *directly* answer such a practical question, because one can always ask oneself the further question 'Shall I do what is the best, most reasonable thing to do?' . . . Since these further questions can always meaningfully arise when the suggested answers are given to the practical question in point, these answers do not themselves imply a commitment to act. (1977, p. 122)

The same argument tells against the widely held view that 'the strongest desire' (or aversion) commits one to action. For according to Aune: 'No matter how strongly a rational person may want something, the question can (indeed, should) always arise: "Shall I take steps to satisfy my want?"' But to commit ourselves through an intention is already to have answered this question affirmatively (1977, p. 136).[3] This may also help to explain why, as I shall show much later, commitment, unlike desiring and other propositional attitudes, is closed under implication.

Aune has some further remarks on the nature of the commitment in which passage he invites us to ask ourselves what we would make of a case in which someone intends to do A but does not do it (assuming that the opportunity for so acting is present and the conditions on the intention, if any, have been satisfied). Thus he says:

> If in deciding to do A [where it is understood that deciding is one way of forming an intention], I fail to do it on the appropriate occasion, then *unless*

---

[3] The most systematic defense of the strongest desire theory is offered by Richard Brandt in *Theory of the Good and the Right*, (1979, Part I). Criticisms of the general theory can be found in Nagel, 1970; Brand, 1979, pp. 137–40; and (the most celebrated) in Davidson, 1973, pp. 137–56.

I have changed my mind [emphasis added], or do not realize that the occasion is appropriate, I am subject to criticism: I am being *practically* [original emphasis] inconsistent; I am not doing what I have, as it were, agreed to do. *In this respect a decision is like a promise: appropriate behavior is required* [emphasis added] as long as the mandate [i.e., the intention] is in effect.

(1977, p. 118)

Aune's remarks, however, are not as clear as they might seem. For they seem to trade on a certain ambiguity as to whether an intention is the kind of commitment that need be honored. The main thrust of the passage takes the commitment to be normative, but how does that jibe with the suggestion that one is permitted to change one's mind, i.e., change one's intention? If one is allowed to change one's mind at will, what remains of the commitment? Notice how very different this is from a promise, in which case what I am committed to is precisely not to change my mind, or at least not to except for a weighty reason.[4] But perhaps Aune has in mind another sense in which the commitment need be honored, the causal sense. In the next section I examine this causal sense with an eye to its adequacy for explicating intention.

I.   The causal theory of commitment

i.   Causal sufficiency vs. temporal discontinuity On the causal theory of commitment, intention commits one to *act* in the sense that if it has not changed, and is occurrent, if the conditions on it are satisfied, the opportunity is at hand, and known to be such, then it essentially causes the appropriate bodily movement. (A variant on this is that it causes a mental event called a 'trying' or a volition, which in turn causes the appropriate bodily movement.) The act of intending then is essentially the exercise of a causal power: it is a setting in motion of a train of events that results in, loosely speaking, an event that satisfies the semantic content of the intention. Of course, like all causal powers, it requires other enabling conditions in order to be strongly sufficient. These include such factors as indicated above: that the intention remain unchanged, be occurrent, the opportunity be present, etc.

There is a useful analogy to a more ordinary exercise of a causal power. This would be one in which I intentionally squeeze the trigger of a loaded gun, with the further intention to cause the gun to

---

[4] This formulation was first suggested by Rawls (1955), and forms the basis of my own views, especially discussed below in Chapters 4 and 5.

fire, and this with the still further intention that the bullet reach the target. Now even though the bullet's reaching the target is an event remote from my body, and not (at least not under that description) an act of mine, its occurrence is nevertheless something to which I am *committed*. For this is what it means to bring it about intentionally. Again, following Aune and others, this is in contrast to a desire, etc., which presumably does not involve the setting in motion of a train of events.

The trouble with this analogy, however, is that if the intention is formed in the present and the act is to take place in the future, as it invariably is, then apart from other things that can go wrong, it is always possible for the agent to change his mind, that is, abandon his intention. If so, there is a gap between the act of intending – the exercise of a causal power – and the action that can be closed only by something that still appears to be up to the agent and (which is to say the same thing) does not appear thereby to be causally determined in the act of intending. This is nothing else but the capacity on the part of the agent either to abide by his intention or to change his mind. And inasmuch as this appears to be up to the agent, it cannot convincingly be written off as another enabling condition for the causal efficacy of intention, as, for example, the lack of opportunity or ability can be written off.

In order that this argument carry conviction I must explain more precisely what is meant by the phrase, 'being up to the agent.' There are two interpretations, the negative and the positive, and it is the positive that seems to be required by the argument. On the negative interpretation, the agent in the act of intending sets in motion a train of events which will eventuate in the intended result *unless* he interrupts that causal chain. This interpretation would not threaten the causal role of intending because it seems no different than what can be said about causal chains in nature. A ball rolling down an incline, for example, will continue its downward path, unless interrupted by any number of things, including a person standing nearby, but that does not mean that its motion cannot be caused by gravity, friction, etc.

In contrast, the positive interpretation of 'it is up to the agent' seems to be quite another matter. It is not that his intention *will* be followed by the appropriate action unless he interferes; it is rather that his intention *will not* be followed by the action unless he does something positive to *make* it follow. Suppose today that I intend to

23

get up tomorrow at 6.00 a.m. to do two hours of strenuous exercises. When tomorrow comes, it saps my strength just to roll out of bed. To claim that the act of intending yesterday has a causal role in my getting up today (if I do) strikes me as the motivational equivalent of making water flow uphill. Notice that I need not deny at this point that my effort in getting up is caused by *something*; indeed I think it is (see below, pp. 50–9). I only wish to deny that it is caused by the original act of intending. To think it is seems just a shade less fanciful than thinking that an act of promising causes the keeping of it.

Some defenders of the causal theory of commitment point to as evidence the fact that their position is supported by counterfactuals:[5] if S did not intend to φ, S would not have φed (intentionally). Waiving the cavil perhaps that intentional action need not be preceded by an act of intending (about which I am unsure), I find this piece of evidence inconclusive. It is certainly compatible with the weaker, and, I think, more plausible view that intending is only an enabling condition for other events or things (like volitions or agents) that cause actions. But it is also compatible with a non-causal, conceptual relation between intending and acting, a view perhaps closer to the one I shall defend.

Other causal theorists have attempted to close the temporal gap between intending and intentional action by eliminating in effect the time difference, the result of which is either to make the causally relevant part of the intention simultaneous with acting, or if not simultaneous then close enough so that it is essentially too late for the agent to change his mind. Brian O'Shaughnessey, for example, begins by talking about the act of intending, but is really concerned with the causal connection between the realization that the act intended is to occur *now* and the doing of A now. He writes:

If there occurs the realization that [the present instant] is an instant at which one intends to act, then that instant is the one in which the will is beginning to move. . . .
    Yet it is natural to think that something more needs to be interposed between intending and trying [where for him 'trying' is a volition that causes bodily movement]. But that creates a gap that could never be closed. . .
    For the instant in which actual time and intended time are seen to

5 For example, Gilbert Harman, in an unpublished lecture and in discussion. See also Lewis, 1973b, for the most well-known attempt to model causations on counterfactuals.

24

coincide, there is nothing left for one to do but to act. But it is a parody of this position to suppose that one has lost the power of choice, for that is precisely what one is exercising. We are running up our head against nothing but – *commitment*! [emphasis added].   (1973, pp. 380–2)

Perhaps we can strengthen O'Shaughnessey's position on the causality of intention by making one important revision in it recommended by the more recent theory of Brand (see 1979, pp. 131–52).[6] According to him, no action will issue merely from the cognitive act of recognizing that the act is intended now (more precisely, was intended to occur now). In order to trigger action, the 'recognition' must itself be another act of intending, i.e., a *conative* rather than a cognitive act. In this fashion, an immediate intending, an intention to do something here and now, is said to be the 'proximate cause of action.' And it is too late to change one's mind because this immediate intending is, conatively, a 'moving to act' (1979, pp. 147–9) such that it is *simultaneous* with at the beginning of movement.[7]

There are two related difficulties with these proposals, however. The first is that if we try to understand the concept of intention in terms of exerting a causal power on action (either with or without the intermediary of volition), we lose the sense in which intention is meaningfully a commitment. For the 'commitment' signifies a relation between two time periods: the time in which the intention is originally formed and the time of acting on it. But the causal relation alleged between intention and action does not, correspondingly, span these two periods. Instead of running from the original act of intending A to A (or even from the intention to A to the doing of A, which intention may span the two periods), the causal relation occurs (on O'Shaughnessey's view) in an instant, from the realization that A is intended now (however far in the past was the act of intending it) to the doing of A now. And on Brand's view it runs, simultaneously, from the immediate intending of A here and now, to the doing of A (or the beginning of such a doing) here and now. On either account we are left with the problem of how the causally

---

[6] Brand's theory differs from O'Shaughnessey's, first, in that Brand eliminates the middleman, volition, between intention and action, and, second, in that he takes the causal connection between them to occur simultaneously. See below, p. 25 n. 7.

[7] See his paper, 'Simultaneous causation,' (forthcoming), in which he argues that the causally relevant parts of all events are simultaneous with the causally relevant parts of their effects. It might be useful to compare G. H. von Wright's analysis of an intending to do something *now*, which is such that 'you cannot slice it up into an earlier part of which it is true that the agent did not *begin* to do A, and a later part of which it is true that he then did A' (1978, p. 54).

efficacious part of the intention is related to the earlier, original act of intending, which is where the commitment begins. The problem, I think, is that if we grant that some intentions are *causally efficacious* on an *action*, they are not the intentions we identify with the *commitment* to it. The *causation* occurs either simultaneously or in close contiguity with the action, whereas the *commitment* is not contiguous, or at least discontinuous enough to allow the agent enough time to change his mind.[8]

ii.   Deviant causal chains The second, and opposite, problem arises for the causal theory if we *do* allow the causal relation to run from the original intending at t_i to the action at t_j. I am not referring to the obvious objection that the intention may fail to be causally efficacious.[9] The nature of the difficulty is introduced by a writer who himself is a causal theorist:

> Intention commits one to *act* [emphasis added]. And it is for this reason that it is counted as a peculiar sort of failure when what a man intends to make true is made true though no action of his (or what amounts to the same thing) is made true by something he does unintentionally.
>
> (Danto, 1973, p. 24)

The passage indicates that if intention is a commitment to *act*, then it is not satisfied merely by the occurrence of an *event* which answers to whatever specifications were in the intention. No, after the intention is formed, it can be satisfied only by the agent's own action – and an intentional action at that.[10]

Now suppose that our movements *are* caused by the intention. Is that enough to make those movements an intentional action? The causal theory of commitment that we have been considering is really part of a larger theory – the causal theory of action, whereby action is nothing but an event with a certain kind of causal antecedent whose

---

[8]   O'Shaughnessey's whole position on intention trades on the confusion between the original commitment and the causally efficacious mental act immediately preceding the 'willing.' Since we already made a choice to commit ourselves at t_i to do A at t_j, no further 'choice' or 'willing' is needed at t_j to bring about the act of trying to do A. But the *cause* of the trying to do A at t_j was not, after all, the act of commitment at t_i, but the non-actional mental event of recognition at t_j.

[9]   Causal theorists hedge against this somewhat in the reference to enabling conditions, see above p. 22.

[10]   This insight seems to be in the part the basis of Castaneda's analysis of intentions, whose semantic contents are not propositions, but practitions, and whose reference to the first person is *de se*. (See 1975, pp. 25–52, 169–75.)

26

semantic content it satisfies, namely, an intention.[11] Let us assume that the intention precedes the action in time. The adequacy of the theory is challenged by a class of counterexamples known as deviant or lunatic causal chains and which reveal felicitously the second difficulty. It will pay us to study these counterexamples somewhat because we shall find that they can be more easily accommodated by the theory of commitment than we shall defend.

A deviant causal chain is simply an instance, possibly alluded to in Danto's passage (above, p. 26), whereby an intention to do A causes exactly an Aing, but in an odd or deviant way, and therefore it is questionable whether the Aing is intentional even though it was caused by the intention to do exactly that. For example, suppose that a golfer, standing at the tee, intends to drive the ball onto the middle of the fairway. His intention causes him to swing in the appropriate way, but his swing causes the ball to veer to the side, striking a tree, which in turn deflects the ball right towards the middle of the fairway, exactly in the spot where he intended to hit it. Intuitively, we may say that 'his making the ball land in the middle of the fairway' was not an intentional action, even though it was caused by the intention to do precisely that. We may say it was unintentional because it got there by a deviant, unanticipated route. Now, it seemed obvious what else the theory required for successful intentional action: that the act and its causal milieu be anticipated; that in the golfing case (and other non-basic actions) the intention include an 'action-plan' as to the causal route and that the ball actually follow that route. From this the general theory was modified to make the semantic representation of the intention include the action plan as well as the (intended) result. The action must not only be caused by the intention but conform to it.[12]

But is this enough for an account of intentional action? Not if our movements can conform to our plans, be caused by our intention to make them occur, and still occur deviantly, i.e., unintentionally. The following famous counterexample is offered by Davidson, one of the founders of the causal theory! Although it is couched in terms

[11] Other famous versions of the causal theory involve interpreting the antecedent as a desire and belief. The most celebrated of these are that of Goldman, 1970, pp. 49–169; and Davidson, 1963.

[12] For Danto intention causes action by being a representation of it, as distinguished from the way that shouting causes an echo or a sexual fantasy causes tumescence (see 1973, p. 190). Also see Goldman (1970, pp. 56–62, 71–2, 78–9), on action-plans.

of wants and beliefs as the causal antecedents of intentional action, his point can be preserved by substituting the word 'intention' and its verb forms in brackets where he uses the word 'want':

A climber might [intend] to rid himself of the weight and danger of holding another man on the rope, and might know that by loosening his hold on the rope he could rid himself of the weight and danger. This belief and [intention] might so unnerve him as to cause him to loosen his hold, and yet it might be the case that he never *chose* to loosen his hold, nor did he do it intentionally. It will not help, I think, to add that the belief and the [intention] must combine to cause him to [intend] to loosen his hold, for there will remain the *two* questions how the belief and the [intention] caused the second [intention], and *how* the [intention] to loosen his hold caused him to loosen his hold. (1973, pp. 153–4)

The point of the example for our purposes is that an intention can cause *uncontrollable* bodily movements which otherwise (behavioristically) satisfy the content of the intention in every particular. But because uncontrollable they are *eo ipso* unintentional. Thus it does not do any good to think that the problem can be circumvented by filling in the 'plan' in more detail, by adding some exacting specification that will exclude what we want to exclude. Suppose that the climber intends to loosen his grip, *slowly* and *unobtrusively*, exactly at *t*, exactly when his companion is at a certain distance from him on the rope. The fact remains that all of this can be caused by the intention to happen exactly in this way, but the movements can still be uncontrollable, more like movements that occur as *events*, rather than *actions*, let alone intentional actions.

As I see it, what has been left out of the causal analysis and what is a breeding place for these kinds of counterexamples, is what takes place *while* these movements are occurring: they must be under our direct control if they are to qualify as actions, to say nothing of intentional actions. The usual vehicle for such control is a volition, which on some interpretations may imply not only the power to guide our movements, but also the power to stop them in their tracks. On this reading, we are thus driven to countenance volitions as one of the elements of intentional action. And historically, volitional theories are usually offered as a rival account to the causal theory of action because they undermine the functionist motivation behind it (see, e.g., Frankfurt, 1978; Chisholm, 1976a, pp. 53–88, 1976b).

iii. *The dilemma for the causal theory* This difficulty, together with the first, reveals the implausibility of the causal theory of commitment. For if the intention that is causally efficacious does correspond to the original act of intending that is the commitment (and is causally efficacious through some causal chain spread out in time), then it provides a model of commitment whereby commitment is the exercise of a causal power at t_i to bring about the *occurrence* at t_j of some event which is a movement. We *commit* ourselves to the event in the causal sense by setting in motion (perhaps irrevocably) at t_i a chain of events which result in its occurrence at t_j. But this view of commitment leaves out whether the movements that occur at t_j are controlled at t_j. All that seems required is that they occur according to the specifications (the action–plan, etc.) that set the process in motion at t_i. And it is just this which gives rise to the problem of lunatic causal chains.

The other horn of the dilemma is that if the causally efficacious part of the intention is something that is immediately contiguous with action or simultaneous with it – supposing even that the immediate intending of Brand might be the medium through which we exercise control – then it leaves unexplained the *relation* between what happens when the action occurs and what went on in the original past act of intending.

Commitment, then, seems to have an irreducible, *double* indexical, temporal reference: the reference to the time at which we are committing ourselves *and* to the later time we are to honor it. Any adequate theory of commitment has got to accommodate both, and that is exactly what the causal theory of commitment seems unable to do.

II.   *The normative theory of commitment*

i.   Mistakes in intention vs. mistakes in performance A better theory, I suggest, is the normative theory of commitment. This is best introduced – though unintentionally, to be sure – by that same pregnant passage of Danto's, to which we now return:

Intention commits one to act. And it is for this reason that it is counted as a peculiar sort of *failure* [emphasis added] when what a man intends to make true is made true through no action of his (or what amounts to the same thing) is made true by something he does unintentionally.   (1973, p. 24)

I emphasize the word 'failure' this time rather than 'act,' in the sense that it is a *failure* on the part of an agent not to satisfy his intention

29

with the matching intentional action. What we need to develop, as a rival theory to the causal theory, is what kind of failure this is; but a clue to it is to ask *when* the failure occurs. In reading Danto, does the failure occur at t_i when the act of committing ourselves occurs (which would make it a failure because it fails to yield an action that satisfies it); or does the failure occur at t_j in the *performance* (or lack thereof)? It seems to be the latter. For what Danto is saying is that when a man does not satisfy his intention, something is *wrong* – not simply because what happened did not fit an action plan (at t_i) – which is the way the causal theory would interpret it (and the way Danto himself ultimately construes it) (1973, p. 193), but wrong at t_j because the agent did not *do* something he was *supposed* to do![13]

Thus it looks as though the normative theory makes intentions stand to action in a normative relation: the intention 'binds' the agent to act at a later time or – if we introduce volitions as I believe we must – it binds the agent to later exercise his volition, to 'try' or to 'will' the appropriate bodily movements. (As to whether this binding relation is *really* incompatible with the causal view is a question I wish to sidestep in this book. They certainly *appear* to be incompatible – but then so do reasons and causes. In what follows I shall in effect indicate how they run along different tracts and how the normative view of commitment can do the work set out for it in this book.)

Before we examine the nature of the volition to which one is bound, we have a more immediate question: what kind of bond is an intention, and how strong? For example, is the agent *allowed* to change his mind, i.e., his intention? The causal view (when it took the causally efficacious intention to be contiguous with the action) was entirely too relaxed with respect to the original intending. We must therefore develop a rival account of this, but in doing so we must steer between Scylla and Charybdis, between allowing for the changing of one's mind in a wholesale fashion and ruling it out so stringently as to assimilate intentions to vows. I think that a reasonable middle course – and one that is not ad hoc – is suggested in a gloss on a famous example of Anscombe's (1969, pp. 56–7). The essential point of it is that, pursuant to Danto's remarks (see above, p. 29, it will allow us to distinguish between a mistake in performance and a mistake in intention (although the latter phrase is not her terminology).

[13] Cf. Aune's remarks about the agent 'being subject to criticism,' above, p. 22.

Suppose, then, that a man writes out a shopping list for himself. When he gets to the store he is followed closely by a detective who is jotting down everything that he buys. Suppose now that the man buys nectarines, but the detective writes down 'peaches.' This is a mistake in the detective's list; he simply corrects it by crossing out the word 'peaches' and writing in the word 'nectarines.' But what if the man who was shopping discovers after leaving the store that it was he who made a mistake, that he bought peaches instead of nectarines? This is a mistake in performance, not a mistake in anyone's list. And because it is a mistake in performance, he cannot make it right by afterwards crossing out the word 'nectarines' and writing in the word 'peaches.' For what happened was a mistake in what he *did*, not, as in the detective's case, a mistake in what he had written down.

Now let us alter the story in one particular. Before the man is about to buy the nectarines, he looks at his list – an expression of his intention – and simply changes his mind: he buys peaches instead of nectarines. Having changed his mind *before* buying, is the buying of peaches still a mistake in performance, or does it reflect a mistake in making up the list, or neither? And what about the act of changing his mind itself? More information, of course, is needed. Suppose that he changes his mind because he finds upon getting to the nectarine section that they have been picked over and that the ones left do not look very good – something he did not know when he drew up his list. We can see that this way of changing his mind is perfectly permissible – permissible in the sense that crossing out the word 'nectarines' and writing the word 'peaches' simply corrects a mistake that was made in his list, a mistake really in his intention. More precisely, it was a correction of a mistake in the belief component of his intention, or the belief premise of a 'practical inference' on the basis of which his intention to buy nectarines was formed. If he is still 'subject to criticism,' it is not because he failed to honor his intention, but because he had an intention he should not have had in the first place, one that was formed on the basis of a false belief. This is the only kind of change of mind that Anscombe discusses (1969, p. 56).

In passing it would be well to mention a more controversial case of mistaken intention discussed in a recent paper by Michael Bratman (1981) in which the intention to buy nectarines is contrary to the shopper's preferences. We might imagine that he puts nectarines on his list either because he is mistaken about his preferences or *akratically*. In either case his intention is mistaken, and to keep things simple we can treat it like the case above.[14]

I am now going to lead up to a kind of *akrasia* that is almost never discussed in the literature, one that takes place between intending and acting (whereas it is typically thought to take place between judging and intending). Imagine that our shopper prefers nectarines slightly to peaches, but knows that this is offset by the fact that they are harder to get to than the peaches. Perhaps, unlike the peaches, they are several aisles away from anything else on his list. These two facts, let us say, cancel each other out so as to make the choice a toss up. However, we may suppose that he has to choose between them: his list is already long enough without complicating it with disjunctive intentions, and he wants to have his mind settled before he enters the store, if only to conserve energy while shopping.

The next scene finds him in the store, conveniently located close to the peaches. Contrary to his plan, he buys the peaches. To make this clearly a case of *akrasia*, we would have to add that right before he buys the peaches he is reminded briefly of all the considerations that resulted in (not to say 'warranted') his intending to buy the nectarines. Moreover, it is essential that in ruminating over these facts he does not discover anything that he did not know before – in the occurrent sense of 'know' that includes not only awareness of the relevant items, but also with the desired degree of vividness. (It might be thought that he acts contrary to his plan in another way: he renews reflection on a question he thought was already settled. However, it is important that my account does *not* count this as part of the *akrasia* or even consider it a mistake of any sort. The reason I exclude this is that I do not want to confuse simple intending – which is what we have here – with deciding, which I take to be different; see Chapter 4.) Our question is, given the way the story is told, is the buying of peaches a mistake in performance?

Will the answer be clearer if we have it that he changes his mind formally, i.e., right before he buys the peaches he crosses out the word 'nectarines' and writes in the word 'peaches?' If he is mistaken in the first case, does this get him off the hook, or does it compound the error? In the first case we were imagining that he is intentionally acting against his intention without explicitly changing it – at least

---

[14] Once we get a better handle on the commitment in intentions, we might have to handle this *akrasia* case differently.

not changing it by a new act of intending. In the second case he does change it by a new act of intending, viz., intending to buy peaches now. It might be puzzling that there can be a mistake in performance in either case if the intention to buy nectarines was arbitrary to begin with.[15] If you may form the intention arbitrarily, may you not change it at will?[16]

I shall argue that you may not change it at will, that intentions, even arbitrary (preferentially indifferent) ones, may not be changed arbitrarily. This will not become clear until we see how intentions behave differently from, say, desires. In a recent paper, Michael Bratman showed how the forming of an intention, no matter how arbitrary in the above sense, gives you a reason to do things that you wouldn't have a reason to do without the intention (1981, pp. 252–4). The first thing he mentions is that of choosing the means to satisfy that intention. If I *intend* to buy nectarines, do I not, in virtue of that intention, have a reason to choose the means to satisfy it? (The shopper in our example had already chosen the store in which to buy them and how he was going to get there.) Why does intending to buy nectarines give him a reason to choose the means to it? To begin with, the explanation is that if he failed to opt for the appropriate means, he would be guilty of a practical incoherence in his intentions (1981, pp. 252–4). This is an incoherence of intending some end, seeing that to achieve it he must decide on some means, but yet having reached no such decision. 'Since [he] avoid[s] such incoherence by opting for some means, [his] intention [to buy nectarines] gives [him] a reason for opting for such means' (1981, pp. 252–4).

The observation that intentions themselves, independently of desires, create reasons for choosing the means to them is important in contrasting them with desires and, perhaps, hopes. Suppose alternatively that the shopper does *prefer* nectarines to peaches tout court, and that because of this he forms the intention to buy nectarines. While his preferences no doubt give him a reason to buy nectarines[17] it is not at all the same kind of reason that is created by his intention. If he did not yet *intend* to buy the nectarines, and does not intend to pursue the means to buying them, he is *not* guilty of *any* incoherence

---

[15] Meaning by that that he was preferentially indifferent.
[16] I am very grateful to Gilbert Harman and Páll Árdal for helping me to frame the issues here and in the ensuing discussion.
[17] Which Bratman (1981, pp. 252–4) calls a 'desiderative reason.'

for failing to pursue the means. Intentions have special means–end coherence requirements which do not seem attributable to desires and hopes. If he *intends* to satisfy his preferences, it is his intention that creates the same reason–giving force (to choose the means) as when he forms a preferentially indifferent intention.

This is about as far as Bratman takes the reason–giving force of intentions. I would like to extend it two more steps. The first is that if an intention gives one a reason to choose the means to satisfy it, it must give one a reason to satisfy itself simpliciter. This is because the reasons you have for choosing the means must derive from the reason you have for satisfying the intention in the first place. The whole point of choosing means is to satisfy intentions.

The next extension is, however, quite difficult. Many thinkers might concede that intentions do have this reason–giving force, but add the clause: only if they are in force. If the agent changes his mind, he wipes it out. I can think of some reasons behind this intuition. One is: 'He who lifteth himself by his own bootstraps [referring to the bootstrap rationality that has been created] hath the power to topple over.' More precisely, 'He who hath the power to create reasons hath the power to remove them.' I will argue that this is incorrect. One thing that may seem to support it derives from a plausible conception of intention, viz., that to *have an intention* (whether occurrent or standing) is *to intend*. Since it is the *intention* that creates the reasons, if you change your mind, you no longer intend, and therefore, no longer have the reasons!

I think that the inference implicit in the last principle is faulty, however. I will concede that to have an intention does imply that you intend.[18] But it does not follow from this that to *have* presently the reasons that were created when you inten*ded*, implies that you *still intend* to do the thing that created them. The faulty inference stems from the failure to notice or appreciate that intending is doubly temporally indexed – a fact on which we have already relied. Suppose that I intend now to do something tomorrow. If the act of intending creates a reason, what is the temporal index of the created reason: today or tomorrow? It seems to me that if the act is to occur tomorrow (and if there are no preparations I might have to make for it today), I intend or at least expect that I will have those reasons

[18] This is not as obvious as it seems, not only because of my earlier uncertainty whether an intention is necessarily preceded by an act of intending, but also because one should be mindful of Myles Brand's observation that one can recognize an intention as a cognitive act without conatively re-intending it. See above, p. 25.

tomorrow. In fact, if the act intended is like waking up early tomorrow, there is nothing I have to do today to prepare for it. Now if I am right, this means that I expect that my *intending today* will create the reasons for me *tomorrow*. If I thought that I *also* had to *intend* the act *tomorrow in order that* I will *have* a reason *tomorrow*, then what will be the point of intending today? Isn't the point to settle for both today and for tomorrow that I *will* have a reason tomorrow?

If this is so, then I will *have* the reason tomorrow whether or not I still intend to act tomorrow. This, of course, does not imply that I may not change the intention tomorrow, but it does, I think, imply that I may not change the intention tomorrow simply by disregarding, ignoring the reason that I *intend* today to then go into effect. The upshot is that there is important asymmetry between forming intentions and changing them. One can form them arbitrarily (i.e., while being preferentially indifferent), but one may not change them at will. On my analysis one may not change them without showing that the intention is mistaken.

Our last point in this section is to say what is behind the reason-giving force of intentions. Bratman's first explanation in terms of means–end coherence does not take us very far (as he admits) because it simply shows that intentions have special coherence (and, I might also add, consistency) requirements not attributable to desires, hopes, etc. The question becomes: why do they have these requirements? Various explanations have been proposed (see Bratman, 1981; Harman, 1976, 1980a), which I shall later contrast with the present theory that intentions are normative commitments to bring about their satisfaction conditions. This idea is best developed, as we have said, by showing that we are susceptible to a kind of *akrasia* relative to our intentions.

ii. Akrasia Return to the shopping story. So far we have said that if the shopper intentionally does not buy the nectarines (which were written on his list, and if the original intention to buy nectarines was not mistaken), then he has made an intentional mistake in performance. We must now clarify more precisely why this is a case of *akrasia*. We might define *akrasia* in the present context by saying that it is an act of intentionally going against one's intention[19] for reasons

---

[19] Here I am following Davidson in construing *akrasia* to be a kind of intentional mistake (*mutatis mutandis*) in his examples about intentionally going against one's best judgment (see 1969b). The *mutatis* in the present case is that it amounts to intentionally not abiding by one's intention (or former intention, as the case may be).

that, from the agent's point of view, do not aim at correcting a mistake in intention.

One way of intentionally going against one's intention is explicitly to change the intention in a new act of intending to do something incompatible with it (changing the shopping list from nectarines to peaches). But if an intentional act need not be preceded by a separate act of intending, then another way is by not explicitly changing the intention.

But however we construe intentionally not abiding by one's intention, the thing that makes it *akrasia* is that the shopper does not act against the intention in order to correct a mistake in it. An intention can be mistaken, we noted, if there is some oversight of fact (including facts about one's preferences) or logic which occurred at the time of the original intending. Changes of mind, changes of intention, to correct these deficiencies, we have noted, seem perfectly in order. But if you change your mind for reasons that, from your point of view, do not correct an error in the intention, you are essentially in the position of the *akrates*. In our example, the *akrates* changes his mind essentially out of laziness: he knew that he had not uncovered some new fact of which he was formally uncognizant; yet he bought peaches because he was too lazy to buy the nectarines.

But is it true that he had not uncovered some fact of which he was uncognizant? What about the very fact that he feels lazy? Is this fact anticipated or unexpected? If the latter, then when he does change his plans out of laziness, why not say that instead of exhibiting 'weakness of the will' he is simply responding to new information about how he feels exactly when arriving at his moment of truth? Without begging the question, one may dismiss this as *akrasia* only by taking the former alternative: that at the time he intended to buy nectarines he fully *anticipated* that he would later feel lazy, and so did not discover anything new when he later *did* feel lazy. But our detractors may wonder whether a case can be presented in which the shopper fully anticipates this or anticipates this with the desired degree of vividness?[20]

There is a grain of truth in drawing attention to the shopper's inability to anticipate fully how it will feel when he arrives at 'his moment of truth,' but just for that reason the objection is highly seductive, in fact, fundamentally confused about the whole topic of

---

[20] I owe this objection to Andrew Altman.

akrasia, not just my conception of it. The grain of truth is that how the shopper will feel and act is not, cannot be, exactly represented in his intentions, beliefs, and judgments, but the seduction lies in the innuendo that *therefore* those representations are somewhat defective or incomplete. But if when we form our practical judgments and intentions, our representations were 'complete' in this fashion, then the classical problem of *akrasia* would not even *appear* as a possibility. No representation, however accurate, is exactly like the thing it represents (as we know from a long tradition in the philosophy of language and work on intentionality), and this is especially so when the representation is cognition and the referent is in conation or willing. The very possibility of weakness of the will grows in the space between the two, which is why, following Davidson again, it should not be forgotten that weakness of the will appears to be weakness of the *will*, not weakness in cognition or reason. And so when I say that *akrasia* does not occur unless the situation was anticipated with the desired degree of vividness, I mean vividness as befits representation and mental imagery, not vividness as befits the thing represented. (Any residual problems in this caveat, especially about mental imagery, are addressed in Part II of this chapter.)

As a final postscript on laziness, we should not, however, think that it *is always* on the side of weakness. Davidson offers a telling example in which laziness is on the side of rationality but is overcome by conscious habit (1973, pp. 101–2). That is why I believe that a working definition of *akrasia* is that of intentionally acting against one's intention which does not aim at correcting a mistake in that intention. And lest anyone not recognize the *akrates* here, and think that changing one's intention before acting always averts a faulty performance, he would be committing a third kind of mistake: the mistake of not seeing that an intentional mistake in performance can masquerade as a correction of a mistake in intention.

If this is roughly right, we have extracted a sense of commitment in which intending commits one to act in the normative sense. Included in binding oneself to act is the binding of oneself not to change one's mind owing to considerations of *akrasia*, but permitting the changing of one's mind to correct faulty intention.

iii. The is-ought question We must now deal with an objection to the very idea of a normative sense of commitment. It is clear that this position presupposes that we *ought* to honor our (non-defective) intentions. And whence comes this normative principle? Either the 'ought' of 'honor' has been derived from the 'is' of 'commitment' or 'intention,' or it has been smuggled in by equivocating between the descriptive and normative sense of some critical terms. For example, when I say that we commit ourselves through our intentions (as opposed, say, to our desires, etc.) I am using 'commitment' in a simple descriptive sense. But when I go on surreptitiously to infer that we *ought* to honor our 'commitments,' I am using 'commitment' in the normative sense. Similarly, when a performance 'fails' to match an intention, or vice versa, and that therefore something somewhere is 'wrong' or 'mistaken,' I am simply using those words in the descriptive sense. They mean no more and no less than that the performance simply does not match the intention. And even if the intention also *fails* as a causal power, again, that simply means that it failed to become a cause, as when we say that the rock that the vandal threw *failed* to shatter the glass window. To go on from this to the thought that something is 'wrong' or 'mistaken' in the normative sense is to equivocate on those words. And if this is the foundation upon which the normative conception rests, then the only mistake in performance that exists (normative sense) is in embracing that position.

These objections, however, reflect a misunderstanding of the justification of the normative conception. No equivocation has taken place, because the whole point of that conception is to use those words in the normative sense throughout. Nor is an 'ought' being *derived* from an 'is.' That we ought to honor our intentions is not being *derived* from anything. Rather, it is *justified* by its close connection to the intelligibility of intentional action and, ultimately, to agency. The justification is that (1) our understanding of intentional action is irreducibly normative, which in part explains the folly of understanding it purely in terms of the causal view, and (2) more strongly, if the concept of agency were not normative, i.e., were not recognized as the source of values and obligation, then rational and free agents would look unrecognizably different. The latter point places the justification in the spirit of a transcendental argument, while stopping short of the letter. It is in spirit because it construes a substantive (and also normative) conclusion to be a condition for the intelligibility of a familiar and indispensable concept (agency or intentional action); but it stops short of the letter because it fails to impart any *necessity* to that conclusion. To make peace with Quine, (who eschews any such necessity), the argument does not, and does not have to, deny that there is a possible world in which the concept of agency is not normative, but only that if there is, the concept would look unrecognizably different.[21] Calculated not to satisfy purists of any persuasion, this hybrid view has the greatest chance of approximating the truth. And finally, it is because obligation is a product of the will, mediated by the concept of commitment, that such obligations can, as we shall see, become woven into an objective moral order.

iv. *Rival explanations of the reason-creating force of intentions* Suppose that the reader accepts at least the data that my theory seeks to explain, namely, that intentions have special coherence requirements and create special reasons for acting over and above desires. Suppose further that he accepts that because of this we may not change our intentions arbitrarily even if they were formed arbitrarily. My theory is that intentions are normative commitments in the sense described, the justification lying in something like the transcendental argument sketched above. As I had suggested earlier, some people agree with these data but offer rival theories to explain them. One comes from Michael Bratman (1981), the other from Gilbert Harman (1980a).

Consider Bratman first. His explanation avoids any mention of commitment; instead it serves up a straightforward pragmation justification. The special coherence requirements and reason-giving force of intentions are derived from our interest in getting what we want, and to the extent that we breach those requirements, we fail to maximize desire satisfaction (1981, p. 262).

The trouble is that the first part of his paper draws attention to the *conflict* (which he thinks is only apparent) between the rationality requirements of desires and beliefs, vs. the requirements of intentions. For example, my intention to ϕ can be irrational in relation to my desires and beliefs. But *once I intend* to ϕ, and believe that ψing is a means to ϕing, then it may not be irrational, in fact it may be *rational*, to intend to ψ. It may be rational in relation to the totality of my desires, beliefs, *and intentions*, (which include the intention to ϕ) although irrational in relation to the sub-set of just my desires and

[21] Cf. Nagel's justification of rational motivation (1970, p. 19).

beliefs. But whether the conflict is formally apparent or real, there is still a tension, which he admits, between the rationality of intending to ψ, and the rationality, say, of intending to ω, where ωing, being incompatible with ψing and φing, *would* maximize desire satisfaction. If the *source* of the rationality requirements of *intentions* derives from that of desires and beliefs, then how could the rationality of the one conflict with or be at odds with the rationality of the other?

Bratman's 'solution' is not so much an answer as it is a statement of his problem. For he says that this tension or conflict is analogous to the familiar one between rule utilitarianism and the principle of utility (1981, pp. 262–3). Although the normative force of rules supposedly derives from the principle of utility, those very rules sometimes conflict with that principle. Suffice it to say, this analogy is an apt one indeed, but hardly in a way that gives any comfort to Bratman's position!

My own theory, in contrast, is not saddled with this problem because it takes the source of normative character of intentions to lie elsewhere than in desire satisfaction.

Turning to Harman, he also believes ultimately in a pragmatic explanation for our data, but this plays a relatively negligible role in his discussion of these phenomena (1980a, 1980b).[22] Instead his is a richer theory that ties the reason–creating force of intentions to his conception of 'methodological conservatism.'

According to this idea, intending, like believing, involves a primitive notion of 'full acceptance,' which means that you are not only going to rely on the thing accepted, but also henceforth terminate your inquiry into the truth or desirability of it. Terminating your inquiry means that it is not to be reopened unless there is a special reason for doing so. A special reason for reopening inquiry need not at all be like a reason not to close it, once it is on-going. Using the case of belief, for example, suppose that I know that someone down the hall has some information about the thing I am investigating. If I have not closed my inquiry, then my knowledge of this is a reason to check out that information. But if I have closed the inquiry, it is not a reason to check the information.

Harman's explanation of why I cannot arbitrarily change my intention even though I may have formed it arbitrarily, would be that in intending I am closing inquiry, and in arbitrarily changing it I

[22] Some of the points of Harman which I shall address were made in his NEH Summer Seminar at Princeton University, 6 August 1982.

am acting as if it were not closed, so there is a kind of inconsistency. To some extent this dovetails with the Bratman thesis that intentions have special coherence requirements, but the explanation of those requirements is the 'methodological conversativism.' Its justification in turn is the background pragmatic one that it is useful to be able to rely on things accepted without continuing to inquire into their truth, and useful to be able to store them in long term memory without also storing all the intermediate steps in their justification.

For reasons that will become obvious in Chapter 4, I am quite sympathetic to the emphasis on closing inquiry. But even if it admits of a pragmatic justification, I do not see how this does not include the presence of a normative commitment – at least in understanding *what* it is to terminate further inquiry. Since the temporal indices of closing and reopening inquiry are different, there is not a formal contradiction between them. After all, when I reopen inquiry that earlier I intended to close, why can I not just say that I have changed my mind? As I see it, the normative commitment in my sense is just what is needed to blunt this maneuver and to bridge the two indices.

Another difficulty with this account is that the characterization of simple intentions as implying the closing of further inquiry strikes me as too strong and too strained. Too strong because I do not see that once you intend to do something (as opposed to *decide* something), you have closed inquiry in Harman's sense. For on my account, something that might have a bearing on the rectitude of the thing intended has that bearing both *before* and *after* the intending of it. This is the kind of thing that, in my terminology, would reveal a mistake in intention, which, I have held, does warrant the changing of the intention.

'Closing inquiry' strikes me as also too strained because (and this is related to the point above) it implies, implausibly, two levels in the conceptualization of intending: first level reasons that bear on the thing intended, and second level reasons relating to the inquiry into those first level reasons. But when I change my intention, do I separately consider *whether* I will consider changing my intention (reopening inquiry) as well as reconsider the thing intended? I do not mean to suggest that Harman takes these levels to be necessarily psychologically real; I am only questioning their adequacy for third person conceptualization. In this sense, it seems that in the shopping story, one simply reconsidered the thing intended.

As I see it, Harman's two levels analysis gets its plausibility from

41

the fact that it *does* appear to fit something easily confused with intending, namely, deciding or vowing, which, as I said, I take up in Chapter 4. (The story of the shopper *choosing* between nectarines or peaches indeed fosters this confusion, but the choice was merely a literary device for making plausible the idea of an *arbitrary* intention, and the point of this in turn was to isolate intentions from desires so as to focus on the normative structure of the former.) Our tentative conclusion regarding intending is, I think, more straightforwardly explained as a commitment that rules out only *akrasia*.

v. Intentions as normative commitments vs. causal powers and predictions
We are now in a position to draw out some further critical differences between the normative and causal theories of commitment and intention. I want to show here how only the normative sense of intention as commitment can make sense of the idea that, relative to intention, there can be a mistake in *performance* in the first place. Consider how the two conceptions would try to handle this. Recall that Anscombe's original example had two lists: the shopping list and the detective list. If all goes well, i.e., if the shopper buys what is on his list and if the detective accurately reports this, then the two lists will match. Nevertheless, the lists are very different and the challenge of her example is to say which theory, the normative or the causal, best explains that difference. Searle made a good beginning when he said that they have a different 'relation to fit' (1979, pp. 3–4, 12–20). In the detective's case, there is a world–to–world relation of fit; in the shopper's case a word–to–word relation of fit. In the detective's list, the words have the burden of conforming to the world. That is why when he makes a mistake, he simply corrects the list. But in regard to the shopping list, it is the world, i.e., the shopper's action, that has the burden of conforming to the words. The mistake, as we have said, is in the performance; that is why it can be corrected only by changing the performance.

The causal theory of commitment pays lip service to these different relations of fit by simply making them out to be different directions of causality.[23] In the detective's list, the causality goes from the world to the words (mediated by perception, etc.). In the shopping list it goes from the words (the intention) to the world. But this, I hold, garbles Searle's and Anscombe's insight, because

---

[23] I am grateful to Gilbert Harman and Barry Loewer for clarifying this to me, and to William Richards for discussing with me the point that follows.

42

they should be understood as making a *semantic* point about the contrast between the two lists as *representations* of the world. On the causal theory both lists are representations of the world in similar senses: the detective's list is a representation of the world as it is; the shopping list a representation of the world as it will be. Under the causal theory, when something goes wrong in either case, it is a breakdown somewhere in the causal chain. From the *semantic* point of view, however, *both* lists would be (when something goes wrong) semantic *mis*representations, the detective's list misrepresenting what occurs, the shopping list misrepresenting what will occur. Semantically, an unfulfilled intention has exactly the same status as a false prediction.[24]

Now I want to claim that this misconceives the concept of 'relation of fit,' which I have said, I take to be a semantic, not a causal, relation. When the shopper doesn't buy what is on his list, we cannot conceive the *list* as a *misrepresentation*, as we *can* conceive the detective's list when he misdescribes what was bought. For one thing, to do so would make the *time* of the *mistake*, at least semantically, occur at the time of intending, instead of at the time of performance. More important, the causal view misses the fact that the shopping list is not in error when it fails to match the shopper's performance; it is the performance that is in error in not matching the list. In Searle's words, it is the world that has the burden of conforming to the words. Since the causal theory takes the shopping list to have the same semantic status as a false prediction, observe what happens when the agent becomes aware in the interim between intending and acting that he will not act as intended (for whatever reason). Assume that this realization is causally or conceptually connected with changing his intention (cf. Harman, 1976, and Bratman's rebuttal, 1981, pp. 255–6 n. 4).

Semantically, changing his mind is substituting a new prediction for a faulty one, hoping that the new prediction will prove accurate. The difficulty is that this seduces one to believe that all mistakes in

---

[24] Cf. Harman, 1976. There is an analogous controversy concerning whether an unfulfilled promise has the same status as a false prediction. People like Páll S. Árdal argue (in 1968), that promises are statements (as opposed to performatives), involving a commitment only in the sense that, like all *statements*, they are commitments to the truth of a proposition. (See also Árdal, 1969. Also see Warnock's (1971) predictive conception of promising.) Of course this proposition differs from other varieties by being in the future tense. The discussion that follows in the text, while ostensibly about intention and the causal theory, has a bearing on this controversy as well.

one's *deeds* can be averted simply by drawing up a better shopping list, as if the only source of semantic error lay in the intention or the process of its formation.

PART II
VOLITION

My position thus far is that commitment makes volitions the proper object of intentions. Until recently, volitions have had a bad press through much of analytic philosophy,[25] and so to call upon them to explicate in part the already difficult concept of intention is *explanare obscurans per obscurios*. Nevertheless, I believe that if we approach the subject without prejudice, as exemplified by Goldman's (1975) outstanding article, we shall be able to dissolve many of the puzzles in action theory.

The standard objections to volitions seem to be these. If action is such that it is caused, or anyway, controlled, by volitions, the question remains whether volitions are themselves actions or things that we do. But if volitions are things that we do,[26] and things that we do are caused or controlled by volitions, then there must be another volition through which we cause or control them, and so on, *ad infinitum*. Along similar lines, if these are actions, then do not they take the same adverbs, e.g., are they performed easily or with effort? If they are not actions, we might avoid the regress but only at the cost of some obscurity. Moreover, our doubts about the status of these entities may be reinforced by Gilbert Ryle's famous question: how many volitions are involved in reciting little Miss Muffet backwards (1949, p. 65)?

These questions, however, do have a Lewis Carroll quality about them. For example, the question of how many volitions occur, especially in skilled action, is no more obscure than the question of how many movements occur (see Baier, 1971, p. 165 n.7; Rescher, 1970, pp. 252–3), or, as McCann (1974, p. 468 n. 20) notes, than how many actions occur. As they stand they are suspicious, for example, in the sense that because we may be puzzled about how to count movements we do not think that reason enough to deny their existence. The real difficulty with these questions, however, is not

[25] To chronicle their comeback, see Goldman, 1975, and Sellars, 1975.
[26] That they are actions was maintained by Prichard, 1949, and more recently by Hugh McCann, 1974.

that they are frivolous, but that they are the wrong place to begin the inquiry. Before we can heed Quine's dictum, 'No entity without identity' (1969, p. 23), we first need a theory of volition, and then can perhaps accept some counting criteria as a constraint on the theory.

To that end, it should be noted that the questions about counting, although not the place to begin, are underlain by a question about skilled action that should at the outset guide our inquiry. We know that most of our complex, skilled actions, like riding a bicycle, playing the piano, and tying our shoelaces, consist (because they are complex) of a series of movements. Yet each movement does not seem to have a separate volition. In fact, as has been noted in the literature, the mark of having certain skills is that the practitioner does not, indeed should not, attend to each movement in the way expected of a beginner. Instead, his 'volition,' if he has one, seems holistic. But if it is through volitions that his *actions* are voluntary, what of these *movements*? When a skilled pianist plays, are his *movements*, each of them, involuntary – to be relegated to the same status as his muscular contractions or the neurological events occurring in his brain?

Related to this question is another, equally important, issue with regard to volitions, for those who dredge them up, namely, how they are related to the bodily movements they control. Of course, there is, in my opinion, a less than helpful version of this question too, that occurred on the preceding page, namely, whether the volition is an action, and if so, is it caused by an infinite series of volitions? Some solutions seem merely verbal on their face, e.g., Sellars's, which appears to resolve the puzzle by simply calling them 'acts' instead of 'actions' (1975, p. 48), while others leave the aftertaste that both the answer and the question are verbal.[27] Far more helpful, I think, is the question indicated above: how are these volitions, whether they are themselves actions, related to the appropriate movements? Are they causes of the movements or are they the movements both (non-causal) 'components' of some hideous, two-headed, hybrid monster called 'action'? Either answer appears unsatisfactory. Volitions do not seem to be the first event in some

[27] See Harman's solution of making willing and/or intending self-referential in his 'Willing and intending' (forthcoming), and in 'Practical reasoning' (1976). Harman does admit that there are any number of solutions the choice of which may well be verbal. For other solutions, see McCann, 1974; Brand, 1979; and Chisholm, below p. 59.

causal chain which (at least in the case of basic action) terminates in movement, because they are temporally continuous with movement, and seem to control it through a complicated process of feedback.[28] In the case of simple actions, like moving one's finger, we experience the voluntary movement as a unity and as immediate – too much so to be accommodated to such Cartesian fragmentation. And in the case of a skilled series of movements, once again, it is difficult to believe that the holistic volition is causing each movement, since it does not even represent them in its 'propositional content.' Yet if the two were not causally related, being instead components of action, how would they be related?

The last difficulty has given rise to the problem as to what basic actions are themselves – a question that I have thus far ignored. Intuitively, a basic action is something we do directly, and not something we can do only by doing something else. Thus, moving one's finger seems to be basic in this sense; whereas squeezing the trigger, firing the gun, shooting J, killing J, and causing a panic are all things that we do non-basically. For we may be said to kill J, by shooting him, and ultimately by the basic act of moving our finger. But if we are not aware of our movements in complex skilled actions, are we performing each movement as a separate, basic action or only the whole series?

Moreover, consider Baier's example of a Gestalt lace-tier who can only show you his hand movements by actually tying his laces. And if the lace tying (rather than the movements) seems to be the focus of his attention or volition, etc., then lace tying appears to qualify as a basic action (1971, p. 166). So the question here is whether basic actions are simple or complex. But this prompts the more general question as to what may be taken as the relevant units of action (one movement, a sequence of movements), the importance of which question is necessary for better understanding the principles of their composition.

I.   Volition and intention

I want to argue that we shall be able to find our way through this thicket by a better understanding of what volitions are, and how they are distinguished from other things. With regard to the latter, we have said thus far that a volition is distinguished from an inten-

[28] This assumes, but only in part, that causation is not simultaneous. Cf. above, p. 25 n. 7.

tion (at the time of intending) in that it plays some executorial role with respect to what was intended, and, unlike what occurs at the time of intending, it is co-temporal with the movements it 'causes' or controls. We can make this a bit more precise by saying that a volition and an intention (what is intended at the time of intending) share in common some residual propositional content, but that the volition fills in this residue in more detail. We might even say that an intention (in the sense of what is intended) continues before the mind at the time action is to occur, but continues as the residual content nested in the more detailed content of the volition. My basic point in distinguishing between intention and volition is to demarcate clearly what goes on at the time of commitment and what goes on at the time of its execution. The terms 'intention' and 'volition' roughly demarcate these two tasks even though they share in common this residual semantic content.

II. Basic action and movement

Let us begin by considering this common content. This can best be done by taking the case of a virtuoso who has a holistic volition to play the piano, and by assuming that his holistic volition and his intention have the same propositional content. Our question, now, is how this volition is to be understood with respect to playing each note, but this really is an amalgam of at least two further questions: the question of whether each of these *movements* is an *action* as opposed to 'action' being relegated to the entire process, and the question as to whether each movement is *voluntary* when it does not prima facie satisfy the content of the holistic volition. In this case, there just is not a separate volition in the offing for each movement. These two questions have different, albeit related, answers.

Accordingly, I think it is important to distinguish action from movement. I want to understand action as being related to intention, and its ultimate simple units to be basic actions. But I would like to understand basic actions – at least some of them – to be composite with respect to movements. Sometimes smaller, and simpler, movements will be the simple units in relation to volition. Accordingly, we may say that the virtuoso pianist whose holistic volition governs the entire process, or at any rate large stretches of movements, performs a sequence of note-playing movements as a basic action. The reason is that the holistic volition includes the propositional content of his intention, inasmuch as he is playing the piano intentionally. To whatever extent the virtuoso forms an intention with a complex action-plan, his basic action will be its simple and ground floor level. For a beginner, however, the case will be different: he starts out forming an intention and a corresponding volition to play each note. In this case, each note is played as a basic action.

Now we have intimated that as the beginner becomes more accomplished he can incorporate larger stretches of note-playing into one basic action. In this case his basic action, though simple with respect to his intentional action, is composite with respect to his note-playing movements. The next hurdle is to explain how these movements are voluntary. There are two related ways to handle this. The first is to follow Goldman in distinguishing between the master holistic volition, which is the focal point of awareness, and the non-focal awareness which circumscribes that holistic volition (1975, pp. 74–5). In this we are relying on a well-founded psychological phenomenon that our perceptual field usually occurs as a figure against a ground. The 'ground' includes all the non-focal items of awareness, which, however peripheral and less likely to be stored in memory, are not entirely absent. They are not absent because information about them can be elicited by questioning. As Goldman suggests, it therefore seems likely that the skilled pianist's holistic volition really is the 'figure' in a larger 'volitional field' which includes his movements as peripheral elements. We can say, then, that these movements are voluntary in that they satisfy the propositional content of these non-focal items of the volitional field. Perhaps a phenomenological description of the difference between the expert and the amateur is that the expert need have only non-focal awareness of his sequence of movements, all of which is integrated by a master volition, while the amateur needs to form a separate, focal volition for each one of them.[29]

Against this it might be objected that the figure-ground analogy lets in too much, because it includes the non-focal awareness of many other things besides movements. We might reply, although we cannot defend it here without circularity, that there is a need to distinguish the volitional field from the larger perceptual field, so that peripheral mental contents to which we are referring are part of the volition. I believe this to be the case, but need not amplify it because there is at hand an easier way out of the difficulty.

[29] These points parallel the theories of Jane Martin, 1972, and Ripley, 1974.

We might, accordingly, say that each voluntary movement first occurred as a basic action, that is, as a movement that satisfied the content of the *focal* volition and intention, this being the first step in the learning process which enabled our crude basic actions to recede into the background of occurring as merely voluntary movements. This implies that the prior occurrence of a movement as a basic action is necessarily written into the history of its present status as a voluntary movement.

It might be useful to contrast this historical-genetic link between voluntary movement and basic action with a forward-looking position that alternatively links voluntary movement with its *potential* to *become* a basic action. This would take the form of saying that a movement is voluntary just in case it can be performed as a basic action if we want to, or tried to. But this would be too narrow and too wide. Too narrow because it would exclude as voluntary precisely many of the movements in the skilled complex actions that we have considered. It is, of course, likely that the pianist *can* play each note separately if he wanted to, but think of the Gestalt lace-tier. For the force of Baier's point is that he would have difficulty performing each movement separately, in isolation from the rest of the movements in the sequence. And, of course, if he could perform each movement only by going through the whole sequence, that would make it doubtful that he *has* the requisite *focal* volition and intention.

Certainly the proposal is also too wide because, for one thing, it would count as voluntary some of our present movements which do not seem to be so, and, for another, even some entities which are not even movements at all (let alone voluntary movements). These are things that occur only as parts or slices of movements. The former (non-voluntary movements) would involve such things as shifting in my chair while writing, or stroking my beard while thinking through a philosophical problem.[30] With respect to intentional action, these appear to be 'movements' only in the sense in which a man may move his leg while asleep. We seem either not to be aware of such movements at all or aware of them only as the ground in the larger perceptual field, not the volitional field. Less circularly, the historical-genetic link would correctly rule them out because they didn't first occur as basic actions in the learning process of the (skilled) basic actions I am *now* performing, e.g., writing.

We have said that the forward-looking link is too wide in another

[30] I am indebted to Timothy McCarthy for raising this issue with me.

49

respect in that it lets in slices of movements as well. Consider, for example, an activity like walking. Do our movements consist of taking whole steps or two half-steps? Certainly taking half-steps is something we *can* perform as a basic action. On the genetic account, however, they fail as current movements because they did not figure into the learning process as a basic action.

The above analysis suggests a parisitic relation between the identity conditions for a voluntary movement and those for basic action:

(A) Any physical event, or part thereof, *can* be a voluntary movement for S at t just in case it can occur as a basic action for S at t.

(B) Any physical event (or part) *is* a voluntary *movement* for S at t just in case

  (i) it occurs as a basic action for S at t

     or

  (ii) it occurs as a temporal part of a larger basic action of S at t

     and

  (iii) its first existence was that of a basic action of S's at $t-1$ that was part of the learning process of the larger basic action that S performs at t.

Items that can satisfy (A), but not (B), include non-voluntary movements at t, and certain slices of voluntary movements at t.

Although basic action may be larger than movement, it seems to be the smallest unit of an intentional action. For basic action is any movement or set thereof that satisfies the propositional content of the intention and of the focal volition. The smallest possible units with respect to a volition though are smaller, consisting of a movement which stands to the volition in either a focal or non-focal way.

III.   Causal relations

Regardless of whether volitions are focal or non-focal in relation to movement, we are still faced with the question of explaining how they operate on movements as a causal power. Before we search for this answer, however, a few clarifying remarks are in order. First, the question how they operate as a causal power is ambiguous, because it is not clear whether a philosophical or scientific answer is called for. My answer will involve both, although a scientific answer only in the barest outline. Second, there is a way of construing talk about 'causal powers of volitions' as that of a hopelessly trapped Cartesian in search for a pineal gland! I am unsure whether this interpretation can be sustained, largely because I never underestimate the ingenuity of identity theorists and other physicalists in trying to make such accounts of mental acts compatible with some underlying physicalism (see, e.g., Kenny, 1975, pp. 97–161; Danto, 1973, pp. 145–96). On the identity theory, all of the events I shall describe would *also* have physicalist (probably neurological) re-descriptions. In this sense the causal powers I shall attribute to volitions would be read as in the same spirit as that of recent materialists, like Davidson and Goldman, who trace a causal chain from desires and beliefs to bodily movements.

Where my position seems to rule out such identity theory maneuvers is in two places: one, which we have already discussed, is in the idea that commitment is a primitive relation, allowing for the *ability* to change one's mind, etc., which does appear to embrace a libertarian or contra-causal relation between intention and action. But, as indicated, there is a way that some physicalists have tried to construe roughly similar conceptions as compatible with identity theory re-descriptions (see, e.g., Kenny, 1975, pp. 97–161; Danto, 1973, pp. 145–96). It is beyond the scope of this book to evaluate such claims. All I wish to deny is that there is a covering law or causal relation which preserves my characterizations of the mental acts that I shall employ in this book. The same point applies, I think, to the second place where the identity theory seems ruled out – a place that will emerge from the subsequent discussion of the causal powers of volitions. It seems to involve ultimately a conception of agent, rather than event, causation, much like the position of Chisholm (1976b).

i. *Psychokinesis vs. the ideo-motor theory* In any case, let us begin our search for a plausible account of the causal power of volition on movement. I have suggested that a beard stroking could be a basic action, but wish to add that an ear waggling could not (at least in my repertoire). Neither could the movement of a distant physical object through psychokinesis. To say these cannot occur as a basic action is to say that they cannot satisfy the shared propositional content of a volition and an intention. But why not? Can I not form the intention

51

and volition to move a distant table by psychokinesis? It is interesting to note that in Prichard's (1949) theory of action there really is no difference in content between such an act of will and volition, and since he also claimed that forming volitions is the only thing that we 'do,' it is utterly a Cartesian mystery as to why the act of will to move my arm will usually result in my arm's moving, but not so in the case of willing the movement of a distant table. Others, like Danto and Ripley, have made the more parsimonious suggestion that only things we know we can do can be represented by the content of a volition (Danto, 1973, Ch. 5, pp. 116–44; Ripley, 1974, p. 145). This is on the right track but the arguments for it do not seem to rest on anything more than linguistic intuitions. Goldman, however, provides a much more solid basis for this view by citing James's ideo-motor theory (1975, p. 76), and the recent findings of cognitive psychologists.

According to James's theory, a person can never perform a movement voluntarily for the first time. Instead, once the movement occurs randomly it leaves a memory trace of itself in the form of an image that consists largely of kinaesthetic sensations. Thus James writes: 'We may consequently set it down as certain that, whether or not there be anything else in the mind at the moment we consciously will a certain act, a mental conception made of memory images of these sensations, defining which special act it is, must be there' (1890, Vol. 2, p. 487). Following Goldman it is helpful to label such a representation of sensory feedback a 'response image,' which is taken from such psychologists as Mowar, Anokhin, Adams, and Greenwald (Goldman, 1975, p. 146; and Greenwald, 1970).

ii.   *VIPs and MIPs* This makes clear, I think, that not any old 'act of will' can count as a volition, as on the Prichardian view, which perhaps takes it to be a strong wish accompanied by a high degree of concentration and perhaps mental effort. Instead, we are presented with a concept that makes the past sensation of actual movement imbue the content of the volition with a response image. The occurrence of such an image in an act of volition is not, of course, enough to guarantee that the volition will continue to have its causal power, but it would be well to focus first on cases in which it is causally efficacious and then see if there is an explanation at hand of the degenerate cases. Accordingly, for the causally efficacious cases I want to suggest that if we probe further into a response image, and what it is an image of, we shall find a clue as to its causal powers. Now, with respect to such powers we should *not* expect a one-to-one correspondence between a volition and a (voluntary) movement. That is, to take a simple example, when I 'will' the raising of my arm under the guise of an appropriate response image, I want to reject the view that the causal relation runs from the arm raising volition to the raising of the arm. For this tells against their nomic simultaneity and what we know about feedback processes. The picture instead is that with respect to causal power the simplest volition and the simplest movement are composed of sub-parts, which are the real terms in a causal relation. We can unearth these sub-parts by considering some data about feedback processes. Goldman, for example, cites studies according to which 'for visual feedback the interval for corrections of [a] hand movement aimed at a target is between 190–260 milliseconds. For proprioceptive [i.e., kinaesthetic] feedback, corrections may be made at intervals as short as 112–129 milliseconds' (Goldman, 1975, p. 73; and Pew, 1974). If these findings are true, they suggest that the causal mechanism takes place at a micro-level in units that fill the intervals between feedback corrections, i.e., in segments as short as 112–29 milliseconds!

Since there is not a name for such units, we shall have to invent one. Let us call these very important particles of volition VIPs and those of movement MIPs – acronyms respectively for 'volitional integrated particles' and 'movement integrated particles.' Thus the co-temporality between the 'simple' arm raising volition and the simple arm raising movement is a macro-level description of a micro-level rapid *succession* of causal connections between VIPs and MIPs and in feedback from these MIPs to the monitoring sensations of them. We know enough, I think, to describe this process more precisely. Under this conception, the first VIP sends out an efferent impulse through the nervous system, which very rapidly results in an MIP. The nerve ending attached to that particular limb immediately returns to signal back to the brain which results in a sensation known as afferent feedback. These are the kinds of sensations we get from the movement of muscles, joints, tendons, and in fact are the very sensations from which the original response image was formed. A successful volition, when a VIP causes an MIP, is confirmed by matching the afferent feedback sensations of the MIP with the response image associated with that VIP. Since that response image essentially is a memory trace of prior afferent feedback sensations, the confirmation of a successful VIP consists really of a match between the present afferent sensations and the memory of past afferent sensations of similar VIPs.

The feedback process is complicated by another factor which might help us later to explain the degenerate cases. The complication is that there is another kind of feedback in normal and abnormal cases known as 'efferent feedback' (Goldman, 1975, pp. 81–2; and Pew, 1974). This apparently is a sensation that results directly from monitoring the efferent (outgoing) impulse before it is confirmed by sensations of actual movement (afferent feedback). As I understand it, an efferent impulse (caused by a VIP) is *directly* monitored by a signal sent back to the cerebral cortex. The existence of such feedback has been confirmed in Lasley's experiments 'finding reportedly different perceptions of active movement of a patient's deafferented lower leg, and Taub and Berman's report of a new response acquisition by a deafferented monkey' (Goldman, 1975, pp. 81–2; Lasley, 1917; and Berman and Taub, 1968).

Now, whatever the scientific details, the philosophical case for micro-level causation (of roughly this kind) seems compelling. For how else can we account for the intuitive idea that volitions cause (at least under some description) bodily movements and yet are simultaneous with them (without accepting simultaneous causation)? And the theory moreover fits in nicely with the latest findings of psychology.

There is, however, a strong objection to this approach. To many it might seem that to resort to such micro-level explanations is already to have left the realm of volitions and to enter that of neurological events and the like. I am not sure this objection is correct. On the view I am suggesting, the 'response image of kinaesthetic sensations,' etc., is a Gestalt representation of *sensations* of the causal interaction between VIPs and MIPs, which *sensations* are at highly reduced levels of awareness, but awareness nonetheless.

The arguments for this, though highly tentative, seem both philosophical and scientific. Philosophically, if the ideo-motor theory is viable at all, we have to ask what the 'response image' is of, in the intentionality sense of 'of.' If it is of kinaesthetic sensations, then, at the very least, the Gestalt image is *of* something somewhat composite, leading us some distance, albeit with a good deal of the road (or garden path) left to travel to VIPs and MIPs. Moreover, that the

54

response image is a *memory representation* also suggests that this something it is a representation of must be itself intensional, which in the context confirms that we are dealing with a realm of consciousness. The constituents of the object of the image must be intensional because even if these sensations were identical with neurological signals, they are still represented in the response image under their mentalistic descriptions, not under their (alleged) neurological descriptions. The argument thus far provides some warrant for supposing that the referent of the Gestalt response image – the monitoring (afferent and efferent feedback) sensations of MIPs – is to some degree both composite and conscious. Now what about the Gestalt image itself, which at the outset looked like the content of volition in the macro sense? Are the VIPs of which *it* is composed also conscious (as the theory claims)? To answer this, let us go back for a moment to the monitoring sensations of movement. Assume that those sensations are also understood to be feedback, in which case the very concept of feedback (whatever one's theory) suggests that those sensations are playing a confirmational role to which one responds by making compensatory adjustments. Now would it not be very odd if the *confirmation* in this case were both conscious and composite, but that *that which it confirms* and which is a compensatory response to such confirmation were not equally conscious and composite? But the thing that is confirmed, etc., is the response image on the present theory; in which case the response image qua image is also conscious and composite. So we are thus led again in the direction of VIPs.

The scientific evidence seems to converge with this. The experiments conducted by cognitive and motivational psychologists are aimed at eliciting *sensory* awareness of minute feedback processes and of response images as part of the process that initiates the movements. The assumption behind such experiments is that although these occur in consciousness in a highly reduced form of non-focal awareness, their existence can be discovered by carefully contrived experiments and questions addressed to subjects. Such methods appear responsible for the discovery of *efferent feedback* (Goldman, 1975, pp. 81–2; Lasley, 1917; and Berman and Taub, 1968) – a kind of feedback which seems distinctively conscious because the neurological basis for the normal kind of afferent feedback was completely absent.

iii.   Degenerate cases What has been maintained thus far is that a volition is not any act of will but one that occurs under the guise of a response image, and that a study of such images might fetch us a sketch of the causal mechanism through which volition causes movement. We have also noted that a response image is possible only if the kind of movement that is willed did occur at least once in the past. But, of course, the volition under the image is not enough to guarantee that the volition will continue to be causally efficacious. The interesting cases are those in which a volition (i.e., one with an image) lasts as long as it usually does when it causes movement, but produces none. All that occurs in such cases is the belief that there was movement. Consider, for example, a famous experiment cited by James and Ripley:

If a patient who has lost sensation in one arm is asked to put the affected hand on top of his head while his eyes are closed, and is at the same time prevented from doing so, he will be very surprised, on opening his eyes, to find that the movement has not taken place. This, James says, is the rule rather than the exception in anaesthetic cases. Confirmation of this is also found in medical journals.   (Ripley, 1974, p. 144)

These experiments, and related ones about amputees reportedly willing and feeling the movement of phantom limbs, are puzzling because such cases can engender an awkwardly dualistic picture of volition – a picture in which both the volition (with the response image) and the 'confirming' feedback sensations occur in a world of their own, and have nothing to do with the actual occurrence of the movements which the agent thinks he is controlling. The volition would then appear to be causally connected, not to the movement, but only to the feedback *sensations* of movement, and in turn to the belief in the movement's occurrence. This must then be followed by the question as to whether this is not a better account of the normal 'causally efficacious' cases as well, first appearances to the contrary notwithstanding.

We can block the assimilation of normal cases to the degenerate by finding some neurological and/or conscious difference which sets off the degenerate cases. Accordingly, we might try out two hypotheses explaining why in degenerate cases the agent is tricked. The first, which is purely a neurological explanation, would suppose that the illusory movement *feels* exactly like the actual movement, while the second, not so purely neurological, would hold that the two movements feel only somewhat alike, but enough to fool the agent at the assumed reduced level of awareness. The first (the one which would suppose that both cases feel exactly alike) would have the VIPs stimulate the *afferent* nerves, not in the typical way by routing the impulses through MIPs which then stimulate the attached afferent nerves, but by routing the impulses directly to the afferent nerve track through the other end, viz., some place in the brain.[31] This process, needless to say, would be rather mysterious. But suppose that the illusory case only feels roughly like the actual case. We might then suppose that in the illusory case there is only efferent feedback taking place, whereby the efferent impulses are monitored before they terminate in a MIP, or in a process shortcircuiting that route, and that the agent confuses these efferent sensations with those which result when both kinds of feedback are present as in the normal case. Presumably this hypothesis can be tested by experiments of the kind that confirmed these processes in the first place.

iv.   *Agent causation and lunatic causal chains* The content of volitions that I have so far sketched enables them to serve two roles, corresponding to the macro and the micro world, and to forge the link between them. In their Gestalt representations, they are objects to which our intendings commit us and satisfy the content of these intendings. This is the world of intentions and actions, of conceiving plans and of doing what in the macro sense is necessary to carry them out. The ground floor through which the intention is carried out is the basic action, and the degree of match between the intending and the volition, and again between the volition and the action, takes place above a certain threshold of awareness.

But insofar as these Gestalt volitions exercise a causal power over our movements, through which we execute the intention, the Gestalt image becomes a composite of VIPs, occurring below the threshold of intentional awareness and discoverable by only the most indirect methods of experimentation.

Of course, how such a response image can be both a Gestalt and a composite, can be read as an extension – though no doubt in attenuated form – of the puzzle as to how the pianist's holistic volition can be an image of his discrete finger movements. Hardly 'conjunctive' of its parts in either case, the Gestalt admits of an analysis that has the

---

[31] I owe this suggestion to Michael Bradie.

macro as the 'figure' on the 'ground' of the micro. Another possibility is that the macro is 'supervenient' in some way on the micro, in a way analogous to Jaegwon Kim's conception of the mind as supervenient on the body (1979). This seems, no doubt, to be an area in need of more research.

At any rate, there is one last but important point to be made before leaving the subject of volitions. In this prolix discussion about the distinctive *content* of volitions, it would be easy enough to lose sight of the fact that on my conception they are also mental *acts* through which vehicle we exercise our agency. This is in contrast to James's view, which takes them to be certain kinds of *events*, without any further act of will. For James the occurrence of a response image, whether it is willed or not, is enough to set in motion the appropriate efferent impulses. Goldman, however, disagrees, taking the response image only to give rise to the feeling of acting voluntarily, without its actually being so. This occurs, for example, in the passenger seat of an automobile when certain stimuli elicit the involuntary movement of one's foot as if to apply the brake, but elicit it under the appropriate response image. This, he suggests, accounts for its 'feeling' voluntary in a way that twitches and reflexes do not; but, according to him it is not voluntary, because it was not caused by an appropriate desire and belief. This is a version of the causal theory of action which I have not discussed, but it seems in any case that his 'volitions' are going to be just as vulnerable to the lunatic causal chains as was seen in the case of intentions. In Davidson's example about the mountain climber, assume that everything is the same as before: that he formed the intention to loosen his grip, that the intention was caused by the onset of a belief and a desire, that the intention caused a 'volition,' and that the volition caused the appropriate movement of loosening his grip on the rope. But what is meant by the 'volition' as a link in the causal chain is that the intention caused the movement under the guise of a response image which is co-temporal with the movement. Now does this make any decisive difference? Is it now impossible that the intention 'unnerved him to make a movement that is still uncontrollable' and *involuntary*?[32] The answer seems to be no. Thus 'volition' as a content and a mere event is no less open to lunatic causal chains than any other mental event, and the causal link from intention (or desire) and volition just underscores the point. But on my view (whatever its

[32] See Michael Corrado (unpublished), which emphatically makes this point.

58

other difficulties) such counterexamples cannot arise. A volition is more than a mere content, more than an event characterizable as a response image. It is instead a willing of an action under the guise of a response image. The willing is a causal power of an *agent* as a separate act in the service of his commitments. As Chisholm indicated, the agent does not have to do (will) something else to bring about his willing (1976b, pp. 204–5).[33] Rather, the appropriate relation between an agent and his volition is in the idea of agent or imminent causation, which is taken to be a kind of causation irreducible to the more common event or transeunt causation. In the former conception, agents, or more generically, substances are the causes of things, while in the latter, it is events, or the changes the substances undergo, that do the causing. The chief obstacle to reducing agent causation to event causation is that when an agent is said to be the cause of his willing, there does not seem to be another event or set thereof that is its *sufficient* condition, whereas the notion of one event causing another event does (at least on a common analysis) imply that the first event is a sufficient condition for the second. Under agent causation, at the time the agent sets in motion and controls the causal mechanism that will execute his intentions and plans – the setting in motion and the control being the volition – he always has at that moment the power to change his mind, or as Chisholm would put it, the power of being able to do otherwise (1976b, pp. 200–7). This whole idea is a direct result of my claim that an act of intending to do something in the future does not causally determine, under any description that preserves it as a mental act, the act that is to execute it, and this because it is still up to the agent whether he will act as he so intended. Thus the act of intending, or any other mental event preceding the volition that starts – controls – the action, does not seem to function as a sufficient condition. It is beyond the scope of this book to develop the concept of agent causation beyond this.[34]

Let us return for a moment to commitment. If it is a primitive relation in connection with basic action, it will prove equally ineluctable for the concept of non-basic action, to which we must now turn.

[33] This, obviously, is an attempt to answer the infinite regress argument about volitions (see above, p. 44) which appears to presuppose the concept of event causation repudiated below.

[34] Although interested readers are referred to Chisholm's (1976b) work above, p. 59, and to his more thorough treatment of it in *Person and Object* (1976a).

3

The normative stratification of non-basic action

If the intention to perform a basic action commits one to a mandate or an imperative, what can be said about the intention to perform a non-basic action? Non-basic actions occur, we have said, when we successfully intend our basic action to achieve a significance beyond the bounds of our own body, to achieve that significance by embracing portions of the world as well. Such actions occur, for example, when we satisfy our intention, not only to move our finger, but to flip the switch or to turn on the light; they occur when we do such things as sign a check, cross a river, assert that it is raining, or end a war. One controversy in action theory is whether these verbs really name *actions* over and above the basic bodily movement they encompass. For we perform a non-basic 'action' ultimately by performing a basic one; we turn on the light by flipping the switch, and this, ultimately, by moving our finger against the switch. Thus, when we are *turning* on the light, are we *doing* anything more than moving our finger? We shall be able to take a position on this, as well as sharpen the distinction between basic and non-basic action, by again examining the concept of intention, this time in a non-basic context.

I. *The similitude theory*

Our quarry is this: if we perform the act of ψing intentionally by φing intentionally, where ψing is ostensibly the non-basic action and φing the basic one, what is the difference between φing intentionally by itself, and φing intentionally with the further intention that it constitute ψing? Many of the causal action theorists who have tackled this and related questions have thought that an answer in large measure can be extrapolated out of the received analysis of intentional basic action, expounded in Chapter 1. That conception characterized intentional basic action, not only to be caused by the intention, but to match the intention as well, the match consisting of the correspondence between the intention and the movements (at least in their Gestalt conception). It is then thought that intentional non-basic action consists of a similar match between the non-basic intention and the non-basic action. Since the non-basic action is related in a special way to the basic action (roughly in the by-relation), the theory implies that that relation must also be duplicated in the non-basic intention. Under this conception, to intend a non-basic act is to conceive of a plan as to how it will be brought about by the basic action; and in whatever way the non-basic act is related to the basic must also be duplicated in that action–plan. If all goes according to plan (as well as caused by it), then the non-basic act is intentional, otherwise it is not.

The basic thrust of this position is that an intentional non-basic action consists of (a) an intentional basic action, (b) a certain connection in the world (viz., the by-relation) between the basic action and the non-basic action, and (c) the cognition or awareness of this connection in the intention to perform the non-basic action. There is, however, a basic flaw or rather lacuna in this conception. Successful intentional non-basic action depends as much upon us as it does upon the world. For example, suppose that I intend to start my car this morning. Roughly speaking, I intend to do this by turning the key, and turning the key by moving my hand and wrist with key in hand. Now, I may *do* everything right, but still fail because of the condition of my car, the weather, and so on. On the other hand, the condition of the car may be perfect, the weather hospitable, but yet I may fail to start the car because it is *I* who fail. I may turn the key the wrong way, or not enough, or perhaps fail because I just do not really know how to start a car, or at any rate *this* car. In order to have successful intentional non-basic action, we need both the co-operation of the world *and* to *perform* or *contribute* as required. Now the problem with the similitude theory is that it does not indicate just what part is up to us and what part is up to the world. There are in fact here two areas of vagueness: for the part that depends upon us is both of a cognitive and a conative nature, each of which the theory sometimes leaves unspecified. The cognitive contribution requires of us some knowledge, background beliefs, etc., as to *how* the act of turning the key causes the car to start. The conative contribution requires of us not only that we perform the lower level act of turning the key (which is included in the standard notion of an action plan) but also that we do it in a certain *manner*.

That both of these are left seriously unspecified in the similitude theory can be shown as follows. Start with the cognitive contribution. In our example starting the car is the result of a causal process or mechanism that begins with turning the key. So intentionally starting the car should be such that the 'intention' mirror that causal mechanism; otherwise even though I may have 'done' all the right things in turning the key, I may have started the car only by dint of luck. But the question arises: how much do I need to *know* about that causal mechanism in order to intend to start the car (and if it starts, to be credited with an intentional act of car starting)? If my intention must duplicate fully that causal mechanism, then I cannot intend to start the car without a mechanic's knowledge of the internal combustion engine! This is absurd. Yet it seems that *some* understanding of the causal connection between key turning and car starting is needed to distinguish between intentional acts of car starting, and car starting by deviant causal chains. In not telling us how to make this distinction, the similitude theory does not say where our own cognitive contribution ends, as it were, and where the cooperative role the world begins.

The other area of vagueness, the conative one, can be exposed by fixing on our main question: what is the difference between intentionally turning the key in the ignition without the intention to start the car and intentionally doing it *with* the further intention to start the car? Now the similitude theory is silent on whether there is any difference in manner in (the lower act of) turning the key in each case. All that the theory implies is that in the latter case, key turning be done with the further intention that it generate starting the car, the intention, in turn, encompassing some further cognition (still unspecified) of the causal connection between key turning and car starting. And these are all the elements that the standard notion of an action plan consists in, viz., (unspecified) cognition of causal or other connections between events, together with a (type) description of the lower level act token that is to generate the higher level one (see, e.g. Goldman, 1970, pp. 41–4, 56–62, 75). These two elements are sometimes collapsed into the one notion of Goldman's known as 'level-generational processes' (Goldman, 1970, pp. 50–60).

We can readily see, however, that these two elements are not enough; more emphatically, that the lacuna about the manner of the lower action is just as egregious as the one about cognition. For suppose that the cognitive contribution were completely specified to a degree approaching the maximum. To return to the car starting case, ask yourself whether it is enough to have even a mechanic's knowledge of the internal combusion engine, and to know simply that (in order to start the car) you are to turn the key (in the ignition).

But suppose that this is a new model car, basically with the same engine design, but which requires that the key be turned, say, in a counter-clockwise direction. Obviously if you still turn the key in the normal, clockwise way, then all your theoretical knowledge and your action-plan will not enable you to start the car intentionally, which, of course, does not rule out the possibility of starting it anyway by a 'deviant causal chain' or more precisely by a deviant performance of the lower level act. And even in the ordinary case, if you turn the key in the right direction, but not quite enough, you will just normally succeed in turning on the accessories (unless, again, you are lucky).

The problem with the similitude theory, then, is that (a) it does not tell us how much background knowledge of causal or other level generational connections we are supposed to have, and (b) it does not specify what modifications of our lower level act (types), if any, are sometimes required in order to generate the higher order, but which are not required if we intend to perform those lower level acts themselves.

These lacunae are more than of just academic interest. For if we cannot get a clear conception of the part of successful intentional action that depends upon us (both cognitively and conatively), as distinguished from the part that depends upon the world, then we will not be able to tell when our non-basic intentions are satisfied intentionally and when they are satisfied by dint of a deviant causal chain. To take an example of Castaneda's (1979, pp. 254–5), if Francesca intends to kill Romeo by shooting him, does she have to intend to shoot him through the heart instead of the brain? And suppose she intends the one but gets the other; does she then fail to kill him intentionally? And to consider another example of his, does her action-plan have to include the intention to use her right index finger with which to squeeze the trigger? And if everything goes according to plan, except that she uses the wrong finger, does she fail to kill him intentionally? It would seem, then, that a better understanding of the division of labor between ourselves and the world would give us a handle on the limits of intentional non-basic actions as well as resolve other related issues.

II. Goldman on level-generation

The view that I should like to defend is that the part that 'depends upon us' in performing an intentional non-basic action can be specified by the theory I call the normative stratification of non-basic action. This theory is best regarded as a supplement to the similitude theory because both the cognitive and conative (manner) contributions can be understood as adverbial modifications on all the lower level act (types) which an action-plan might specify as necessary for generating the higher order act (types). I call them adverbial requirements because these modifications can be regarded as more specific recipes for intentionally producing the higher order act. The normative stratification theory shows how such requirements group themselves around the different strata in a recursive pattern which culminates in a rather special way in the basic action or movement. An adverbial requirement on basic action is something indeed whose fulfillment is up to us, for whether it is satisfied is as much within our *direct* control as the basic action itself. The essential point of this adverbial requirement is that although it modifies the basic action, it derives completely from the intention to perform the non-basic action. The best way to locate these adverbial requirements is within a larger structure reflecting the manner in which non-basic actions are built up out of basic ones. And the most systematic account of this available is Alvin Goldman's theory of level-generation (1970, pp. 20–85), which is his name for the 'by-relation' between higher order and lower order acts. To be sure, Goldman's theory has been the target of considerable controversy, largely because of the contentious metaphysical thesis to which he is committed.[1] I shall attempt to dodge most of those issues because I believe, although I cannot argue it here without taking the reader too far afield, that the theory of adverbial requirement can be accommodated to the rival metaphysical positions as well. As it stands, Goldman's account is the most thorough and provides the best background for introducing my own theory. In particular I shall be following his taxonomy of kinds of level-generation, or, in other words, kinds of by-relation.

As a brief introduction, recall that non-basic action is something that one does by doing something else: one turns on the light by flipping the switch, kills someone by shooting, and signals by

[1] Namely, that the higher order act is really a different act than the lower order one, that, for example, signaling is a different act from hand waving, and similarly killing from shooting. For critical discussions of this 'multiplier' position, see Thomson, 1970; Thalberg, 1977, pp. 85–130; Davis, 1979, pp. 27–41. For a defense of the rival position, see Anscombe, 1969, pp. 37–47; Davidson, 1969a, 1967, 1971; Bennett, 1973; Volrath, 1975; Grim, 1977, p. 221.

waving one's hands. Hence the 'by-relation.' There are initially two things that make the by-relation worthy of philosophical study. The first is that when we do one thing by doing something else, it is not like doing one thing *and then* doing something else. The latter involves clearly *two* acts, as when we mix the batter and then bake the cake. But when S kills J by shooting him, even though *death* may occur after the shooting, it is not the case that S shoots J *and then* kills him. For the killing began at least when the shooting began. But neither is it the case that S shot J *while* killing him, as, for example, when I drive a car while talking to a passenger. For although the killing began with the shooting, it lasts longer than the shooting (because it includes dying, but the shooting does not).

In both of the other cases (of temporal succession and simultaneity), it is pretty clear that there are two actions involved. But since both simultaneity and succession are ruled out in the by-relation, it is not obvious that two acts are designated. Is, for example, signaling so obviously a different act from hand waving? The idea that they may not be different is underscored by a third consideration: if I signal by waving my hand, what *more* do I have to *do* to signal except just wave my hand? If killing can be achieved by shooting, and this ultimately by moving a finger against a trigger (the basic action), what more does the killer have to *do* to kill other than move his finger?[2]

Goldman, however, advances several arguments to show that these are two acts.[3] The most important idea here for our purposes is in his theory of level-generation itself. According to his scheme, there are four kinds of level-generation: causal generation, conventional generation, simple generation, and augmentation generation (1970, p. 22).

---

[2] This argument was made famous by Donald Davidson, in the following passages adopted from a story from Hamlet:

> The queen moved her hand . . . thus causing the vial to empty into the king's ear . . . thus causing the poison to enter the body of the king . . . thus causing the king to die. . . . The queen moved her hand thus causing the death of the king. . . .
> Is it not absurd to suppose that, after the queen has moved her hand in such a way as to cause the king's death, any work remains for her to do or complete? She has done her work; it only remains for the poison to do its.   (1971, pp. 22ff, 21)

[3] The most famous is that they are two acts because they may admit of different causes and/or effects (1970, pp. 1–10). This argument is tangential to this chapter and in any case is adequately treated in the literature. See p. 64 n. 1.

i. Causal generation The examples cited about starting a car by turning the key, and killing by shooting are cases of causal generation. In the car starting case, begin with the basic action, the movement of the hand and wrist. In causal generation, this action causes another event, the rotation of the key, such that I can be credited with the higher order act, turning the key. This in turn causes another event, starting the car, which then allows me to be attributed with the still higher order act, starting the car. More generally, whenever I perform some basic act of ɸing such that ɸing causes another event *e*, I can be credited with the act of doing *e*.[4]

ii. Conventional generation This, the second type, is like causal generation except that the conditions that make it possible involve the existence of a convention instead of a causal relation. In the latter case my lower level act causes some other event, *e*, which makes possible the higher order attribution of doing or bringing about *e*. In the convention case there is a conventional connection between the lower level ɸing and the higher level ψing. Thus if I want my hand waving to count as signaling, I must have satisfied a convention in virtue of which hand waving counts as signaling.[5]

iii. Simple and augmentation generation A different kind of level-

---

[4] Goldman was the first to point out the difference between causation and causal generation (1970, pp. 23–4). If the latter were assimilated to the former, then it would be a case of one event following another, as when the cause occurs *and then* the effect occurs. But we have said that when shooting causally generates killing, it is not a case of the one following the other. The *causation* takes place not between the act of shooting and the act of killing but between the act of shooting and the event of the victim's dying. This causal relation in turn allows the act of shooting to *causally generate* the act of killing. Similarly when one *act* causes another *act*, as, for example, when the act of tickling oneself causes the act of laughing, it does not causally generate the other.

Goldman, however, overstated this point, when he claimed in his general characterization of level-generation that the lower order act is not a 'temporal part' of the higher act (1970, pp. 21–2, 35–7, 43, 45–6). What he meant was that we do not perform the lower order act and then perform the higher order act, but he is mistaken if he is implying that the two acts take roughly the same time. See above, p. 64, n. 1 and also Thomson, 1971; Thalberg, 1975; Bennett, 1973; Volrath, 1975; Grim, 1977; and McCann, 1974.

[5] This notion is closely akin to the concept of constitutive rules in John Searle, 1969, pp. 31–41, 50–3, 175–98, and John Rawls, 1955, in which, to use their terminology, a brute fact, say, moving a piece of wood is said to constitute an institutionalized fact, moving a chess piece. One of the main points of constitutive rules, according to Searle, is that they make it possible to create new forms of behavior, which, but for the constitutive rule, would not exist (1969, pp. 50–3).

generation occurs in the following examples: I cross a stream by jumping over it, tie the world record for mountain climbing by climbing Mt Everest, answer S's question by asserting that p, and hide from S by standing behind a tall hedge. This is really a miscellaneous class which Goldman labels 'simple generation' (1970, pp. 26–7), for the conditions under which the lower level acts generate the higher involve a variety of special circumstances and/or intentions. Other purposes, perhaps, would be better served by dividing this class still further; what they have in common is that they are non-causal and non-conventional. (Their lacking these is what inspired the name 'simple' generation.) Actually, though, Goldman does mark off a sub-class for special treatment to which he gives the name 'augmentation generation' (1970, pp. 28–30), because he claims it to be so common, but which many believe (including myself) to have special problems. This is a case in which although the lower level act simply generates the higher one, the lower is entailed by the higher – entailed by it either semantically, but more often by surface grammar. The former occurs when S stutters by speaking, the latter when S speaks loudly by speaking (although we shall note below the 'by' locution does not quite fit there).

This seems to be the least intuitive of the foregoing types – especially when the augmentation involves surface grammar. For it is not apparent that speaking loudly is a different *act* from speaking, and, as noted above, and by Goldman himself, it does not easily admit of the 'by' locution (1970, pp. 28–9). I do not speak loudly by speaking as much as through or in speaking.[6] Likewise, it is counterintuitive to suppose that I perform as many different acts as there are non-equivalent adverbs that truly apply. On the other hand, the augmentations of our actions in some cases seem to be important enough to consider them to have generated a different act. For example, playing the violin may meet with a range of responses from boredom to interest. But playing the violin like Yitzhok Pearlman is so utterly different as to constitute it a separate act. From the latter I may win a prize, earn a living, and achieve international eminence; from the former I do none of these.

[6] This point is inconclusive, however, in that the distinction between 'by' and 'in' was at least a tentative grammatical criterion for Austin's distinction between the illocutionary and perlocutionary acts, and yet both were genuinely different non-basic acts from the lower level, locutionary act from which they were level-generated. See Austin, 1965, pp. 120–31.

The problem of augmentation generation is a difficult one, but I believe, once again, that it can be resolved by the forthcoming theory of adverbial requirement. If I am right, then we shall be able to assess this without getting embroiled in the more abstruse metaphysical dispute which seems to surround this, e.g., act individuation and multiplication.[7]

III. The basic idea of normative stratification

From the foregoing examples we can give the notion of level-generation the following characterization: φing level-generates ψing, only under certain conditions.[8] The means that φing by itself is insufficient (either logically or causally) to level-generate ψing. Instead, the success of generation depends upon the satisfaction of *other* conditions. What are these conditions? Goldman's taxonomy of different kinds of level-generation is really a classificatory scheme of these conditions. In causal general it is causation. That is, if a lower level φing is causally to generate a ψing, and if ψing is the act of bringing about a certain event *e* (like killing's being the bringing about of death), then it must be the case that φing causes *e*. To say that causation is a condition for causal generation is to say that in order for φing to causally generate ψing, the act of φing must have actually been causally efficacious. Similarly, for conventional generation the condition is the existence of a convention; for in order for φing conventionally to generate ψing, it must be the case that my act of φing actually satisfies a convention in virtue of which φing counts as ψing. In simple and augmentation generation to conditions under which φing generates ψing are a miscellany of circumstances that are non-causal and non-conventional.

It must be noted that the conditions for successful level-generation say nothing yet about intentional level-generation. The aim of Goldman and others like him is rather to sketch a general theory of action and then derive from it as it were the theory of intentional action. That is why Goldman takes intentional level-generation to be something that can be superimposed on the more general theory. Accordingly, in order for an intentional act of φing to generate ψing intentionally, the intention to ψ must 'mirror'

[7] Some of the major articles were cited above, p. 64 n. 1. See also Thomson, 1977; Aune, 1977; and Danto, 1973.
[8] This is hardly intended as an analysis in the traditional sense. A fairly rigorous one is provided by Goldman, 1970, pp. 43–5, although he does not completely avoid the problem of circularity.

whatever conditions in the world allowed the φing simpliciter to generate the ψing simpliciter. And we have suggested that this similitude theory of intention is incomplete because, while it correctly recognizes that successful intentional action depends upon the world, it is fuzzy on the degree of contribution that also must be made by us.

We are now ready to see what additional work can be done by the theory of adverbial requirement.[9] This requirement, I have indicated, is normative and really attaches to all non-basic acts that are lower level with respect to a generated act. That is, any act that is lower level relative to a generated act admits of its own adverbial requirement. For this reason these requirements are part of a total conception of action which I have called the normative stratification of action. The special role of the requirement on basic action cannot be understood until this is developed.

Accordingly, the schema for the normative stratification can be set forth as follows. Consider any two acts (types) φing and ψing, such that φing is lower level than ψing and such that they are connected in the by-relation. It is important to consider here act types and not tokens, even though during the fact it is tokens that will stand in the by-relation to other tokens. The reason is that the flow of intentional action from intending is a flow of performing act tokens from thinking about act types. Intentional action is in some sense concurrent or retrospective, intending prospective. Thus consider the difference between intending to φ (as a type) and intending to φ with the further intention that it constitute ψing (as a type). The normative stratification theory holds that the further intention to ψ imposes on the lower level φing type an additional adverbial requirement of either of two sorts: as to the *manner* of the φing, and/or as to the requisite degree of knowledge of the level-generational conditions, where 'the requisite degree of knowledge' will emerge when the entire structure is laid bare. Again, it must be emphasized that this requirement is in addition to φing by itself and derives completely from φing with the further intention that it be level-generational. For this is how the scope commitment of intention is extended in non-basic actions.

Thus, consider again the case of starting a car by turning the key.

---

[9] First presented in my paper, 'Deviant causal chains' (1980b). A more extended treatment can be found in my 'Deviant causal chains and non-basic action' (forthcoming).

According to this theory, to turn the key with the further intention to start the car is to impose on the act of turning the key the additional requirement to do it in a certain way. What the certain way is can in general involve some complex questions, namely about the connection between level-generational knowledge and practical reasoning. But the short answer is that the certain way is the outcome of the practical reasoning concerning the way that turning the key causally generates starting the car. This reasoning will typically yield a modification of key turning that is a necessary condition for car starting, and in cases where the higher order act can be achieved by one among a set of alternative modifications, it obliges us to select one. In the present case we saw that not any old way of turning the key is necessary to start the car, but turning it in a certain direction, etc. In addition, there are cognitive requirements on key turning which are transmitted to it from our general understanding of the causal mechanisms. Applied to this lower act, these requirements take the form of knowledge of the circumstances under which it is to be performed, more generally, circumstances as to time and place. Thus I am to turn the key, for example, *when* I believe that the engine is in working order, that the gas tank is not empty, that the oil and other fluids are at sufficient levels – although these last ones may be more appropriate only for the further intention of *driving* the car a distance or safely. Again, just how much or how little we can know about these circumstances in order intentionally to generate the higher order action is a question that we shall shortly be in a position to tackle. For the moment, we must extend the analysis.

Accordingly, we have thus far taken the terms of 'lower order' and 'higher order' only in the relative sense, by which we mean that the same act that is lower order with respect to one thing, say, the act of key turning, can also be 'higher-order' with respect to something else, e.g., the basic action of moving the hand and wrist. But, if the concept of adverbial requirement really applies to *any* lower level act, even if that lower level act is higher level relative to the acts beneath it, then we must, we have said, extend the analysis to the whole structure of a multiple tiered hierarchy of intentions that terminate in some higher order act.[10]

To see this, suppose that starting the car is done with the still

[10] On Goldman's terminology this is a single, multi-leveled *act-tree* – so called because one basic action, represented as the trunk, can have many boughs, and these in turn many branches (see 1970, pp. 32–5).

higher intention, say, to test the ignition timing. Then the act of starting the car admits of *its* own adverbial requirement owing to the intention to test the ignition timing; and if 'testing the ignition timing' is done with a still higher order intention, then it, too, admits of a requirement owing to that higher intention. The process continues up the hierarchy of intentions, until the highest stratum is reached. The highest stratum, though, in turn does not get modified, but instead dominates all of those under it.

An examination of this domination or downward stratification will ultimately reveal the special pattern in which the requirements are formed, and this will have, among other things, some implications for the contours of the cognitive requirements. Consider the act of turning the key. Although it is lower order with respect to starting the car, it is not a basic action, but, as indicated, was generated out of the basic act, the movement of the hand and wrist. If turning the key is adverbially modified in the way we suggested (i.e., adverbially modified in order to start the car), this requirement is also transmitted to the basic action as well. The general picture is that any requirement attached to level n is transmitted recursively down to level $n-1$, and from level $n-1$ to $n-2$, and so on until the basic action, which bears the weight and cumulative effect of them all. This structure can be depicted in Figure 1. The shaded box represents the action simpliciter at the various levels; the unshaded box the adverbial requirements. Looking upward, the number of requirements at any level is at least one more than the level immediately above it. This is explained by the fact that a requirement at level n is derived only from the further intention that n generate an act at $n+1$. Looking downward, the structure is such that the intention to perform an act at level n does not impose an adverbial requirement at level n, but at level $n-1$, and to all the levels beneath it, stopping at the basic action, depicted as level 1.[11]

To take a different illustration, suppose that the starting of the engine causes the radio to play. If this is something I intended to happen in this way (that is, intended to turn on the radio by starting the car, without first turning the knob), then again, I must know or

[11] I am indebted to Nancy Cunningham-Butler for help in conceiving this graph. It should be interpreted to represent not the maximum number of adverbial requirements attached to any level of action, but the minimum number owing to the intention to level-generate higher orders of action. This obviously produces some complications in the case of augmentation generation, which I discuss below, pp. 78–82.

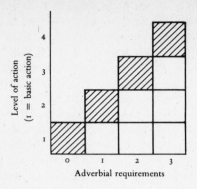

Figure 1

believe that I am to start the car *when* the radio knob is on the 'on' position, this being the adverbial requirement on starting the car. But this must get transmitted to a requirement on turning the key, and finally on moving my hand-wrist.

i.   The special normative role of basic action I now want to draw attention to the fact that the adverbial requirements from all the higher levels ultimately find themselves attached to the basic action. This is but a consequence of our intention to relate our bodily movement to the world through the mediation of non-basic action. For as the scope of our intentional actions reaches outward from our body to embrace increasingly larger portions of the world, it imposes, ultimately, on our bodily movements new constraints and new skills as to both the manner of the movements and as to cognition of the proper circumstances under which they are to be performed.

It seems that the normative role of basic action in this suggests some parameters for the limits of the cognitive requirement, that is, sets limits, maximal and minimal, on how much we can be expected to know about the level-generational processes that make intentional non-basic action possible. The reason for this, in broad outline, is that any knowledge that is necessary or sufficient for performing a non-basic action will ultimately have to transmit to the basic action at least an adverbial requirement as to time and place and more often an additional adverbial requirement as to manner.

72

ii. Maximal and minimal limits Let us now utilize this theory to determine for any possible item of knowledge *k* whether it *can* be included under a maximal specification of the cognitive requirement or whether it *must* be included under a minimal specification.

Start first with the question of *k*'s inclusion under the maximal specification. Consider as an example that you are intentionally firing a gun with the further intention that the bullet hit a target, and that, unlike other marksmen, you have a precise mathematical understanding of the bullet's trajectory. Does such an understanding imbue your action-plan, ostensibly at the cost of opening up new possibilities for deviant causal chains? The first question here is whether this knowledge transmits any requirement as to manner: does it, for example, offer any *special instructions* as to *how* you are to move your finger against the trigger, aim the gun, or so on? This, of course, all depends upon the trajectory. But it should be noted that if the knowledge did transmit a manner requirement, that would pre-empt in the affirmative the question of its inclusion in the action-plan. The assumption behind the pre-emption is that manner requirements are necessary to achieve the act under that specification, which implies that if you fail to move your body *in that manner*, then you either fail to achieve the act period, or fail to achieve it under that specification. And if you achieve it anyway via another specification or route, then that route is *ipso facto* a deviant causal chain. For if that alternative route were not a deviant causal chain relative to the specification, then its not being so would violate the assumption that the 'manner' modification is *necessarily* implied by the specification.

In any case, suppose that in the trajectory case there is no manner requirement in the offing. To be included in the action-plan, it must then transmit a cognitive requirement as to the time and place of the basic action. For example, the trajectory may require you to press your finger against the trigger (in the regular way) *when* the wind is blowing in a certain direction and velocity, or *where* your altitude is within a certain range. If the trajectory description transmits such requirements, then it gets admitted in your plan; if not, it is nugatory. It must be noted, though, that 'circumstances' as to time and place are relative to the agent (as well as to the specification). Two people might say they have the same plan but only one of them may have a keen enough sense or perhaps the scientific hardware to detect the differences in 'circumstances' modifying the basic action which the

73

specification requires. Thus only for the more sensitive agent is the specification integrated in the plan. If the less sensitive agent still satisfies the plan, to what can that be attributed other than to lady luck? So unless a given specification makes a difference in circumstances on basic action to the *agent*, it cannot determine whether he acts intentionally or by luck. This is nothing more than a demand that the details of an action-plan be practical.

When the mathematical description does not give the agent any special work to do, then it is perhaps a mere re-description of his ordinary background beliefs. Much scientific knowledge could be just that, for example the knowledge also that the travelling bullet will move molecules of air – to say nothing of smaller particles.

Let us turn to the question of k's inclusion in the minimal specification. A challenging example is offered by Lawrence Davis (1980, pp. 59–60). Suppose that Mary wishes to kill Jane, and believes that she can do so by pushing a certain button. Must her intention, as opposed to a mere wish, include as a minimum more than just button pushing and killing, which operates as a requirement on the button pushing? On its face this appears to be a case in which there is no requirement as to *manner*. Button pushing is not the kind of action that requires much dexterity. But that does not mean that her intention to kill Jane does not contain some cognitive requirement, viz., some background beliefs, k, about the nature of the causal connection between button pushing and death. Such background beliefs would focus on the *normal* and/or *sufficient* conditions obtaining in the world through which our intended movements achieve their causal efficacy.[12] As noted above, these beliefs would transmit to the

[12] Why do the *cognitive* adverbial requirements refer to the normal or *sufficient* conditions, but the requirements with regard to *manner* apply only to *necessary* conditions (see above, p. 73)? The reason seems to be that in the case of the latter, we can hardly learn how to perform a non-basic intentional action unless we learn what modifications of our basic movements are necessary to achieve this, or necessary to achieve it in a certain way. These modifications, together with the causal processes in the world, will be sufficient to generate the non-basic action.

But in the case of cognitive requirements there are all kinds of necessary, technical conditions which must obtain in order for the causal mechanism to be efficacious in the world, and yet a knowledge of each or even of many of these appears unreasonable and onerous: the failure to imbue one's intentions with academic physical theory hardly relegates one's normal intentions to the domain of luck or of miracles. The typical case need only refer to the normal conditions in the world that common sense requires. (No doubt the reference to normal conditions involves an element of convention and perhaps conceptual relativity.) These normal conditions, though, need not be sufficient, the standard of knowledge being set by convention. On the other hand, knowledge of sufficient, non-basic action the adverbial requirements as to time and place, to perform the lower level act when and where certain normal conditions for generation are believed to be satisfied. Thus if Mary *intends* to kill Jane by pushing a button, is she not required to push the button *when* she believes that the machine or whatever it is is plugged in, or turned on, or has its battery charged up? Is she not *also required* to push the button roughly *where* she believes Jane is? Must she not, for example, push the button when she believes Jane to be in the same room, the same building, the same city, or the same country?

Because our background beliefs about these normal conditions are so commonplace, we tend not to notice that they are there. But such an omission is not likely to be made by a developmental psychologist. For these background beliefs seem to be exactly what infants must acquire when they intend to exercise a causal power beyond their own bodies. They do not automatically find that they have this power in the way that they find that they can very early perform intentional *basic* actions. If they did, then non-basic action would be more like discovering a natural gift of psychokinesis, than discovering by trial and error the normal causal connections between one's body and other objects. It is precisely because the concept of an intention to perform a non-basic action is imbued with such normal level-generating conditions that, once the basic action is correctly performed, we can still distinguish between intentionally performing the non-basic action and performing it by a deviant causal chain.

Nevertheless, it might be objected that the minimum background beliefs need only involve something like an inductive warrant, rather than knowledge of the nature of the causal connection. If Mary's pushing the button is regularly followed by a person dying,

---

necessary, conditions in the world does seem to be required if we intend to accomplish an ordinary task in an unusual way.

The comments above about *normal* conditions raise still another problem. Notice that the general conundrum about the boundaries of deviant causal chain is sometimes referred to as the problem of defining the limits of causal *normalcy* (as distinguished from causality by a fluke). Now if we define causal *normalcy* in intentional action as involving cognition of the normal conditions for generating it out of our basic action, then there appears to be an element of circularity in the analysis. This is true, but it is not a vacuous or even a vicious circularity. For the analysis would show that causal normalcy (in intentional causal generation) is parasitic upon a different kind of normalcy involving the cognitive requirements that an agent can be expected to satisfy, and this normalcy may in turn be analyzed as relative to a conceptual scheme. (See my paper, 1980a, pp. 68, 69–70 n. 2.)

need she believe anything about batteries, electricity, etc.?

The difficulty with this conception can best be appreciated by switching examples. Suppose that you have repeatedly witnessed magicians waving their magic wands over a hat invariably being followed by a rabbit climbing out of it. If one of these magicians offers the wand to you, do you have enough on which to form the intention to make the rabbit appear? Suppose, just to strengthen the adversary case, that you actually try it a few times and succeed. We might imagine that the magician or his assistant is sitting behind a curtain pulling strings and levers to make the rabbit appear. And the story may be completed by having the man behind the curtain receive a signal when you wave the wand, either from the magician on the stage or electronically, thus completing the causal chain that began with your wand movements. You certainly have your inductive warrant, but did you make the rabbit appear intentionally or by luck? And what else can be required in the minimal specification of intention except some knowledge of the causal connection, as well as an inductive warrant?

IV. Adverbial requirements for varieties of level-generation

We must now determine briefly whether all of the varieties of level-generation admit of such a normative stratification. A cursory investigation should turn up some confirmation for the theory, but it will present some challenges as well. As for causal generation, we have already taken that up as an illustration of the theory. Let us, then, look at the other types.

i. *Conventional generation* This should be the most transparent confirmation of the theory, although it does not yet quite fit into our general plan of this book because conventional acts are social, whereas we are first trying to provide an account of non-social intentional action, out of which social acts will be constructed. Nevertheless, it will, perhaps, still be in order to indicate how the normative stratification generally applies, even if a full accounting for the *source* of the conventional adverbial requirement must await the later chapters. Accordingly, take as an example signaling by waving one's hand. It does seem clear that to intend that the act of hand waving *count* as signaling is to impose on the act of hand waving adverbial requirements as to manner, time, and place. To be credited with an intentional act of signaling, the convention must be known in virtue of which hand-waving counts as signaling, and to have this knowledge is to know *what* adverbial requirements are to be satisfied.

ii.   Simple generation In approaching this, it would be well to remind ourselves that in any form of level-generation the lower level act is insufficient to bring off the generation: it is also required that the world cooperate and that the agent do certain further things construed as modification of the lower level act. Now, what role does the 'world' play in simple generation? One might say simply that the right circumstances or relations have to exist in order for the generation to be possible. These, of course, can neither be causal nor conventional in nature, for the intention to perform an act via simple generation is not to attempt to exercise either a causal or a conventionally enabling power, but simply to commit oneself to bring it about that the lower level act achieve a certain significance that could not be achieved in other circumstances.

As for the part of simple generation that depends upon ourselves, it is more difficult to characterize this in the abstract. Instead let us consider a few challenging examples. Suppose that I perform the lower level act of asserting that p with the higher level intention to generate the act of answering S's question. Once again we shall note the paucity of any adverbial requirements on the lower level act as to manner. For we do not necessarily answer a person's question by making an assertion in a certain way. In fact, like one of the cases we discussed (see above, p. 74), the absence of a requirement as to manner might make it look to the casual observer that answering S's question just *is* asserting that p! (Compare the familiar argument: inflicting capital punishment just *is* murder, and so the executioner is no better than the criminal!) But if this position is wrong, what more does one have to *do* to answer S's question other than simply asssert that p? And the answer is that here, as elsewhere (see above, p. 74), the only adverbial requirement is of a cognitive kind, and these are the ones we tend to take the least notice of. Yet from the standpoint of developmental psychology, this kind of cognition should be no less significant than the kind required for causal generation. The cognitive requirement on the assertion would be something to the effect that one is to assert that p *when* and *where* one knows that the context that generates it to be an answer is present. This context would include the fact that S recently asked a question

77

and that the semantic and speech-act properties of the agent's assertion are such that it can count as an answer, and that the facts, as the agent believes it, are such that it is an answer.

Consider, next, a case that appears to be a counterexample to the theory of the normative stratification. Suppose that I intend that *playing* the piano generates the act of *practicing* the piano.[13] The question is, what adverbial requirements does the intention to *practice* impose on *playing*? Sometimes the requirements as to manner are quite apparent. If we hear someone playing scales, or playing the same passage over and over, then it is obvious how the playing is modified in the practicing. But sometimes there is not any difference in manner between playing and practicing, for sometimes one may want to practice the piano just by playing it in the ordinary way. Are there, then, any cognitive requirements in the offing? Again, there are cases in which *these* would be obvious. If I intend to *practice The Warsaw Concerto* in just the way I am to *play* it for a recital tomorrow, then practicing would consist of playing it in the ordinary way *before* the recital. That seems crucial, for notice that we do not *practice after* the concert. But this may seem too strong. Can I not just play the piano in order to practice it, period? If asked the difference, cannot the reply be that the latter consists of playing, plus the *intention* to practice? If so, we have a counterexample to the normative stratification of action, for we would have a case in which a lower level act could be performed with the intention to generate a higher level act without the interposition of an adverbial requirement.

But the simplicity of the above account is deceptive. Is not my intention to *practice* founded on the belief that I will be playing the piano some time again; and I intend to practice now so that I will play it better when I play it again, or at least no worse than I would had I not practiced now. This means that I just do not play, but play *before* I believe I will play it again, *and* when I believe that my present playing is likely to have some effect on my future playing. Notice that if I do not expect to play ever again or do not believe that my present playing will have any effect on my ability, I cannot be *practicing now*.

iii. *Augmentation generation* Let us finally turn to the most recalci-

[13] The example originally appeared in Goldman, 1970, p. 27, to illustrate simple generation.

trant class. Suppose that I am pulling a heavy wagon and now intend to pull it up a hill. Suppose further that I can do this without any help from others; I just pull it up the hill myself, by pulling it in a certain way, namely, by pulling on it harder than when I am just pulling it. So far so good. This seems to be a bona fide case of augmentation generation, for I can pull it up the hill only if there is something else I have to do to my pulling, namely pull on it harder. And the pulling on it harder is at least a partial description of the requirement. (Notice that the by-relation fits the φing as modified by the requirement, but not the φing itself. I pull it up the hill by pulling on it harder but not by pulling on it simpliciter.)

But what about pulling on it harder? Although this is a requirement on the pulling of it, is it also a new augmentationally generated, separate act from the pulling of it? If it were, it would have to give rise to a *further* adverbial requirement on the pulling of it. But what *else* do I have to do to my pulling on it (either conatively or cognitively) in order augmentationally to generate pulling on it harder? (We cannot mention – at least not yet – that we pull on it harder by gripping on it a certain way, while walking a certain way, for these are augmentations of lower level acts. Our thesis, though, commits us to the view that for any two acts, φing and ψing, in which φing generates ψing, the ψing gives rise to a further adverbial requirement on the φing. This is a different claim, also endorsed by the theory, that that requirement is transmitted recursively down through the lower levels, if there are any.) But this poses a serious dilemma. If there is nothing else I have to do to my *pulling* on the wagon in order to pull on it harder, and if pulling on it harder is itself a bona fide augmentationally generated act, then I can intentionally level-generate a new, higher order act without the interposition of an adverbial requirement – another ostensible counterexample to the theory. The other horn is even worse: if there is something else between the pulling and the pulling on it harder, and if this something is another augmentationally generated act, it would impose a further requirement which is then a new act between *it* and the original. But this would impose still another, and so on, *ad infinitum*.

This regress may have a familiar ring to the reader familiar with Danto's seminal papers on basic action, which in part inspired the following solution to it (1965, and 1963). The short answer is that although the pulling on it harder is a genuine *requirement* on the pulling of it, the act of pulling on it harder is not, contrary to grammatical appearance, a bona fide augmentationally generated act, distinct from the pulling simpliciter. More generally, not every adverbial requirement on a lower level act need involve the satisfaction of another, more primitive adverbial requirement. Instead, *pulling on it harder* essentially belongs to the act of *pulling on it*, having been level-generated by a corresponding requirement or modification on the preceding lower level act of gripping on the handle, namely, the gripping on the handle tensely. Likewise, although the gripping on it tensely is the requirement on the basic action of gripping on it, it too belongs to gripping as an essential aspect of the basic ability to grip simpliciter. Hence the modifications of basic actions that satisfy adverbial requirements attached to them are reflected in a corresponding modification of each of the higher, generated levels up the hierarchy of intentions. But these modifications do not mark any new augmentational generation from any of these levels.

The long answer involves referring to the theory of basic action that was outlined in Chapter 2. Recall that they were such as to allow under their umbrella complex movements of a kind that involved developed skills, but also gifts (in Danto's sense) (1965, 1963; see also 1973, Chapter 5). These movements, however, were counted as *one* basic action (roughly) if they were governed by one holistic volition and satisfied the propositional content of the corresponding intention. We must now note that basic actions are complex in another sense as well: the descriptions of them may take the grammatical form of augmentationally generated acts, but they are still performed as basic actions. By this I mean that the adverbial modifications of them are performed as basically – and as much as an extension of our normal basic abilities – as the simpliciter action that is so modified. Take, for example, raising one's arm and raising it quickly. For most people, raising one's arm quickly is as much a basic action and as much within one's direct control (involving VIPs and MIPs) as the raising of one's arm as such. Yet the grammatical structure makes it look as though it is augmentationally generated from raising the arm, which on my view implies that one has to do something *else* to one's act of arm raising in order to raise it quickly. But this, of course, is nonsense. One just raises it quickly, just as one can raise it slowly, these modifications occurring as part and parcel of one's direct control over an arm raising and as a manifestation of the basic act abilities in one's repertoire.

On this conception, bodily movement is the stuff of basic action, but when we intend to level-generate any variety of non-basic action we must learn to move our bodies in certain characteristic ways and under certain required contextual conditions. When we have such non-basic intentions, the way that we move our bodies satisfies adverbial requirements in my sense: as such, the relevant modifications of movement remain part of our basic actions because of our direct control over them; we do not bring them about by doing something else. (For this reason such requirements do not admit of any by-relation, but I remain hesitant to invest very much credence in this grammatical criterion.)

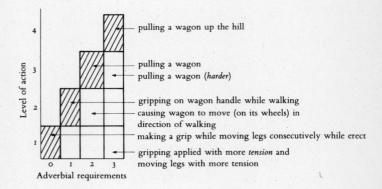

Figure 2

The next point is that this holistically modified basic action can be traced through all the various levels of the non-basic action so built up, but such modification will be traced up as a corresponding modification of each of the higher generated levels, and not as an augmentationally generated act, separate from each of these levels. Thus, referring to the graph in Figure 2, each adverbial requirement is on the same level as the action it modifies, whereas a genuinely augmentationally generated act is depicted at the next highest level. Returning to the wagon example, assume that I know how to pull a wagon (level 3) and would like to generate pulling it up a hill – augmentation generation (level 4). My level-generational knowledge informs me that this is done by pulling on it harder, which is an adverbial requirement on level 3. (It is precisely because of this requirement that we are justified in placing 'pulling the wagon up the

81

hill' at level 4.) But because I know that pulling on it harder is not itself an augmentationally generated act on the pulling on it simpliciter (both are depicted at level 3), I have to know how I am to generate pulling on it harder from the lower levels that generated pulling on it in the first place. We note from the graph that pulling on it was generated from level 2, which involved gripping on it while walking, and this in turn was generated from the basic acts (level 1) of making a grip, while also moving one's legs consecutively while erect.[14] What I need to know next is what modification of the gripping and the leg moving will generate pulling on it harder. Eventually I learn that it is gripping tensely or more tensely (and a similar modification on the leg movements). I then know (or assume that I know) all I need to know. I subsequently grip tensely, but I do this as a basic action in the context of the requisite level-generational knowledge.

From this we can see that the distinction between adverbial requirement and augmentation generation is what keeps the regress from getting started. It also avoids the other horn of the dilemma, viz., that higher order (augmentationally) generated acts would not place requirements on lower acts, because only genuine higher order acts, not spurious ones, involve the requirement. The difference between augmentation generation and adverbial requirement (really the difference between *any* higher order act and adverbial requirement) can be sketched along the lines indicated (see above p. 80). While the performance of the higher act involves, in part, the satisfaction of conditions in the world, outside my own body, and hence not within my direct or complete control, the satisfaction of requirements does depend only upon my body and is as much within my control as any basic action. Assuming that my gripping has already simply and causally generated pulling, I need only grip more tensely (and walk in a certain way) in order to generate pulling *harder*. But in order to generate pulling the wagon up the hill, I need to do all of these things, plus depend upon being in this relation to the hill.

V. *Intention and normative stratification*

If the thesis of stratification is correct then the matching theory of intentional non-basic action involved in the causal theory and alluded to earlier (see above, p. 60) is in need of supplementation. This is not to deny that intentional non-basic action is action level-generated

---

[14] So there are really *two* basic actions at the bottom of this: making a grip while moving one's legs, etc.

according to plan. It is rather to suggest that as we intend to bring a basic action under an increasing number of higher level acts, under, perhaps, act trees increasingly multi-leveled, our very planning, intending itself, imposes on the basic act a litany of requirements. These requirements will correspondingly increase in number and sometimes in the degree of dexterity of the movements that must satisfy them. Thus, sometimes moving our body in these various ways and circumstances is a fairly easy task, sometimes a delicate balance between too little and too much, as in a difficult golf putt, and sometimes – however much it may be up to us – is an achievement to be had only by a lifetime of continuous practice. But as we make the scope of our intentional actions reach outward from our body to embrace an ever-increasing portion of the world, we weave around ourselves a web of adverbial requirements. It is a web, though, of our own making, or rather intending. Its source lies in our intentions, its prescriptive force in requirement, and its bond in commitment.

4

Vows: the bridge between solitary and social acts

In the previous chapter, it was argued that the intention to perform non-basic actions committed us to new mandates beyond those involved in basic action. These amounted, ultimately, to further constraints on the way we are to move our bodies, and this because of our further intention to relate our bodies to the world through non-basic action. Non-basic action, then, enlarges the mandate in *scope*, though not in *strength*. However many adverbial requirements may be attached to our (basic) movements, these requirements amount to no more stringent a commitment than that found in basic action. In the present chapter, however, we want to consider how it is possible to extend the mandate along the dimension of *strength*. As we shall see, these two dimensions, scope and strength, work together to provide all of the raw materials for the possibility of social acts, and with them the existence of moral obligation.

I. *The strength of the commitment*

Bearing in mind that our focus presently is still on solitary, non-cooperative, intentional action – the 'state of nature' – we must ask whether it really is possible for our intentions to give rise to a stronger commitment than was sketched in Chapter 2. Let us review the conclusions that were reached therein. We said that an ordinary act of intending was the most primitive kind of commitment on the part of the agent – a commitment of an essentially normative kind which on the one hand bound him later to exercise his volition to effect the appropriate bodily movements at the appropriate time and in the right circumstances (the time and circumstances being essential for non-basic action). It was argued that because intention was a normative *commitment*, the failure to effect such bodily changes can be considered a prima facie mistake in *performance*, instead of the failure reflecting a previous mistake in intention. On the other hand, this 'commitment' would appear to be meaningless if it did not *also* rule out changing the intention in some way. The thought was that

84

such prohibited changes are limited only to *akrasia*, which we construe as an intentional mistake in performance. As for other kinds of changes in intentions, these were perfectly permissible, in fact even desirable, in that they were merely attempts at correcting what look like mistakes in the original intention.

It seems, then, that if it is possible in purely solitary intentional action to buttress the mandate along the dimension of strength, it must be possible to commit ourselves, in some act that resembles intending, not to change our mind in the way allowed for in ordinary intending. This would mean that there is some special kind of intending that prohibits or at least limits the changing of our minds even for reasons that we think *would correct a mistake in our intention*! What we would be doing is committing ourselves not to change our mind even if it later turned out that we were wrong to have made the commitment in the first place![1]

II.   Vows and promises

What, then, can such a mental act be like? I want to suggest that it is of the nature of a vow. Vows seem particularly apposite for a variety of reasons. First, a vow intuitively creates a stronger commitment than a mere intention. In this respect vows seem like promises (and in fact have often been confused with them). But vows differ from promises and serve our purposes much better in that, unlike promises, *they need not be essentially social acts*. As indicated in Chapter 1, vows differ from promises in the crucial respect that they do not constitute the undertaking of an obligation to someone else, who then enjoys the power of releasing the vower from his obligation. Vows, on the contrary, are not obligations to anybody; there is no 'vowee' as there is a promisee, although vows can, of course, be communicated to others and may have others as beneficiaries, as is typical of promises. Instead, the nature of vows is that of a self-imposed commitment to do something, which creates a right on the part of nobody.

---

[1] We must be careful not to read the prohibition on changing our mind as so ironclad as to allow for no escape clauses, just as we must not be fanatical later about promises. A more reasonable reading is that we are placing certain limits on the changing of our mind which are otherwise allowed in the case of intending. The force of the commitment is that it still allows escape clauses, but yet is stronger than intending. This is a problem most often discussed in terms of promising and prima facie obligation, which I tackled in my 'Practical inference, necessity, and defeasibility,' 1983.

The difference between vows and promises can be illustrated in the case of a marriage ceremony. Notice how the nature of the commitment differs depending upon whether the marriage ceremony is a mutual exchange of vows (as it is often so characterized) or a mutual exchange of promises. An old-fashioned view of marriage, which takes dim view of divorce for reasons of mutual consent, would be sustained on *this* point if the commitment were that of a mutual exchange of vows. For as we have said, this would confer no power on each partner to release the other; there simply would be no waivable right on the part of each to demand continued fidelity. A more contemporary view, which does sanction divorce for reasons of mutual consent, regards the commitment as that of a mutual exchange of promises – and some social thinkers have even promoted the idea of an explicit contract.[2]

There is another sort of example that is elucidated by the distinction in question – the case of the so-called death-bed promise. This is a promise that is given to a man on his death-bed, typically to look after his children, with the mutual understanding that the promise can be kept only after the promisee is likely to be dead. Despite the perennial fascination this case has held for philosophers, I think we would do well to characterize it to be a death-bed vow rather than a promise.[3] For the 'promisee' is not expected to have the power to release the 'promiser' at the time of performance, because, again, he most probably will be dead. To suppose that one can nevertheless undertake an obligation *to* someone who is not expected to enjoy the power of release is not a little fanciful. Why not simply regard the dying man as the beneficiary of the act of *communicating* the vow, as

[2] Haskell Fain makes a similar point about the interpretation of treaties. Accordingly, he claims, if treaties were exchanges of vows, then the non-performance on the part of one country could not release the other from its obligations, whereas it would supposedly release the other country if it were a promise. But this point misfires. What Fain has confused, I think, is the non-performance of the one party voiding the obligation of the other and the power of the other not to demand, for whatever reason, the obligatory performance of the other as in waiving his right. Vows and promises alike can be such that their obligations are *conditional* upon the performance of the other party. Although a vow would not give the other party the power of release, it can render his non-performance such as automatically to void or fail to bring into existence the obligation of the first party. (See Fain, 1978.)

[3] I myself have been guilty of this mistake in my article, 'Hare's golden-rule argument,' 1974. The more general confusion of promises and vows underpins my paper, 'The primacy of promising,' 1976b. Melden's recent treatment of the death-bed 'promise' would have saved him from needless embarrassment had he simply made the distinction indicated here. (See 1977, pp. 48–52, 147.)

distinguished from the children, who would be the beneficiaries of the vow itself?

Concerning the nature of vows, it is important to emphasize that although they can be communicated in language, they need not be (unlike promises which do have to be communicated). They thus do not necessarily give rise to expectations on the part of others. Hence, if we are to make sense of vows intrinsically, we cannot appeal to these and other social dimensions that are often closely associated with promises. Because vows are not inherently social acts, and seem in the above sense logically prior to language and convention, some have characterized the Hobbesian state of nature as one in which only vows, not promises, are possible (cf. Fain, 1978, pp. 345–6) (ignoring Hobbes's admonition that without the sword, promises are but words (1958, Part I, pp. 115, 119–20); on this interpretation it would *not* be the case that without the sword, vows are just intentions).

Vows, then, provide the most intuitive link between solitary intention and social acts. Once mankind has reached the rung on the evolutionary ladder in which vows are possible *in* a state of nature, he will provide therein the instrument for getting himself out of a state of nature. As I shall argue in the next chapter, social acts proper presuppose promising, but promising is parasitic upon vowing, in the way that vowing, as I shall argue presently, is upon intending. If I am right, then each level of the architectonic is unintelligible without the more primitive, adjacent, lower level.

III. *Vowing, intending, and deciding*

Our task, then, in this chapter is to characterize the way in which vows are built up out of intentions, with the upshot that the vows that result will carry with them the desired degree of commitment. As indicated, this amounts to finding a way in which we can commit ourselves, in a mental act involving intending, to limit changing our mind, even if we think of the change as correcting a mistake in the intention. We can begin to make some headway if we can discover a process, involving practical reason broadly conceived, which will have as its conclusion not only an ordinary intention, but also a second order intention not to change that first order intention – even if it may prove faulty. And this, I think, can be made perfectly intelligible if we first derive *deciding* from intending, and then vowing from deciding. In doing so, we shall be following closely Raz's theory of exclusionary reasons (1975b, pp. 35–48) (although we shall come to see that 'exclusionary intentions' will better serve our purposes). This also obviously dovetails with Harman's two level analysis which he suggested for simple intentions (discussed above, pp. 40–2, see also Harman, 1976, 1980a, and 1980b). However, some differences from both of these views will be noted.

Concerning the relation between intending and deciding, it can be seen that although a decision is a kind of intention, an intention need not be a decision. For a decision is an intention that was arrived at by some process of deliberation between alternatives.[4] Making a decision, whether or not it is logically implied or rationally warranted by the preceding deliberation (as in some Bayesian fashion), is (a) forming of an intention to act, and (b) resolving to terminate deliberation. I say 'resolving to terminate deliberation' because, obviously, one may later reconsider one's decision or 'reopen inquiry,' without defeating the attribution that one had earlier made a decision. What seems to have made it a *decision* was the *intention* at t_i not to reconsider (or to place limits on reconsidering) it at t_j. It is for this reason that I take this resolve to be an intention that pertains to future deliberation, just as the first order intention pertains to action. This seems to make that resolve a second order intention not to change the primary intention.

This follows Raz except that, as indicated, he prefers to make the point in the idiom of 'reasons for action.' Accordingly, an intention is something like 'a reason for action,' and the resolve not to continue deliberating is a second level exclusionary reason, i.e., a *reason* not to give consideration to any subsequent first level reasons for (or against) so acting. Thus he writes: '[An intention] is always (unless based on a decision) open to competing claims of other reasons. [But] to decide what to do is to rule out such competition or at least to limit it' (1975b, p. 67).

This fits the account offered in Chapter 2 rather well. For it was envisaged there that ordinary intending did allow for what Raz is calling competing reasons, and which I took to be reasons which would reveal oversights in the original intention. My difference with Raz here is one of style and emphasis rather than substance. For

[4] It must be noted that 'deliberation' is a somewhat idealized term for some decisions; all that seems to be required is that the intention in question be the product of some 'consideration' of at least one alternative, even if 'consideration' may have only amounted to having it before one's mind, before opting for one among the set. Even this minimal sense is not, as we shall see, implied in a vow as such.

I believe that the concept of an exclusionary intention captures better the idea that a decision is a second level *commitment* than does the notion that an intention is a second level exclusionary reason (although it can hardly be denied that both kinds of intentions function as reasons).

It would appear to the casual reader that this two level analysis is exactly the kind of thing that Harman has in mind in his 'methodological conservatism,' (see above, Chapter 2, pp. 40–2). But this is not so. In fact the proverbial shoe is on the other foot, because he has suggested that my conception of *decisions* is too strong[5] – the very charge I leveled against his conception of *intentions*!

Thus he claims that when one fully accepts something (his term covering both practical and theoretical decisions) one does, of course, terminate further inquiry unless there is a special reason to reopen it, which means that one is not to reopen it without a special reason for doing so. But this doesn't imply that one *intends* not to reopen it without a special reason, etc. This is too artificial and dogmatic. Too artificial because, for example, when I close the door, it may be that I am not to reopen it without a special reason, but it is doubtful that I have a further intention not to reopen it in the absence of a special reason. Well, whence derives the thought that 'I should not reopen it . . .'? The answer I suppose is that intending to close inquiry (methodological conservatism) implies that I should not reopen it, whether I intend to or not. 'Intending not to reopen it . . .' is also too dogmatic because the *intention* not to reopen inquiry without a special reason is an *intention* not to consider possibly defeating evidence, which is certainly more dogmatic than as a matter of fact not considering further evidence, perhaps, by turning one's attention to other things.

If I have Harman's argument right, I find it unpersuasive. It seems to me that while closing inquiry (without a special reason, etc.) does entail not reopening it (without a special reason), the argument denies that intending the one *entails* intending the other. The missing premise – as far as I can tell – is that intending is open under implication – a point I have repeatedly endorsed myself. But that principle cannot be used to block the transmission of intention in the above case. Propositional attitudes are generally open under implication either because one might not be aware of the implication or, being

---

[5] In comments and conversations about this section.

aware, one might refuse out of *akrasia* to take the appropriate attitude towards them (see Goldman, unpublished). Neither of these rifts in transmission is appropriate for the above. *Psychologically*, how could I intend to close inquiry without *being aware* that I am intending not to reopen it, or how could I intend the one, but waffle out of *akrasia* at intending the other? All intending is, logically and psychologically, doubly temporally indexed so that when I intend at t_i to close inquiry, *my* concept of closing inquiry necessarily is indexed to include t_j.

Note that as a fallback measure, even if the argument above fails, it would at least follow that intending to close inquiry *commits* one not to reopen it, because commitment is not open under implication (see below, Chapter 6, pp. 149–50). So at the very least, a decision would be a second level exclusionary commitment, which, I think, is all that is necessary to support the argument of this chapter. I shall, however, refer to decisions and vows as exclusionary intentions.

i.   The epistemic rationality of exclusionary intentions We have said that the second order intention which is the distinctive mark of a decision has a connection with deliberating or inquiry – at least the consideration of alternatives – which is far from accidental. For one thing, this suggests that the ability to make decisions must have come later in our evolutionary history than the ability to form intentions, the former coinciding with the development of the capacity to carry on deliberation. For another, the connection with deliberation does mitigate somewhat the prima facie irrationality connected with exclusionary intentions. The irrationality seems to surface at the point where these intentions commit the agent to exclude *in advance* any consideration (or to exclude full consideration) of further reasons that may seriously bear on the proposed action, even reasons that may well warrant a contrary action!

But if such exclusionary intentions grow out of deliberation, then they can, in varying degrees, be *justified* by that deliberation. Moreover, assuming a certain conception of justification described below, we may say that a decision that is so justified is *less likely* to be mistaken when acted upon than one that is not. The conception of justification being presupposed is the practical analogue of the reliabilist position in epistemology, whereby there is some direct relation between the justification of a belief and its truth, the connection being that the more justified the belief, the more likely it will turn out to be true – at least in the long run.[6] And this in turn implies that a justified decision (in this reliabilist sense) is one which makes it less likely that we will be discounting a reason that may later prove defeating.

But even if this is all correct, does it not just underscore the charge of irrationality? For the reliabilist conception entitles one to say at most that a justified decision is less likely to rule out future consideration of a defeating reason, not that it is never likely to rule it out. And when that occurs, what then? Isn't it still irrational? *Why* should we *ever* put ourselves in such an untenable position?

The force of this objection brings out just how different a decision is from an ordinary first order intention or a belief.[7] As an ordinary intention, the decision is like a belief (although we shall note a difference below) in that it can be justified at the time it was formed by deliberation or evidence, but as a decision it *also* commits one to the further act of not deliberating any further (or to restricting such deliberation). And this is what appears so irrational, as Harman already intimated. It is that, unlike beliefs and ordinary intentions, decisions necessarily go beyond their epistemic justification, and are at bottom incompatible with the spirit of openness and free inquiry.[8]

This would be a fault grievous enough, but there is even more askew. The case against decisions as exclusionary intentions is reinforced (if that is necessary) by noting that a decision also implies as we have said, a first order intention to act, and this importantly distinguishes intending from believing.[9] The distinction is that while we may assume that both intentions and beliefs may be fully justified at the time they are formed, an intention commits one to act, and once so acted upon, is relatively irrevocable. In contrast, a belief, however fully justified, is always open in principle to revision, viz., when disconfirmed or proven false. However, actions (to which intentions commit us) are not 'revisable' in the same way: once

---

[6] See Goldman, 1979, and 1980; and Armstrong, 1973. This doctrine is opposed to that of Chisholm, who denies any direct connection between such epistemic notions as 'justification,' 'confirmation,' and even 'probability' on the one hand and truth on the other (see his 'Transcendent Evidence' (1979) and cf. Keynes, 1952). This is hardly the place to defend the reliabilist conception against the Chisholmian one, although I am doubtful that the latter is even a coherent conception. In any case, we may take the reliabilist conception as an assumption relative to my argument above.

[7] At least a conception of belief unconnected with methodological relativism.

[8] Cf. Chisholm on 'the right to be sure', 1977, pp. 116–18.

[9] Even the conception of believing on methodological conservatism.

done, they cannot be undone. The most we can expect is compensation, contrition, or even liability to punishment, but none of these, of course, is tantamount to revision.

These considerations demonstrate that decisions and even intentions do not admit of epistemic justification in a way servicably like that of beliefs. They differ from beliefs in that they both go beyond the evidence. Decisions do because they involve the further commitment to discount possibly defeating reasons, and intentions (first order) do because they involve a commitment to something (namely action) which is not even in principle revisable by such reasons.

ii. Practical rationality Such obstacles to decisions as exclusionary intentions need not, however, be taken as insuperable. Instead, they can be removed, in my view, by noting that the conception of rationality at issue may be appropriate to our role as knowing subjects, but at bottom it is incompatible with our *other* role as *agents*, incompatible with our *conative*, as opposed to our *cognitive*, nature. In our cognitive role, it may or may not be appropriate never to resolve the termination of further inquiry depending upon, again, the endorsement of methodological conservatism. Not resolving to terminate inquiry may insure, as much as humanly possible, the avoidance of error. But with respect to our other role as agents, such a drastic policy would produce a palpable state of paralysis. For if the policy tells us that it is wrong to *commit* oneself to something which may irrevocably prove mistaken, then further deliberation should never be terminated or even restricted. The result, however, is that intentional action, which can only be the outcome of such termination (once deliberation has started), would be postponed forever. We cannot, therefore, accept such a standard of rationality and also accept the possibility of *acting* as rational agents.

Is there, then, a conception of rationality that is appropriate to this role? If there is, it might be one which derives from the practical demands of agency instead of the epistemic concept of evidence (Firth, 1978). Certainly, that deliberation be terminated or restricted at *some* point can already be justified from the things we have noted about agency. But we can do much better than this. We can offer a schema that would justify stopping deliberation at t_i rather than t_j. It would be a justification of a 'utilitarian' or 'cost-benefit' kind, according to which deliberation should stop at the point where the cost of pursuing it further, gathering more information, etc., would exceed the expected utility of anything new that would be discovered.

If these points are sound, we may say that, for one thing, rationality is not incompatible with the concept of exclusionary intention – i.e., once our role as agents as well as knowers is recognized – and for another thing, a suitably practical concept of rationality can offer guidance in the prudent deployment of this intention. Yet it should also be recognized that an exclusionary intention serves the same function whether it was formed rationally or not. For even a silly decision is one with a second order commitment not to change a possibly mistaken first order intention. This is no more revolutionary than saying that a promise that should not have been made still creates an obligation. (In this sense, the doctrine defended in this chapter parts company with 'utilitarianism' – or at least with the 'act' variety.) The point is that it is precisely because this second order commitment is so much stronger than an ordinary (first order) intention that it ought to be made with care.

We are now in a position to consider the relation between decisions and vows. It would simplify matters if we could identify them, as Raz comes close to doing (1975b, p. 70), but I don't think that will quite do. My suggestion rather is that a vow is an exclusionary intention that does not, like a decision, imply that it was necessarily the product of deliberation.[10] I would thus want to classify all decisions as vows (because of the exclusionary intention), but not all vows as decisions. In fact when both elements are present, as in a decision, calling it a decision merely emphasizes the backward-looking aspect of its having been the product of deliberation, whereas characterizing it as a vow underscores the forward-looking aspect of the exclusionary intention.

Accordingly, a vow that is not a decision is the forming of an exclusionary intention without even having 'deliberated' in the minimal sense, i.e., without even having considered an actual alternative. All that need be before one's mind in an act of vowing is the *concept* of an alternative, for that, after all, is what one in the act of vowing intends to exclude. The *concept* of an alternative is, of course, different from any particular alternative, even though a vow is a commitment which, being closed under implication (see above, Chapter 1, p. 15 and n. 13, and below, Chapter 6, pp. 149–50, may

---

[10] Recall that 'deliberation' is an idealized term for what might minimally be the mere awareness of alternatives. See above, p. 88 n. 4.

later commit one to exclude some particular alternative. But the commitment's being closed under implication no more requires awareness of that alternative at the time of vowing than does the act of believing require awareness of all the other beliefs that may be implied at the time of believing. We shall discuss this complicated matter more fully in Chaper 6 below, pp. 149–50; 156–63, in connection with derived obligation. As a caveat we should note, however, that nothing much turns on whether vows and decisions have precisely the relation sketched herein or whether they are identical. The essential idea is that both involve the concept of an exclusionary intention.

IV.   *The scope of the exclusion*

However, the concept of an exclusionary intention, especially when it is encased in a vow, raises still another question. If the exclusion on changing the intention is not ironclad as we have said, then some such changes *are* allowed. Which ones? What are the boundaries of the exclusion and whence do they derive? This is especially puzzling in a vow because we have just said that there need not be any awareness of what alternatives are being excluded (or allowed). But however critical this question is, it must be deferred. It raises essentially the same issues as the previous paragraph concerning the scope of the commitment not being packed into awareness at the time it was undertaken. These are complicated matters really about the nature of practical reasoning (and to some extent, reasoning simpliciter) which can be systematically addressed only in Chapter 6. As a preview of that discussion, however, it should be said that the boundaries on the scope of vows do not differ structurally from those on promises, even though other kinds of differences will emerge to the extent that promises do differ from vows. The boundaries on the scope of both will prove to derive from the nature of practical reason rather than from the specific nature of promises or vows.

V.   *Vows and non-basic action*

There is one last point. We began this chapter by indicating that we were concerned with extending commitment along the dimension of strength, just as the previous chapter extended it in scope. The latter, we have said, occurs in the intention to perform a non-basic action, while the former occurs in a vow. We can now see how these two dimensions work together. They are coordinated in this sense: the commitment does not approach the strength of a vow until its scope has involved a non-basic act. We do not, in other words, vow unless the action vowed is taken to be non-basic. We do not, for example, *vow* to raise our arm, even to raise it quickly. At most we can *intend* to do this. But we may *vow* to threaten someone or to seek recognition (in a meeting) by raising our arm. These two dimensions work together, we have said, to provide the basis of genuine social acts, which are to come next.

5

Promising, social acts, and convention

> Integrity is inseparable from commitment ... which is to human institutions generally what truthfulness is to the institution of language ... [and] what fair play is to games.
>
> Winch, 1972, pp. 70–1

We have seen how there is a natural line of development from intention to vows, the idea being that at some point in the transition it must be possible for an agent to form an exclusionary intention not to change his first order intention. At the same time, it was implied that this new-found intention would be unintelligible unless it were built upon the more primitive sense of commitment that is the *sine qua non* of intention as such. How the primitive commitment gets transformed into the new variety is explained by the new circumstances, new demands which the environment makes upon the agent, wherein he finds it necessary to use some kind of deliberation, perhaps even Bayesian reasoning, to arrive at his intention.

In any event, this is the strategy I shall follow in the derivation of promises from vows. Given that we can make vows, we shall soon find ourselves in novel circumstances in which we wish perhaps to form special bonds with other people, or to create the conditions necessary for cooperative behavior. When such demands impinge upon us, we shall have to find a way to transform our vowing commitment into a promise. On the view that I shall defend, promises are but vows with the social dimension. Once promises are possible, we will effect for the first time a *social act*; and from this it is but a short step to establish other forms of conformative behavior: rules, conventions, institutions, games, etc. The direction in which we shall aim is to show that inasmuch as all of these later trappings of human intercourse are attended with a sense of obligation, they need to presuppose as more primitive the concept of promising and not the other way around. It might be unclear why I am insisting that conventions presuppose *promising* rather than the simpler concept of *vowing*. Indeed, if the order between promising and convention is reversed such that promises cannot be derived from vows without the interposition of a convention, that is still no threat to the thesis defended here. For the concept of vowing would still remain the primitive presupposition behind promising. My reason, however, for defending the priority of *promising* over convention is simply that I take it to be true that conventions presuppose not only the commitment of vows, but also the social dimension of commitment that promising represents. This will not, of course, become clear until the analysis of both promising and convention is laid bare. On the other hand, this is somewhat an ancillary issue in the overall derivation of social acts from vows.

I. *Promises, vows, and the social context*

The path that we shall follow is that promises create social relations that did not exist before, but if there is any magic in this, it is to be found much earlier along the way in the primitive concept of commitment. It is to the concept of intention that the truly creative act must be traced.[1] The chief virtue of the account that follows is that promises, and everything else that I believe flows from them, can evolve naturally from a pre-promising society, ultimately from the state of nature. As we shall see, rival accounts have foundered on the attempt to explain this; they have either generated an infinite regress à la Prichard (1928, p. 179) or have had to smuggle in something like the relatively primitive concept of commitment that vows represent in order to explain the obligation to keep a promise (see Searle, 1969, pp. 189–90, 194–5; Rawls, 1971, pp. 112, 343–6; MacCormick, 1972; Narveson, 1971; Lewis, 1969; McNeilly, 1972; and Brandt, 1979, pp. 286–305).

If promises are vows with a 'social dimension,' it would be tempting to explain this new element in terms of 'reliance' or new 'expectations' which the promise induces on the part of the promisee. For such expectations do not attend private vows. But would the expectations be produced by publicly expressed vows? This question, I think, exposes the futility of this approach, and, as we shall see, the more general idea that expectations can do any of

[1] Cf. Prichard's solution in 1928, p. 179. For him the genuine creative act is in the general promise to keep our promises in virtue of which ordinary promises are binding.

the essential explanatory or justificatory work. For the answer to the question is 'yes': the expectations that would be produced by publicly expressed vows would be of exactly the same strength (given the explanation of the intelligibility of vows offered in Chapter 4) as those attending promises. To get any mileage out of expectations would, I think, collapse the distinction between public vows and promises, and more generally the difference between a social act like a promise and a private act that is just publicly expressed. In saying that promising is an essentially social act I mean that the promisee must play some crucial role in the act of promising, beyond being the passive recipient of information.

To this it can quite correctly be objected that a publicly expressed vow is itself a social act, as is any act of communication. What would be meant by this is that any act of communication engages a speaker–hearer pair in an essential social relation so as to be constitutive of certain rights and correlative obligations. The most obvious of these is that if the speaker successfully asserts that p, he *entitles* the hearer to assume that he is telling the truth, has sufficient evidence to believe that p, and so on.[2] Of course, I hardly wish to deny this. I only wish to maintain that promising is a social act in the sense that the essential role of the promisee goes beyond what can be attributed to communication. Promising is more than an act of communication, just as it is more than a vow. That it involves more than communication can be easily seen from a case in which A intentionally communicates to both B and C his promise to B. If B enjoys some right which C does not, then there is rather something special going on besides communication.

This leads me to another important point. If there is something special going on besides communication, then the degree to which promising presupposes communication and possibly with it communicative conventions becomes somewhat nugatory. The claim above that promising can be derived from vowing without the interposition of convention is meant to deny the existence of conventions other than those associated with communication. We might designate the former to be *local* conventions because they would supposedly be necessary for the *special* function that promising is to serve. These would be marked off from whatever *global* conventions that may underpin communication as such. The separation of con-

---

[2] See Holdcroft, 1978, and 1977, for a subtle analysis of these and other speech-act entitlements.

ventions from any possible communicative ones is a distinction, then, between the local and the global. It is not a distinction, *pace* Quine, between questions of substance and questions of meaning. We can follow Quine all we want in allowing that the global background conditions necessary for promising are now conditions of meaning, now conditions of substance, and that such conditions are, for all we know, fraught with the same implicit conventions which make possible the very propositional structure of thought and language, even apart from communication. Still, these matters are neutral as to whether there are any special conventions implicit in promising, as there are, say, in baseball.

It is apparent to virtually all writers on promising that the special function of promising is that it creates a right on the part of the promisee to demand performance. It is a special right on the part only of the promisee because, as indicated, it is only he who holds it, as distinguished from anyone else to whom it might have been communicated. We can also distinguish the promisee from anyone else who might be the beneficiary (if different from the promisee). (This last point is what has caused so much difficulty for the death-bed promise.) No less essential to the right of the promisee is that it be waivable at his option, and in this respect it differs from what many have regarded to be the case of some natural rights, like the right to life and liberty. This gives us a good sense of the formal structure of the special relation which the promise sets up between the promiser and promisee; somewhere it has been said that the latter holds the former on a string.

What more can be said about the content of the right? I think a good characterization of it can be found in A. I. Melden's recent work (1977, pp. 32–55). The thrust of his remarks on the nature of the right is that the promisee has as much right to rely on the action that is promised as he does on his own future action. Prior to the promise the right is held by each person in relation to his future action. It is a given, for Melden, that each person has the right to do as he pleases (1977, pp. 45–6). What the act of promising does is transfer to the promisee the promiser's right to choose his own action. It is not the promiser's actual reliance on his action that is transferred but only his right to choose it. That means that while the promisee has a perfect right to be assured of the performance of the promiser, the promisee also has a perfect right not to have it performed when he so chooses. When the prospective action is the promisee's own and he decides not to do it, he just refrains from doing it. But when the prospective action is the promiser's and the promisee decides that it is not to be done, he releases the promiser from the obligation to do it. Accordingly, to break a promise is tantamount to interfering with the right of the promisee to do as he pleases (1977, p. 47).

Where Melden's account is silent is on the question of the genesis of promisee's right from the act of promising, i.e., *how* the act of promising effects the transfer of rights that he describes. We must now remedy this defect. Our task can be described as one of explaining how an exclusionary intention on the part of A, the promiser, can commit him, not only to ϕ, but also commit *him to B*, the promisee, to do ϕ, and this by creating at the same time a waivable right for B to demand the ϕing by A. The solution I think is that A wants to communicate to B not merely his unilateral commitment to ϕ, but somehow involve B in that very commitment's taking effect. The first thing that comes to mind accordingly is that B's involvement is his acceptance of the commitment, such that his acceptance of it is at least one condition upon which the commitment is in effect. As a rough approximation, A might say the following to B, based upon their common knowledge that A can make vows.

(1) I vow (to ϕ, if you, B, accept).

This however, is strictly nonsense, because if (1) is a promise then it cannot be a vow. But the faulty nomenclature in (1) obscures the basic truth that the vowing element, the exclusionary intention, is common to both promises and vows, and is what is being communicated in (1). Thus a more correct representation is

(2) I intend to communicate to you, B, my exclusionary intention (to ϕ, if you, B, accept).

The first intention (to communicate) looks like a Gricean one (see Grice, 1957), and should not be confused with the second exclusionary intention. But strictly speaking, it is otiose to represent the communicative intention in a separate way because the exclusionary intention to ϕ, conditional upon another's acceptance, already implies that it is to be communicated. This, of course, is not the case with a vow. Thus a less pleonastic version of (2) is

(3) I intend, exclusionarily (to ϕ, if you, B, accept).

There are several points in need of clarification about B's acceptance. As stated, (3) is misleading because it looks as though once B accepts (at the time the promise is made), then A's requirement to φ is irrevocable – or at least irrevocable on B's part. But given B's acceptance, cannot he (as opposed to A) change his mind? Of course, he can. That is what we have been saying all along about his waivable right to φing by A. And this just underscores the point that a promise is a commitment only on the part of A, not on the part of B. That is what makes it so one-sided. The following analysis, then, captures the waivable right better:

(4) I intend, exclusionarily (to φ, conditional upon your, B's, continuing acceptance).

'Continuing acceptance' raises a point about the manner in which acceptance must be taken. Unlike the law of contracts, it need not be explicit. Robert Samek makes this point when he says that while both promises and contracts cannot survive explicit rejection, only contracts require explicit acceptance (1965, p. 204). Thus it can be assumed as background information, perhaps as a conversational implicature of the promissory utterance, that B will accept the promise unless he explicitly rejects it. After all, promises do not come out of the thin air; the conversational context that prompts them usually makes B's proclivities quite clear. This account has the advantage of being able to explain why A continues to be bound by his promise in the absence of anything definite on the part of B, even if B might have forgotten it and it is known to A that he has forgotten. Only if B wishes to release A need he do anything definite. This can be contrasted with the rival view of Fain which makes the analysis of promises parasitic upon the supposedly more fundamental notion of A giving B *permission* to *require* A to φ (1978, pp. 332ff). But this, I think, raises a few difficulties. For one thing, since a 'permission to require' is not yet a requirement without some definite act on the part of its holder, B, the theory puts too much of an onus on B to do something definite in order to activate the promissory requirement on the part of A. If people prefer to analyze promises in terms of permissions it would be better to think of A's giving B permission to release A from his commitment. But the difficulty with this is that 'permission-to-release-from-commitment' presupposes rather than explains the concept of a promise.

A related problem that is raised by 'permission' as such (whether

101

to require or to release) is that like the concept of a command or imperative, it already presupposes a social relation between A and B. In contrast, the concept of acceptance seems to be at a decided advantage: it can be constructed out of the raw materials existing in the state of nature, bearing in mind the points made earlier about communication. We noted earlier that 'acceptance' does not involve a commitment, as does the exclusionary intention. I propose to understand 'acceptance' as reducible to something like 'assent' as in assenting to a proposition, except that the mood of *what* is assented to is not the straightforward proposition that A *will* ϕ (for that is connected with expecting A to ϕ), but something normative like A is to ϕ or is required to. (There will be subtleties as to the content of the assent, but that is a different matter which is best handled under an analysis of the content.) Some philosophers take this normative mood to have a different copula than that of a propositional content. Castaneda calls it a practition, as we have said (see 1975, pp. 16–18, 43–4, 90–130, 149–238), and Raz and von Wright a norm kernal (see Raz, 1975b, p. 50; and von Wright, 1963, p. 70). The essential point is that the content of the assent is normative, signaling that in our theory a promise is parasitic upon a vow. But the mood of the content of the assent should be carefully distinguished in this fashion from the act of assenting itself, which I take to be as primitive, as 'pre-social,' as that of believing and intending. Finally, we must resist the temptation to link the act of assenting to *wanting* or something similar, for this would be open to numerous counter examples involving successfully promising the unwanted (see Raz, 1977, pp. 213–14; and Carter, 1973).

Our attempt to get the acceptance condition straightened out has not, however, addressed the somewhat different question of *how* the promisee's acceptance is related to the promise's taking effect. What I mean is this. So far we have

(5) I intend, exclusionarily (to ϕ, conditional upon your, B's, continuing assent).

But this crude conditional form still does not capture the idea that the promisee holds any *right* to A's ϕing. All that it shows is that he has the *power* to negate it by not so assenting. The following counterexample to (5) should make this clear. Suppose that a college student, who has not yet severed the social umbilical cord, presents to his parents the following proposal:

> (5₁) I intend, exclusionarily (to go to Europe this summer (but) conditional upon your, B's, continuing assent).[3]

His exclusionary intention signals a resolve not to let very many other things stand in his way, but the protasis indicates that his parents are to have veto power over it at any time. (He probably intends this as a bi-conditional, if, that is, we set aside the general constraint on an exclusionary intention as a defeasible concept.) If his parents assent, has the student *promised them* that he will go to Europe? No mere verbal matter, what we are asking is whether they have any right to his performance over and above their power over it; whether he owes them anything (if they assent). The answer cannot be but negative. In fact, all that we have so far is a certain kind of conditional vow.

What is missing is something that can be gleaned from Melden and others on this subject. It is that promising is *transferring* something to the promisee, this being perhaps what generates his holding of a right. But *what* can the promiser transfer from his impoverished holdings in the state of nature? Rights do not even exist yet under the present theory, so how can they be transferred? Intentions exist, of course, but they appear logically inalienable.[4] There is, however, something else; it is the very thing that the promiser intends to create by his exclusionary intention. We may call it his exclusionary requirement or mandate. Recall the double, temporal, indexical reference of intentions and commitment: the reference to one's intending at t_i to commit oneself to a requirement to do something at t_j. The thing that can be transferred is the mandate or requirement for the act that comes into being at t_j. Accordingly, A can say the following to B:

> (6) I intend, exclusionarily at t_i (that you, B, will hold the exclusionary requirement for me to φ at t_j, conditional upon your continuing assent).

We now have all of the elements to represent in logical form both the common origin and difference between vows, and promises. The

---

[3] I am much indebted to Andrew Altman for this example as well as the whole line of criticism that follows.

[4] In the present context, this may be the real lesson in Castaneda's work on quasi-indicators (see 1975, Ch. 6, 1967, and 1968).

common structure is

(F) $EI (I,\pi)$

where EI is the exclusionary intention operator, I is the first person agent, viz., A (the referent of the quasi-indicator), and π is a proposition. It can then be seen that for vows

(F_v) $\pi = ER_2(I,\phi)$

where ER_2 is a two-place exclusionary requirement, and ϕ is the proposition to whose satisfaction A is committed when he refers to himself in the first person. Now, in order to see the real difference between promises and vows, it would be best to represent next the logical form of a vow that is not only conditional but conditional upon the hearer's continuing assent (as in the college student case). Thus

$(F_{v'})$ $\pi = $ continuing assent $(B,\phi) \supset ER_2(I,\phi)$

where continuing assent (B,ϕ) is read: B continuingly assents to ϕ. The contrast with a promise, which necessarily has this same condition, is now apparent:

(F_{pr}) $\pi = $ continuing assent $(B,\phi) \supset ER_3(B,I,\phi)$

where ER_3 is a three place relation between B who 'holds' it, I who is the person over whom he holds it and who is necessarily identical with the person who has the exclusionary intention, and ϕ the proposition promised. The difference in logical form, then, comes down to the difference between the three-place relation ER_3 and the two-place relation ER_2.[5]

---

[5] If the exclusionary requirement in both promises and vows is normative, as it must be under the present theory, then what is the logical role of the obligation to keep promises or vows? Is this the same requirement as ER_2 or ER_3 or a different one? If I am right, the latter answer should be opted for. Hence the obligation to keep one's promises (or that one ought to keep them) is written:

(O_{pr}) $[EI$ (continuing assent $(B,\phi) \supset ER_3(B,I,\phi))$
          & continuing assent $(B,\phi)] \rightarrow O(I,\phi)$

where $O(I,\phi)$ is read: I ought to ϕ, and the same for vows, *mutatis mutandis*. It is true that there are *two* normative concepts here, the plain old ought operator $O(\phi)$, and the ER_3 or ER_2. But there is no oddity or paradox. The one, ER_3 or ER_2 is within the scope of the intentional operator, EI; the other, $O(\phi)$, an implication of intend-

To many readers there is something exceedingly artificial and formal about the transition from vows to promises. The most obvious gap in my account thus far is my silence heretofore on why anyone would want to enter into so one-sided a relation. I have in a word sidestepped the question of motivation. This contrasts markedly with the more standard fare in the literature on promising and consent theories (cf., e.g., Rawls, 1971, Sec. 52, pp. 342–50; Hume, 1888, Part III; Lewis, 1969, pp. 45, 83–8, 188–9; Árdal, 1968; Narveson, 1971), in which the supposed background for agreement making is some kind of conflict or prisoner's dilemma. In such a situation the parties are motivated to invent promises – and with them mutual trust and reliance – as a compromise solution, as a mandate of rationality in the service of their mutual interests. The *mutuality* is the essential motivational structure that keeps the practice going, and this mutuality is true no less of the special bonds between, say, husband and wife, friend and friend, than of citizen and citizen.[6]

My account is not incompatible with such background motivation. All that I wish to deny is that any such considerations should find their way into the *analysis* of promises and the obligation to keep them. As an analytical model this approach, I believe, is mistaken because, for one thing, it has a tendency to assimilate promises to a contract. Of course, many promises are part of a contract, but need they be? Most important of all is the question, what is the more fundamental notion? I am assuming that contract is a mutual exchange of conditional promises, and if so, is it not our

---

ing it. The point can be underscored by noting that although there is a conspicuous ought in 'One ought to keep one's promises,' there is another, *'de dicto'* ought hidden in *what* a promise is. The hidden one comes to the surface when a promise is analyzed as the intention to create an ought. This ought, to reiterate again, is in the content of *what* we intend; the other (as we have said) an implication of our intending it. Stated in ordinary language, the two oughts come out thus:

(O–OL$_{pr}$) One ought to conform to the ought that one intends to create.

This point also receives some reinforcement from the oft-noticed analytic or *pleonastic* character of 'One ought to keep one's promises.' Cf. Searle, 1969, Ch. 8; and Hamlyn, 1962, pp. 179–80.

[6] Rousseau is the most extreme in making the mutuality of the agreement carry almost all of the justificatory burden. See above, Chapter 1, p. 16.

analytical task to explain promises first? Otherwise, what is it that makes a *contract* binding?[7] We shall henceforth examine attempts which directly or indirectly treat the notion of contract as more fundamental. For the moment, let the reader take my word that it cannot give an account of the binding character of such agreements without smuggling into its motivational structure the primitive concept of commitment. The motivational structure has a place in normative theory, but it is one of explaining why we *make* promises and agreements, not why we are obligated to *keep* them. (To see the difference, do we not sometimes assent to our obligation to keep a past promise which we concede should not have been made?)

The second problem with this rival view of promises was brought to the fore by Melden (1977, pp. 35–6, 56–80). Some promises are offered as part of a *quid pro quo*, as in Hume's rowers (1888, p. 490), but can they not be made simply out of our own good will toward or affection for the promisee? Are they any less binding than the shrewd bargain? The motivation for making promises seems in fact to be as varied and as complex as human nature generally, and so that is reason enough to avoid tying any particular view of it to the general account of promises.

The third point I wish to make is this. Quite apart from the motivation to make a promise, quite apart from the intrinsic desirability of the thing promised, the act of promising always seems to carry some weight of its own. Take any act you like, no matter how intrinsically desirable, and you will find that it always makes a difference if you add to it the further fact that it was promised. It is this difference – the 'content independent' justification – that my analysis is intended to capture. This point in fact seems to account for much of the intuitive appeal of consent theories and of traditional (as opposed to 'hypothetical') contractarianism: that no matter how 'rational' the motivation may be for entering into an agreement, it is the *actual* promise that seems to ensure the creation of an obligation and a right.[8] (Notice also that an analogous point can be made about the concept of intention vs. the motivation for it.) For it is the *intention*

---

[7] I have made these points against Rawls in particular in my article, 'Promissory obligations and Rawls' contractarianism,' 1976a, who takes contract – or ostensibly so – to be the more fundamental.

[8] Of course in traditional contractarianism, the 'actual promise' may be tacit, but certainly not 'hypothetical.' This point has some implications for students of Rawls. If an actual promise is needed, then the Rawlsian contract, which is only hypothetical and even counterfactual, is not enough to support his point that society is a voluntary, cooperative venture (see 1971, pp. 13–22). The foundational promise estab-

to act, rather than just the ostensible motivation for it, that explains why a certain non-performance is a mistake in performance (see Chapter 2, pp. 36–7; 42–4.

III. Commitment and moral obligation

If we are going to remain silent on the question of the motivation to make promises, are we also going to be neutral on the question of whether the requirement to keep promises is a moral obligation? I do not think so. Notice that when we had spoken hitherto about the commitment and requirement embedded in vows and intentions, we had intentionally avoided the use of the term 'obligation,' let alone 'moral obligation.' Is the matter any different now that promises are social acts? First, let me cite the main reasons against the notion that promissory obligations are moral obligations. To begin with, there are promises and promises. Some are quite trivial, and others are a commitment to do something immoral. (There are two distinctions here: moral vs. amoral, and moral vs. immoral.) The force of this point is that 'moral' is a fairly weighty term, reserved for something regarded to be important. Some people have interpreted this importance 'prescriptively,' to mean that the ascription 'moral' implies an imperative that overrides all other considerations (except other imperatives that are also 'moral'), while other people have interpreted it 'materially' to mean that the thing said to be moral must connect with our basic beliefs about man and the universe, about what constitutes human good and harm.[9] But whatever the analysis may be, not any promise as such can be of such

lishing the society is supposed to be hypothetical to the extent that *if* we were rational and *were* in the original position, etc., then we *would* enter into the agreement 'made in perpetuity' (pp. 176, 195). Since this hypothetical agreement can supposedly be *derived* from the counterfactual original position, Rawls seems to think that not only is it not actual, but, as a matter of fact, it does not have to be, for it carries the same force of commitment as if it *were* actual. Yet Joel Feinberg (1973) finds it misleading to consider such a theory contractarian: any actual choice of commitment is superseded by this kind of 'moral geometry,' which, given the conditions of the original position, can represent the reasoning for any one of the original contractors. Actually though, this is an ambiguity in Rawls which, I believe, he fails to resolve. On the one hand, he does seem to appeal directly to the intuitive force of such concepts as 'agreement,' 'the strain of commitment' (1973), yet the fact that these can be *derived* from a purely counterfactual situation, as a matter of 'geometry,' seems to undercut that appeal and robs the agreement of its independent force.

[9] For a systematic taxonomy of the 'prescriptive' vs. the 'material' approach, see Singer, 1973. Also see Beardsmore, 1969; and Phillips and Mounce, 1969, for thorough discussion of the Foot–Hare debate on when something can become a moral principle.

moment: it all depends upon the content and the circumstances.

Supporting this position with somewhat more rigor is the view that the obligation to keep a promise is a purely formal notion, something that is part of the term's conceptual analysis. Raz is particularly perspicuous on this point by noting that the whole force of a promissory obligation is to take the thing promised out of the normal competition that exists between conflicting reasons for and against the doing of it. For such a conflict is typically resolved in our practical reasoning along the dimension of weight; and among the weightiest reasons of all, we should expect, are moral considerations. But the whole force of construing promissory obligations as 'exclusionary reasons' (his term) is to exclude (or limit) the matter's being decided only by such considerations of weight. Effecting this exclusion, on Raz's conception, is what it is to make a promise, which also explains why promises have a content-independent force. To turn a promissory obligation into a moral one is to fail to appreciate the two dimensions of reasons (for action): first level reasons (which do compete with one another in terms of 'weight') and second level exclusionary reasons (see 1977, pp. 225, 227, and 1975b, pp. 40–8, 69ff). In spirit, this is like Searle's observation that the obligation to keep a promise is a matter of illocutionary force and not necessarily a matter of moral relations (see 1969, p. 188).

There is a different sense of the term 'moral' in which it gets linked, not with 'importance,' but with 'obligation' simpliciter. So understood, to call something an obligation is already to attribute some moral significance to it; and in cases where we wish to withhold the moral attribution (but still wish to imply something normative), we can use a different term than 'obligation,' a term like 'requirement' or even 'commitment.' There is a sense in which the taxonomy in this book is so influenced. Thus, I say that there is only a *requirement* to honor one's vows and intentions, but there is an *obligation* to keep one's promises. The distinction is between private and social acts: requirements turn into obligations when they are *owed* to someone else. And if this sense of obligation already has a moral significance (because of the involvement of other persons), then necessarily promissory obligations are moral. But if 'moral' is reserved only for what is serious or of overriding weight (for Raz it is a function of the content of the promise), then it is false that necessarily promissory obligations are moral.

To some extent this appears to be a verbal question, depending upon how 'moral' is taken. Yet I do not really think that it is. Instead, I should like to defend the view that links 'moral' with 'obligation' as such. My reason for endorsing this is that even if a promise is fairly trivial, a cavalier attitude towards the obligation to keep it is not. It reflects significantly on a man's integrity in much the same way as does cheating at a trivial game. It is difficult not to think of this as a moral failing. This is explained in part, I think, by the fact that a promise *as such* creates a right on the part of someone else. To be remiss in recognizing that right reflects adversely on the promiser's lack of respect for others as persons. On this view, how we regard promissory *relations* between persons reflects how we regard persons, period.[10] Notice also that none of these points seems to apply to self-imposed requirements: a man who doesn't keep his vows is weak-willed, not morally deficient; nor is a man who cheats at solitaire. The idea of cheating at solitaire in fact is likely to meet with amusement rather than scorn. I thus feel compelled to regard the obligation to keep a promise as a moral one, and to suggest that the important distinction that, say, Raz is concerned to make should best be treated as a tension between different dimensions of morality.

IV.   Promising, constitutive rules, and convention

As we have indicated, it is a distinct advantage of the present view that it can account for the not-too-rough transition from vows to promises, from private acts to social ones, without presupposing for the latter any antecedent convention, practice, or rule, etc., of promising. Again, it is emphasized that this view does not necessarily deny the existence of other conventions necessary for communication (although we will later see if we could get by without even these). Now, such concepts as those of convention and rule are themselves fraught with ambiguity in another sense. Pursuant to promising, and even more generally, they are used in at least two distinct senses. One sense involves the notion of constitution, the other expectation. The constitutive sense of 'rule' is crystallized in Searle's epigram that to ask how a promise can create an obligation is like asking how a touchdown can create six points (1969, pp. 35ff): both, according to him, are explained by a rule, or more precisely, a constitutive rule, which makes it a matter of convention that scoring a touchdown, or uttering certain words, counts respectively as

[10] This point is expanded below in Chapter 6, pp. 168–9.

scoring six points or undertaking an obligation. The notion of *constitution* is essential here (and is really a species of level-generation). In this vein, Searle is not merely saying that a convention of promising simply is necessary to clarify to the hearer the speaker's intention to make a promise. This is a convention that I have hitherto associated with communication. It is a convention whereby antecedently existing thoughts, intentions, or states of affairs, etc., are conveyed unambiguously to the audience. Rather, he is saying that the convention creates the very form of behavior that is intended, indeed creates the very possibility of intending it. Without the constitutive convention of promising, he holds, making a promise would be as unintelligible as would be scoring a touchdown without the constitutive conventions of football. Accuracy requires, then, that 'constitution' be contrasted with 'clarification.'[11]

In any case, the other sense of local convention which is contrasted with constitution is the expectation sense of convention, systematically exploited by the utilitarians (see below, pp. 140–3) and by David Lewis (1969). This one fixes on the notion that a convention implies roughly a regularity of behavior produced by a certain system of expectations and which would be pointless without those expectations. Accordingly, a promise would be pointless unless, roughly, the promisee expects the promiser to keep his promise, and the promiser expects the promisee to expect it, and so on (Lewis, 1969, pp. 27–32). In both senses of 'convention,' the issue has been whether promising is parasitic upon convention for its intelligibility or the other way around. Many of the accounts that have taken the former line have foundered, though, in the attempt to make the convention or rule binding without smuggling in either a more primitive promise or vow. Unless either one of these primitives is explained, without appealing to yet another local convention, there is the possibility of an infinite regress. Three philosophers have seen this difficulty in connection with the constitutive sense of convention. Listed in the order of their directness and clarity on the

[11] It is easy to confound this distinction because in order that communicative conventions may succeed in *clarifying what* the speaker is communicating, it may be necessary for them to *constitute how* it is to be communicated. Typically, the rule will say that uttering certain noises or behaving thus counts as intending to communicate this or that concept. But it is one thing for constitution to be an element in the overall effort to clarify the thing communicated; it is another for those rules to constitute the existence of the thing communicated. Constitutive rules may be involved in successfully communicating to you my belief that it is raining, but that is a different matter than their being necessary for even forming that belief. My principal concern is with constitutive rules in the latter case, not the former case.

question, they are Prichard (1928, pp. 172, 177–9), Searle (1969, pp. 189–90, 194–5), and Rawls (1971, pp. 344–50). The difficulty, however, has not been recognized in regard to the expectation sense of convention, but it will be exposed in our later discussion of the utilitarians and David Lewis (see below, pp. 135–7).

For the moment, the best defense of the contrary view that takes promising to be the more fundamental is to continue to derive promises from vows, without presupposing an antecedent local convention. Accordingly, the elements presupposed by promises can be enumerated in the list below. Despite my earlier caveat about communicative acts, it would be best to complete the picture by including these too, but at the same time marking them off with brackets. Because promising does rely on specific communicative acts at various points, which the list below indicates, it would allay some residual skepticism if even these acts could be made out without a global communicative convention. I shall, therefore, attempt to sketch such an account however tentative.

The elements, then, look like this:

(A) The intelligibility of the distinction between exclusionary intentions and first level intentions within wholly private acts.
(B) The common knowledge on the part of a population of (A).
[(C) The possibility of communicating that one has an exclusionary intention, as distinguished from a first order intention.]
(D) The possibility that the exclusionary intention can both have [and be communicated with] the content indicated in (F_{pr}), namely, that of
  (i) transferring the exclusionary requirement,
  (ii) conditionally upon the promisee's assent.
(E) The possibility of the promisee's assenting to (D) [and communicating it].

Can we make sense of any of these without appealing to a convention, considered first in the constitutive sense? I think so. Let us begin with (A). The whole thrust of the account of vows in Chapter 4 was to make this intelligible as a matter of practical reasoning, and not parasitic upon social convention. If the distinction between intending and deciding is intelligible (and if the main argument in Chapter 4 is correct), then it seems to me that we already understand the concept of an exclusionary intention. So there appears to be no new difficulty here.

111

As for (B), the common knowledge that (A) is intelligible, this means – to paraphrase David Lewis's sense of the term – that almost everybody finds it intelligible to ascribe to himself and others the ability to make vows (1969, pp. 56, 76–8). This in turn presupposes some features of a pre-promising society but they are unproblematic: that people can come into contact with, or at least observe, the behavior of others, and can interpret that behavior. Naturally, like any interpretation, this one is fraught with the risk of error, and possibly open to an indeterminacy between rival interpretations, as well as, perhaps, the problem of other minds. But if it is intelligible to interpret the behavior of others as expressing an intention that was arrived at through some kind of deliberation, then we already have in the making the ascription to others of an exclusionary intention.

(C) refers to the possibility of communicating that intention – in a word, to the stage at which private vows can be publicly expressed. How can this communicative act take place without a convention? I suggest the following Gricean account (1957). A intends (i) to bring about on the part of B, the understanding or recognition that A has an exclusionary intention, etc., and A intends (ii) to bring about this understanding merely by means of getting B to recognize his intention (i). *How* can A satisfy his intention (ii), and thereby (i)? How can A get B to *recognize* A's intention (i) that B understand that he has the exclusionary intention (without, of course, relying on a convention whose purpose it is to secure such recognition)? How, in other words, can A secure recognition of his intention to communicate (which concept among others Grice is analyzing)? Notice what we already have. First, exclusionary intentions are intelligibly distinguishable from first order ones (from [A]) and that there is common knowledge of this (from [B]). Now, since the common knowledge referred to is really an interpretation of the behavior of others as expressing exclusionary intentions, it can also be assumed that there is common knowledge as to *when* people are acting on their exclusionary intentions.[12] In these circumstances, one can easily *have* an intention (i) that others recognize both *that* and *when*

---

[12] This kind of common knowledge would be distinguished from, say, that about people having dreams, in which case we can say loosely that we know that others have dreams, but not when – ordinary language philosophy to the contrary notwithstanding. Cf. Austin, 1962; Wittgenstein, 1953.

one is behaving under an exclusionary intention. One can secure such recognition simply by behaving in the typical way which the population through its common knowledge associates with those intentions.[13] It is one thing, however, for *him* to *have* that intention (i) that others so interpret his behavior (i.e., as that of an exclusionary intention); it is quite another for others to *know* that *he* has that intention (i) *that they* interpret his behavior in such a manner. And this would be true, of course, even if they are correctly interpreting his behavior! For they would yet have no way of even telling whether he acts that way *with the intention* (i) that they interpret his behavior as expressing an exclusionary intention, or whether he acts that way simply with the knowledge (i) that they will so interpret it, the knowledge being simply a foreseeable side-effect of what he really intends. So if he does act with the intention (i) that his observers so interpret his behavior, one way (surely not the only way) that he can satisfy that intention (i) is by somehow getting his observers to recognize that very intention (i), in other words, form the intention (ii). Not being able to rely on a convention (for satisfying (ii)), but mindful that his typical behavior is being interpreted by his observers simply as expressing an exclusionary intention, why can he not secure recognition of (i) by doing something extraordinarily conspicuous, e.g., shout while he is so acting? Obviously, both he and they can be presumed to know that this will call special attention to his otherwise ordinary behavior. If there is no apparent other reason why he is shouting, his observers can reasonably suppose that he shouts in order to call special attention to himself. But since they both know that his observers *will interpret* his behavior as that of an exclusionary intention anyway, without the shouting, they can suppose that the shouting was a crude way to secure the recognition of his intention (i) that his otherwise normal behavior will be interpreted in the ordinary way. True, this interpretation of his shouting is defeasible, and offers no guarantee that his intention to use his normal behavior as a form of communication will be recognized. But this defeasibility and theoretical indeterminacy infects conventions, too, although perhaps not to the same degree. The advantage that a convention would offer appears to be only a practical one, that

---

[13] There is a natural suspicion that 'common knowledge' is a dummy phrase for what is really a covert (local) convention, but this doubt should be allayed below, pp. 133–4.

the recognition of the intention (i) can be secured with more convenience and less effort.

(D) is divisible into two elements: (i) the transferring of the requirement and (ii) effecting the transfer on the condition that the promisee gives his continuing assent. Since (ii) presupposes that the promisee can assent [and communicate it], which is really condition (E), we should start with (E).

I have stipulated that assent in (E) was used in the same primitive sense as in assenting to a proposition or a norm-kernel, these being found in such semantic attitudes as believing or intending. Even so, there might appear to be a difficulty similar in spirit to that involving communication. The emphasis this time would be on the conventions that may be implicit in language and meaning in the non-communicative sense – nowadays called the 'computational' sense. The idea here is that the semantic content of thought as a mental representation having truth conditions and the like would require *computational* conventions on simpler word-like elements (see, e.g., Davidson, 1975, 1976; Harman, 1973, Chs. 4–6; for an opposing view see Foder, 1975; for a rebuttal see Dennett, 1978). But again, the reader is reminded that these are still global conventions that, should they be necessary, are equally imbedded in non-social semantic attitudes like intending and believing, and therefore would not be germane in getting from these attitudes to the distinctively social ones. So, again, I set them aside.

(E) also refers to the communication of the promisee's assent, but I suggest that this admits of the same Gricean account that was already sketched for (C).

Finally, we recur to (D). There are still two elements in it, (i) the transferring of the requirement and (ii) intending such transferring to be conditional upon the promisee's continuing assent. Consider (ii) first. Since the promisee's assent was already discussed under (E), the only remaining part of (ii) that is of interest is its conditional form as such [together with a question as to whether such a form can be communicated readily]. Granted that vows and intentions exist in a state of nature, is there any special problem in supposing them to admit of a conditional form? If there is, it is another global matter, because the conditional form seems to be linked to various stages of cognitive evolution that are both non-social and pervasive. In particular it has been linked to a variety of rudimentary forms of inference, both practical and otherwise (see, e.g., Hare, 1971, pp. 59–93, *passim*). The idea in this is that the conditional form of a proposition is best explained and perhaps actually learned by reference to the pattern of inferences it licenses (and is sometimes reducible to truth functions). So it seems plausible to believe that the very possibility of having *thoughts* with the conditional form is tantamount to the development of the capacity for reasoning at a certain level. The capacity to reason is already presupposed anyway – albeit at a different degree – for the emergence of decisions and vows out of intentions. [There is also the other global problem of communicating an intention with a conditional form, but, once again, the elements of a Gricean account seem to be in place: that the recognition of the intention to communicate this form can be realized by relying on the regularities of behavior already postulated to exist (e.g., conditional vows and intentions), the common knowledge of the regularities, and an additional demonstrative way of drawing attention to one's otherwise normal behavior of this kind.]

Finally, we come to (D), part (i), concerning transferring a requirement. Of all the elements we have discussed, this seems the most threatening. In fact, the question as to whether a transfer of this kind can be effected (not just communicated) without a convention seems intertwined with another critical question, namely, whether the concept of transferring presupposes an existing social relation between the participants, which is exactly the same criticism that was leveled against the analysis of promising as giving the promisee permission to require. There is in fact an even more critical problem along these same lines that is indicated in Prichard's observation concerning giving and exchanging, which bear a kinship to transferring (1940, p. 180). It is that these notions presuppose the concept of promising, in which case there is a circularity which threatens this part of the analysis.

Our first response is to the threat of circularity. Assuming that transferring is like giving or exchanging (which it is not), it should be noted that Prichard's arguments at best show that these presuppose, not promising, but the simpler concept of a vowing commitment (presumably to give up control over that which is given or exchanged), the commitment not to interfere with the recipient's control of it, etc.

Promising cannot be involved in giving because, given my con-

115

ception of it as a social act, it would imply that the act of giving would not take effect without the recipient's assent. But I do not think giving is like this. Can I not give something to someone who avowedly refuses to 'accept' it? Such a person may in protest, of course, refuse to exercise his property right in the object, but that does not mean that he does not have it. Moreover, even if the recipient does accept, does he have the power subsequently to void the gift, i.e., to release the giver from the obligation to forbear, by saying that he no longer accepts the gift? I think not. Yet this is what would have to happen if a promise were at work. If a vow instead is at work, it would only confirm the view defended thus far. What we would be saying is that a transfer transaction (which for the moment we are assuming to be like giving) in an act of promising is the means through which the promisee comes to hold the requirement created by a vow. Promising in a word is vowing plus (conditional) transferring.

But may it not be that transferring presupposes social relations in a sense wider than whatever is associated with promising. There are two ways in which this wider sense can be taken: that it presupposes a social relation *antecedent* to the transfer, and that it creates social relations *consequent* upon the transfer. The second would come dangerously close to smuggling in a local convention precisely in the constitutive sense, while the first would rely on distinct social relations prior to promising. These, in turn, would have to be explained in some way, with or without another convention, but either way they would seem to be discontinuous with the ontological inventory in the state of nature. I begin the discussion with the first. The best way to see that social relations need not exist prior to transferring is perhaps to contrast it with a rival concept, giving permission to require, really giving permission, simpliciter. One can hardly give to another permission to do or refrain from *anything* without presupposing, antecedent to the act of giving, some *authority* over another – at least with regard to the thing permitted. In the case of permission to require, one is assuming a prior authority to *prohibit* the other from so requiring, which, I think, is of a piece with some natural order of rights, rights held by oneself against the interference by others. The purpose of the permission is to modify by consent the existing or natural distribution.

But the concept of transferring does not seem similarly to imply a prior natural moral order. Transferring need not assume that the

116

transferer enjoys a prior moral right or authority over that which is transferred. Rather, the concept can get off the ground relative to brute fact of possession or relative to something that is under one's effective control in some sense (as is the exclusionary requirement). Taking the concept of physical control as a crude paradigm, we can certainly see that it by no means implies ownership.

In suggesting that transferring does not imply a prior natural moral order, I am claiming that, on the position defended here, there are no natural rights or obligations prior to requirements that are created by the will. When these requirements first appear on the scene as internal norms of action and of practical reasoning, they are strictly agent-relative, implying nothing normative with regard to other agents. In fact, part of the thrust of characterizing this to be a 'state of nature' is that any actions on the part of one agent relative to another are strictly amoral. The rival conception of 'granting permission' or even 'giving' presupposes that other-regarding actions prior to the act of permission admit of being immoral, e.g., those involving 'harm,' or interference with rights.[14] On my conception, the only way that purely agent-relative requirements can become transformed into social requirements is by an act of will represented in their intentional transfer.

We come now to the other end of the social relations problem, that those relations or some normative entitlement of another person is implied, not antecedent to, but as a result of, the transfer, in which case there would be something creative about transferring which would then be said to be unintelligible without a convention. As we noticed earlier, an example of such an ostensibly creative element can be found in its close cousin, giving. Notice, for example, the difficulty that young children have in learning this concept. While a small child may easily transfer to a companion the physical possession of a toy, it is a difficult lesson for him to learn that he cannot then take it back at will. What he is learning, so the story might go, is that his physical act *creates* for his companion a right to control the object and for him the obligation of forebearance from interference.

The next chapter in this story would be to insist that these rights can be created by a physical act only if there is a convention for doing so, and that is the real object of the lesson. This would appear to make giving exactly analogous to 'scoring a touchdown.' For in one

[14] Another useful contrast to the position defended here is that of Alan Gewirth, 1978.

sense a touchdown is constituted by a collection of brute facts: that a runner has crossed a certain line while holding an odd shaped ball, etc. But the concept of touchdown also implies something normative consequent upon it: that the runner is *thereby entitled* to six points. And the importance of explaining this via a constitutive *rule* is to indicate that the *relation* between the antecedent *brute fact* and the consequent *entitlement* is created by convention, not nature.

This account, however, errs in two principal ways. First, even if transferring were like giving, which it is not, and even if giving does have a genuinely creative dimension, it does not follow that giving is like scoring a touchdown, in that the latter requires conventional rules. On my conception, it is because vowing, as I have said, is necessarily embedded in giving that giving might appear to create something new and normative; but the source of the creation can be traced to the vow. In giving a toy to another child, the giver is expressing behavioristically the vow not to take it back, and it is this – the meaning of a vow – that is the real object of his lesson.

It still might be thought that beyond this a convention is necessary for giving to work, for *how* is the physical, 'brute fact' of a mere change in possession to be linked with a vow not to take back the object given? My answer is that *if* this is so, it is a convention essentially of communication, that is, it is a means for the giver to *express* or *clarify* to the recipient his *vow* henceforth to forbear from interfering with the recipient's possession of the object. The creative element would still lie in the naturalistic vow, not in the convention. And therefore, whether there is such a convention would be a global, not a local, matter (see my discussion of Searle, above, pp. 109–10).

But this is somewhat otiose, because the second way this conventionalist account errs is in confounding transferring with giving. However, I am understanding the former to be simpler than the latter. As I see it, transferring is what is left over from giving if you subtract (1) vowing and (2) antecedent social relations (i.e., property rights). So understood, transferring is an element of giving; it refers to the simple brute fact of a change in physical possession or control in an act of giving. We may say, thus, that giving consists of: (1) antecedent social relations (i.e., property rights), (2) transferring, (3) vowing, and (4) communication. And we can now see why promising, as the first social act, requires only transferring, not giving, because for one thing, the vow that is necessary to create the right is already present in the exclusionary intention (Chapter 4). If, alternatively, giving were an element in getting the mandate into the hands of the promisee, it would produce an undesirable redundancy. For another thing, we cannot in promising rely on any elements that presuppose antecedent social relations.

But even if transferring is distinguished from giving, the concept still might be obscure especially considering that the *thing* transferred, the exclusionary requirement, is so abstract. After all, this cannot be quite like transferring an apple. Part of the obscurity lies in the supposition that this abstract entity is 'held' or 'possessed' or 'controlled' by the promiser and subsequently 'held' by the promisee. But these expressions sound like metaphors for which the reader has a right to demand the cash value. The value of such metaphors can be found by developing the concept of control.

Using this idiom, I shall first re-describe the situation the agent is in when he makes a vow, and then when he makes a promise. In a vow, the exclusionary mandate should be understood as a vehicle of his agency or autonomy. Roughly, this is a way of saying that the agent exercises or expresses his agency through his mandate. If for the moment we identify the mandate with the vow, a more natural way of saying this is that the agent expresses his agency through his vow. And the same thing is also true of his intentions, plans, and promises.

The force of calling this a vehicle of agency is twofold. First, that it is a vehicle *of* agency is underscored by such common possessive locutions as 'my vow' (or for other mandates, 'my intention,' 'my plan,' etc.). Second, that a vow is a *vehicle* is emphasized by the fact that its exclusionary mandate (or, in the case of intentions, its non-exclusionary mandate) is a way of normatively controlling the agent, or placing constraints upon his agency. We may say, then, that in vowing the agent places himself under the normative control of his mandate.

Even though there are two things here, the autonomy and the vehicle for it, both of them are predictable of the agent in a vow (but not in a promise). And this is true even if the vow is conditional upon the assent of another (as in the college student case) (see above, pp. 102–3); no right has been conferred precisely because all of these normative powers are predictable exclusively of the agent. Let us diagram the situation in Figure 3.

119

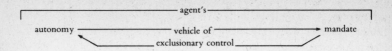

Figure 3

Nevertheless, in another sense, it is precisely the control character of the mandate that enables it to take on something of an independent character. We can see this by noting that (at least the way I am arguing in this book) respecting one's autonomy is really respecting one's vows, or plans, or intentions – in a word, respecting the vehicle. And this is no less true of respecting the autonomy of others. This is further emphasized by observing what happens to respect after the agent is deceased. In a sense – not completely metaphorical – these vehicles of agency appear sometimes to run on their own inertia, or, what is perhaps more appropriate to say considering the death of the agent, they begin to take on a life of their own. If the deceased agent's plans or vows, etc., are unfinished, one can indeed show respect for his autonomy by respecting his plans, etc. And in some cases this may amount to the living finishing what he left unfinished, or at least not undoing it. Now this quasi-independent character of the vehicle of agency is in my opinion the very thing that makes possible the bridge between vows and promises.

When I said, somewhat crudely, that in promising the promiser transfers to the promisee his exclusionary mandate, I mean literally that he transfers to the promisee the (exclusionary) normative control of his agency. Because he had in the state of nature the normative power to place himself under an exclusionary mandate through his intention to do so, he takes it as a natural extension of that power to actually place himself under the normative control of another person.

But this invites the question of how this vehicle is related to the promisee. After all, this relation – whatever it is – is supposed to be the outcome of 'transferring.' My answer – although it will sound paradoxical at first – is that when the promise is completed (that is, when the promisee accepts it in my sense), the mandate is in another sense a vehicle of the *promisee's* agency or autonomy. Because he can void his control of the promiser at any time by releasing him, we may think of the newly acquired vehicle as a place-holder for the promisee's intentions, and certainly intentions are also vehicles of agency. But because in the absence of this the mandate is exclusionary in relation to the promiser, it still is the medium through which he controls the promiser.

What appears paradoxical is that the same thing, the exclusionary mandate, seems a vehicle for *both* the promiser and the promisee! But the paradox vanishes if we note, first, that it is not literally a vehicle of both at the same time. It is a vehicle of the promiser at the time he offers it, that is, at the time he announces his exclusionary intention. But after it is accepted (in the way acceptance is interpreted in this book), it becomes the vehicle of the promisee. Second, even apart from the temporal reference, it is related to the two agents in different ways In relation to the promiser it is exclusionary; whereas in relation to the promisee it is non-exclusionary. These relations are depicted in Figure 4.

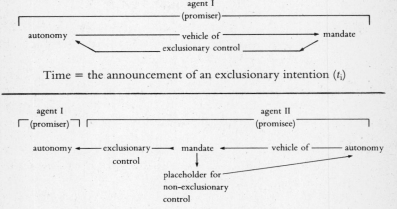

Time = the announcement of an exclusionary intention (t_i)

Time = the continuing acceptance of the exclusionary requirement (t_j)

Figure 4

Some residual skepticism may remain, however, principally, how the two agents can bring about the situation depicted above, the first by announcing his intention, and the second by accepting. Is this not magic? Not if the power of intention described in the earlier chapters is correct. If one has the normative power to place oneself through one's intentions under the normative control of a mandate, why cannot the two parties mesh their normative powers whereby one places oneself under the normative control of another?

121

Well, the next problem, no doubt, is to describe how this 'meshing' is to actually be carried out? When the 'promiser' intends to transfer to the 'promisee' his exclusionary requirement, how does he do this or communicate this to the promisee (without, of course, smuggling in a local convention)? Let me suggest two scenarios.

The first scenario might run like this. First, the promiser would be known to the promisee only as the vower (see above, Chapter 4) and the promisee would be known as an observer of hitherto vowing behavior. Building on the parties' knowledge about vows, conditional intentions, and psychological acts of assent, the promiser can say to his interlocutor that he is going to introduce something new, which once established will be useful and essential for co-operation and mutual reliance. Accordingly, he tells the hearer that he is going to make a vow except that the mandate that it creates is now going to be transferred to the interlocutor, but only if he assents to the thing vowed. If the interlocutor asks 'What do you mean by transferring?', the promiser can say 'It is just like a change in control of a physical object except that the exclusionary control of my agency by the exclusionary requirement is the thing that is being changed: from its controlling me to your controlling me through it. You control me this way because the exclusionary requirement on me structurally is understood as being "at your pleasure": you void it simply by communicating the withholding of your assent. In this fashion, it becomes a way, indeed a vehicle through which, you actually control me.'

Remember that it is safely assumed that the interlocutor understands the building blocks of transferring from his own vowing behavior in the state of nature and from his ability to interpret that of others. That is, he already understands what it is for the vower to be controlled by an exclusionary mandate that the vower creates from his exclusionary intention. And if he also understands what it is physically to transfer possession or control of something as a brute fact, then he has within his ken the ingredients for understanding the transfer of an exclusionary mandate. I just do not see how a *local* convention has to be smuggled in.

The other scenario is what I call the evolutionary scenario, in that these elements of promising, including pre-eminently transferring, emerge as an interpretation of the *de facto* cooperation that may have already arisen. Again, assuming a common knowledge of vows, the elements of promising may emerge as a transcendental deduction of

122

the conditions for the mutual expectations that already would have attended the *de facto* cooperation, however small or sporadic it is. In such a situation, sooner or later the parties to the cooperation will have to ask themselves exactly what their mutual expectations are. Perhaps at first these arise as epistemic expectations that people will continue to behave as they have in the past. But at some point, somebody is going to want to change his mind, and then the question will be whether the expectations of the others should prevent him from doing so. Can the cooperative scheme alternatively be changed only by *mutual* consent; does each party have the power to *release* the other? This would seem to be necessary, they might think to themselves, for otherwise by what right would each party be able to *rely* on the others in the face of some of their number changing their preferences? And without a mutually understood *right* to rely, how would it be *rational* to *continue* to rely? And then, proceeding transcendentally, they would have to ask what is necessary in order to be released only by mutual consent. Rawls's rival view involving the principle of fairness aside (which I discuss below, pp. 127–32, the next thing that suggests itself is the concept of contract. But this could not be the bottom line of the deduction because there would still be a great gap between this concept and the rather thin concept of vows as non-social acts already presupposed. Hence in order to account for the contract, it would have to dissolve into the idea of a mutual exchange of conditional promises, but even so, the concept of a promise, as a one-sided social act, would still be some distance from the non-social vow, and this in turn would introduce precisely the element of transferring already discussed.

I do not see how any step of this transcendental deduction smuggles in a convention except possibly where non-verbal communication comes in, and that, once again, is a global matter. It is true that the mutual expectations that attend the cooperation may already be construed as a kind of convention on Lewis's and Hume's understanding of that term, but, as we shall see more fully, the point of this chapter is that convention appears as the *top* layer of the architectonic, whose infrastructure consists of naturalistic or at best globally conventional elements.

As I have said, the advantage of my naturalistic conception is that it accounts for the way in which cooperation and all its moral baggage arises gradually and perhaps imperceptibly from the state of nature; it accounts for the natural development of social behavior out of solitary behavior. The alternative seems to be the implausible suggestion that any cooperative behavior whereby people have a right to rely on such cannot arise *de facto*, but must first be explained somewhat *de jure* by reference to a pre-existing (local) convention. But this invites the question: how did *that* convention get started? Sooner or later human institutions are going to have to reflect their evolutionary origins, and I suggest that, unlike these rival accounts, my view does this without a trace of infinite regresses (see above, pp. 8–12; 110–11, and below, pp. 124–8).

The chief difference in the two scenarios is that the first is 'bottom up,' while the second is 'top down.' However, both of them are promising routes – if the expression may be pardoned – for arriving at an Archimedean point.

V. Rival positions on the priority of constitutive rules

i.   Searle's speech act theory It might be useful briefly to contrast this account with those views in the literature that make promising parasitic upon a constitutive convention. We shall consider two well-known views in this connection: those of Searle (1969) and Rawls (1971, pp. 343–6). Searle's view makes promising strongly parasitic upon such rules because for him both the social dimension of promising and the creation of a requirement are derived completely from the rule. Rawls's view in contrast accords to constitutive rules this power only if they satisfy other conditions as well. Both views, however, are within the tradition that weaves the commitment of promising out of the fabric of a prior social relation instead of out of that of private vows and intentions. So our task here is to see whether constitutive rules plus whatever other social conditions they are supposed to satisfy can generate the requirements of both vows and promises (although that distinction is not to be found in the literature).

We now turn specifically to Searle, the main contours of whose views were already expounded. As he sees it, saying certain words on certain occasions creates an obligation to do what one said because of the constitutive rule to the effect that anyone who says the words, 'I hereby promise to φ', thereby undertakes an obligation to φ. The emphasis is on the constitutive rule's creating the obligation to keep a promise and not merely clarifying for communicative purposes the intention to do so. The creative dimension is underscored by his insisting that in the absence of such a rule, saying 'I hereby promise' becomes merely uttering certain words or even noises (depending upon how many other constitutive rules have been smuggled in). And this is like the example about striking out in a baseball game generating the obligation to leave the field: without the constitutive rules of baseball defining the situation, striking out would degenerate into merely missing a ball three times with a stick (Searle, 1969, p. 37). On the other hand, it would be more accurate to say that for him constitutive rules simultaneously create the activity and provide the means to communicate the intention to perform it. They are rules for both saying and doing. That is why Searle understands promising to be the name of an illocutionary act (in contrast with the illocutionary act of stating an intention). Insofar as these constitutive rules are rules for linguistic meaning, they stand in stark contrast, he says, to theories of meaning that regard linguistic conventions as a means to some independently conceived natural end – as a matter of strategy, technique, or procedure (Searle, 1969, p. 37).

But our question is, what is it that makes this constitutive convention itself binding? And indeed the thrust of most of the criticism that Searle has received is that an obligation created by a constitutive rule is *only* an 'institutional obligation' – an obligation which is internal to the defining of rules of the institution, but which is not *binding upon the speaker* unless he is a *subscribing* member to it. Thus, for example, J. R. Cameron writes:

What does bind, . . . a promiser, Bridge-player, giver, bridegroom . . ., in the absence of any binding force attaching to the appropriate constitutive convention, is *the person's own will* [emphasis added]: he or she is performing the institutional act willingly, knowing what it imports and entails, and is presumed to have a will to fulfil the requirement he or she is entering into. The facilitating type of practice is founded upon an assumption that the co-operating participants are acting in good faith.   (1972, p. 318)

The force of this objection is bolstered in another objection to the effect that if constitutive conventions analytically entail real obligations, then Searle himself could be obligated by some institution in Australia, wholly unknown to him (1969, pp. 189–90). To this he replied that:

the notion of an obligation is closely tied to the notion of accepting, acknowledging, recognizing, undertaking, etc., obligations in such a way as to render the notion of obligation essentially a contractual notion . . . So unless I am somehow involved in the original agreement, their claims are unintelligible. (1969, pp. 189–90)

Is Searle saying that an institutional obligation becomes a binding obligation only if a contract was made with the subscribing members of that institution? This seems to imply not only that there must be a prior commitment on the part of each participant as a mental act but also that the nature of that commitment is something like a promise. (For each participant seems to be committing himself *to* the others perhaps conditionally upon their acceptance, continued conformance to the agreement, etc.) In the following passage Searle seems to be saying that this prior commitment is not less true of the institution of promising itself:

When I do assert literally that someone made a promise, I do *commit* myself to the institution in the sense that ... I ... undertake to use the word 'promise' in accordance with the literal meaning, which literal meaning is determined by the internal constitutive rules of the institution.
(1969, pp. 194–5)

If these internal constitutive rules can be changed by mutual consent (or become moribund by the lack of regular conformity to them) then it seems that the circle is just about complete: promising allegedly requires those antecedent CRs, defining the meaning of the word 'promise' (as well as the activity it refers to), but in order to understand how those CRs are binding, I must have already made a prior promise to use the word 'promise' in accordance with its literal meaning. It would be useful to compare Searle's final thoughts on the matter (cited above) with those of Prichard.

Promising to do this or that action, in the ordinary sense of promising, can only exist among individuals between whom there has already been something which is really an agreement not to use certain noises except in a certain way, the agreement, nevertheless being one which, unlike ordinary agreements, does not require the use of language. But, of course, it would be more accurate to say that what I am suggesting is not a conclusion but a problem for consideration; viz., what is that something implied in the existence of agreements which looks very much like an agreement and yet, strictly speaking, cannot be an agreement? (1928, p. 179)

Of course, the answer to Prichard's question is the theory sketched in this book, namely, that it is the primitive concept of commitment implied in the existence of agreements in the ordinary sense, and this must be embedded in the concept of intention. But we still have a way to go before this answer can carry much conviction. On the

126

question of the binding character of constitutive conventions, there are still a number of plausible alternatives that I may have overlooked, and which may yet convince some readers that the Prichard–Searle infinite regress can be avoided, and *still* have it that promising is parasitic upon such constitutive conventions. To these we must now turn.

ii. Rawls's principle of fairness Rawls would agree with the above criticism of Searle, viz., that although a promise is defined by a constitutive rule, it generates an obligation that arises only within the institution or 'game' of promising (1971, pp. 343–6). In order for this internal obligation to be binding upon persons, two additional conditions must be satisfied. First, the whole institution – and more generally other institutions which define obligations arising from some voluntary activity – must satisfy his two principles of justice, which, for our purposes, means that the rules constitutive of bona fide promises and those stipulating the excusing or defeating conditions must be such that both parties, but especially the promiser, are free and equal at the time the promise is made. In contrast, promises, he claims, that are extracted by force or fraud are void *ab initio* (1971, p. 343).

The second condition, or rather principle, that validates all voluntary obligations – those arising from rules for the regulation and constitution of some voluntary cooperative activity – is that the parties must have satisfied the principles of fairness. According to this principle, a person is to do his part, as defined by the constitutive rules of an institution, when he has voluntarily accepted the benefits of a cooperative scheme to which others have contributed their share, or has taken advantage of the opportunities it offers in order to further his own interest. The intuitive idea, as Rawls expounds it, is that 'we are not to gain from the cooperative labors of others without doing our fair share' (1971, p. 112). Thus the very rules that make promissory obligations intelligible are precisely of this nature. When accepting a promise and relying on it, I have voluntarily accepted its benefits. Others, in the role of the promiser, have put themselves out, sometimes at great inconvenience. So when *I* make a promise, my turn comes: I am obligated to 'do my fair share,' which, defined by the rules of the promising game, means, keep my promise (unless I can satisfy the excusing conditions for breaking promises – which conditions themselves must satisfy the two principles of justice).

127

Thus we can see how the rules defining a practice can be binding without assuming that we must have made a promise or a vow to obey them, without assuming that we must have made an agreement to keep our agreements. And this would show the principle of fairness to be the more fundamental than the principle requiring fidelity to promises or vows. Or does it?

One of the things that is so confusing about this in Rawls's theory is that he really cannot seem to make up his mind on this point. On the one hand, the constitutive conventions of promising are grounded in the principle of fairness. But on the other, when it is asked what makes the principle of fairness itself binding, Rawls's answer is most curious. Given his general position on the unavailability of necessary truths to ethics and the independence of moral theory from any other 'first philosophy,' the principle is hardly self-evident (see, e.g., 1974). Of course the idea that everyone ought to do his fair share (to maintain a cooperative scheme which he has used for his benefit) does have somewhat of a pleonastic air about it, but no more so than the principle that one ought to keep one's promises. So what is Rawls's answer to the question? It is that the principle of fairness is binding because everyone *would agree to accept it* in the original position! In so agreeing, though hypothetically to be sure, we are, *each* of us, *committing* ourselves to it (in perpetuity)! But if this commitment is either a promise or a vow, we have swung full circle. Promises in the ordinary sense require constitutive rules, and these require for their validity the principle of fairness, but the principle of fairness in turn requires for its validity the principle of promising or vowing – although a special kind of promise or vow that would be made by perfectly rational people in a situation of perfect fairness.[15] Has this special promise been haunted by the ghost of Prichard?

But perhaps the theoretical ax that Rawls had to grind in the last move can be put to one side – as well as the Quinian motivation for it. We still have to face up to the principle of fairness itself to see if the justification for promise keeping can stop with it, and thereby stop Prichard's regress. I do not, however, think that the principle can stand on its own. There is a fatal weakness in it which I believe shows that if the principle is viable at all it is only because it acts as a

---

[15] 'Fairness' as the last token in the above sentence has a different meaning in Rawls's theory than when it occurs in 'the principle of fairness.' A general criticism of Rawls on this whole topic is made in more detail in my article, 'Promissory obligations and Rawls' contractarianism' (1976a).

surrogate for 'tacit promising' or consent, the principle it is designed to support. And perhaps this will prove to be the real lesson in the Rawlsian contractarian move above.

We can begin to see this if we ask just how 'voluntary' the acceptance of benefits on the part of everyone must be. For example, Nozick raises the question, that when I am accepting the benefits, must I also have been *consulted* or have had a fair say in setting up the scheme of cooperation, in order for me to have a binding obligation to do my part in it?[16] And if such consultation is impractical, is my voluntary acceptance taken to communicate the same tacit agreement with the scheme as would be communicated if I actually were consulted? Is this voluntary acceptance to take the form of voluntarily assuming an obligation (i.e., a tacit promise), or merely that of 'acquiescence' or willing enjoyment?[17] Such questions, of course, are difficult in the abstract, so let us take a gloss on an example offered by Nozick (1974, pp. 93–4), already summarized in Chapter 1 above. Suppose that I tune in somewhat regularly to a public FM radio station. As a condition for its continuation, it is necessary that a minimum amount of money be contributed by the community. Am I obligated to contribute my fair share because I have listened to and enjoyed its programs? What about alternatives. Suppose that when I voluntarily tune in to it, I prefer it to the other *available* alternatives: silence, reading, TV, and other radio stations. But suppose that there are lots of other types of radio programs I would prefer to this one, if only they *were* available. Does my tuning in on it *obligate* me to contribute my fair share – supposing it to be twenty dollars a year? As Nozick says, by lending the station my support, I am just making it more difficult to change the status quo (1974, pp. 94–5). He also raises the same point about my contribution. Is there *nothing* else I would prefer to do with my twenty dollars? Suppose that I would rather spend it on something else even at the cost of not having the radio station. Under these circumstances, does the mere act of tuning in on it still commit me to contribute?

[16] See Nozick's discussion in 1974, pp. 90–5. It is true that when Nozick brings up the point about consultation, he says that it is already implied in the institution's having satisfied the two principles of justice. However, I do not see this as implied by the two principles of justice, and even if it were implied, its being so would just muddle the issue before us. So for the purposes of this discussion, let us assume that it is not so implied.

[17] Lyons draws this distinction in discussing the principle of fairness in 1965, p. 191. Lyons takes the voluntary acceptance to mean the latter, but questions whether this can be the basis of voluntary obligations.

There are many unanswered questions here. Actually, I am inclined to think that the cost-benefit considerations that Nozick introduces and which he suggests should be built into the principle as a minimum are somewhat misleading. What I mean is this. Suppose that we know, say, from past behavior, what a person's actual preference ordering is. And suppose that this ordering would warrant his becoming involved in a proposed cooperative scheme. Suppose further that it is necessary to have, say, the first year of contributions before the radio frequency could even be established. Is such a person, then *obligated* to contribute without even having had the opportunity voluntarily to accept the benefits? Could we obligate him because, given his preference ordering, the transitivity of his preferences, etc., we know that he *would* voluntarily accept the benefits in exchange for the contribution? In other words, could the voluntary acceptance be as 'hypothetical' as the contract in the original position? To construe the principle of fairness this way would strengthen the benefit condition (to fit an individual's preference ordering) at the cost of relaxing the voluntary acceptance condition.

Instead, I prefer to construe considerations about an individual's preference ordering as an indicator – and a fallible one at that – of whether he is likely voluntarily to accept the benefits in exchange for the costs of contributing his fair share. This would place the emphasis on two things: (1) actual voluntary acceptance vs. hypothetical, and (2) voluntary acceptance *of* the-costs-in-exchange-for-the-benefits, not just voluntary acceptance of the benefits alone. But since the voluntary acceptance operator in (2) ranges over the entire exchange, it comes uncomfortably close to 'tacit consent,' to assuming an obligation to pay the costs.

This poses a dilemma for anyone who wants to ground the rules governing promising – and other conventions, for that matter – on the principle of fairness – a dilemma over how narrow or broad, weak or strong one is to construe 'voluntary acceptance.' If it is interpreted narrowly enough so as to be distinguished from tacit consent, it becomes too weak to generate an obligation. Alternatively, if it is made strong enough to do so, it merely becomes a form of tacit consent. To bring this dilemma into sharper relief, let us notice that voluntary acceptance can vary along at least two dimensions: strength and scope, which are depicted in Figure 5. Along the dimension of strength, the y-axis, it can range from passive acquiescence – not actively resisting – to willing enjoyment or enthusi-

130

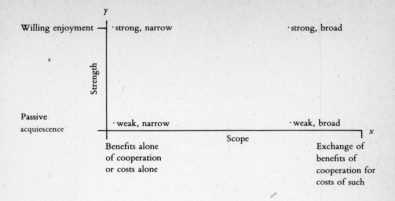

Figure 5

astic endorsement. The scope dimension in contrast, which is represented by the x-axis, draws attention to the variation in *what* is being 'accepted' at the designated level of strength. The extremities in scope are at one end (voluntary acceptance) of just the benefits of cooperation, or just the costs, and at the other end voluntary acceptance of the exchange of those benefits for the costs. Since these two dimensions can vary independently, there are four possible extreme combinations represented in the points 'weak, narrow' (meaning 'narrow' in scope), 'strong, narrow,' 'weak, broad,' and 'strong, broad.' My argument is simply that the first three points in which at least one of the variables is 'weak' are easily distinguished from tacit consent to the exchange, but they also fail, exactly for that reason, to obligate the participant. For obviously, passive acquiescence is too weak, no matter what its scope, so that rules out 'weak, narrow' and 'weak, broad.' That leaves us with willing enjoyment or endorsement, but how can such strong 'acceptance' generate an obligation if it is, say, willing enjoyment of the benefits alone? To sharpen the point, assume that there is not only willing enjoyment of the benefits alone, but willing enjoyment with the knowledge of its necessary costs of cooperation, that the benefit is possible only if a goodly number of people do their fair share. Pursuant to Nozick, assume further that you also know that because of your utility function, you *would* maximize your expected utility *if* you *did* pay your fair share of the costs of cooperation. Yet it still does not follow that you *have accepted, will accept,* or even *ought to accept* your share of the costs. The

131

inference from *knowledge* (of the costs) to acceptance is illicit because 'acceptance' is open under implication.[18]

But, it may be asked, are you not irrational if you do not accept the proposed terms, and unreasonable too, because you have willingly accepted the benefits? Not necessarily. You may not want to *commit* yourself to the scheme because you may want to leave open the possibility of discovering presently unknown alternatives to either the benefits or the costs or both, which could prove even more optimific. Or you may think that your utility function will change. But, then, why accept the benefits – and accept them so willingly? Well, there are many reasons, not all of them immoral. First, few cooperative schemes require even near universal cooperation, so your failure to contribute would not automatically stop the benefits. But second, the scheme may be such that *your* acceptance of the benefits however willingly does not necessarily reduce the benefits available to others. The FM station is the case in point. Under these circumstances, would it not be irrational *not* to tune into your favorite station even though you have no intention to pay a share of the costs? There are, in fact, few schemes whose distribution of benefits is Pareto-optimal.

In contrast, if you willingly accept not only the benefits but the terms of the cooperation, i.e., point strong, broad,' then your voluntary acceptance does indeed get Rawls the benefit of an obligation, but only at the cost of serving as a surrogate for the principle it was designed to support, the principle that one ought to keep one's promises.

It is indeed curious that a principle potentially as complex and/or as vague as the principle of fairness should be thought more fundamental than promising.[19] For notice that similar considerations of the kind just raised are irrelevant to whether there is an obligation to keep a promise. It is, for example, irrelevant to ask whether the thing promised fits the promiser's preference ordering, whether it was the best thing to do given the alternatives, etc. This should be some indication that we are on much more secure ground in taking promising as the more fundamental, and to use it in explanation of obligations arising from fairness, rather than the other way around.

---

[18] Meaning that if I *accept p*, and I *know* that *p* implies *q*, I do not necessarily accept *q*.

[19] As noted above, p. 10 n. 7, Rawls (1971) incidentally distinguishes it from its close cousin, the Rossian principle of gratitude.

One of the advantages of the present account is that it shortcircuits the role of expectations in promises. (Even our discussion of the principle of fairness disregarded the expectations of others that we should do our fair share.) This is because, as I hope to demonstrate here, expectations are too blunt an instrument to perform any justificatory function. The expectations that attend promises fail to distinguish promises from other things;[20] they invariably presuppose something more basic than themselves, typically the more primitive concept of commitment they are supposed to explain; and their normative or legitimizing role for the performance of promises is a mere surrogate for the rights of the promisee and the obligation of the promiser. Nevertheless, promises are accompanied by a strong degree of expectation. For this *is* a way that people can *assure* others that they *will* do their part. Can this be explained without smuggling in a (local) convention, this time in the expectation sense?

I believe that it can. On my view, the degree of expectations that will attend the early promises will be derived from the promisee's background beliefs. This will be of an epistemic, inductive nature; they will depend upon his beliefs about the integrity of the promiser, specifically his integrity in keeping his vows. But even if the promisee is not able to make that judgment, his background beliefs could be built up out of the common knowledge of vow keeping generally in that population. In fact that common knowledge actually precedes the kind of nested expectations that are characteristic of convention. By this I mean that not only does B, the observer, expect A to ϕ, where ϕing is what A vowed, but also that when A announces his vow or believes that somehow B knows about it, A expects B to expect him to ϕ. Likewise, if B believes that A knows that B knows about A's vow, then B expects A to expect B to expect A to ϕ, and so on. The ancillary premises needed to generate these higher level expectations are already present (see Lewis, 1969, pp. 55–8; Lewis's theory is discussed below, pp. 135–7). But it is emphatically *not* the case that this practice of vow keeping is a *convention*. For the element that is missing is any warranting role these expectations on the part of others may play in the

[20] See our early criticism about promising vs. advising above, p. 8, and Raz in his criticism of MacCormick (1972, pp. 99–101) and in his article, 'Promises and obligations' (1977, pp. 216–17).

keeping of one's vows. The fact that *A* expects *B* to expect *A* to keep his vow does not have any special *claim* upon *A* to keep his vow, any more than that *A* knows that *B* knows that *A* takes a walk at 5:00 everyday, and therefore that *B* will expect *A* to take a walk tomorrow places any normative demand on *A* to take a walk tomorrow. These systems of expectations are but side-effects of everybody's common knowledge about vowing. And the practice of vowing itself is a mere regularity.[21]

To this there are two important objections. The first is that the expectations associated with promising are decidedly different from those associated with vow keeping and their difference is accounted for by the fact that promising is parasitic upon an antecedent convention. The difference in the nature of the expectations is that promissory expectations are cited in the warrant for keeping a promise: witness the plausibility of act-utilitarianism. But in vows they are not. As noted earlier in the case of promising, they become legitimate expectations in the sense that we say that the promisee not only expects the promise to be kept, but is *entitled* to do so (see above, p. 133). But the entitlement is no mere induction; it actually is thought to make a claim upon the promiser. But the nature of *these* expectations is precisely of the kind associated with conventions and rules. When a rule is practiced and accepted, it likewise not only generates a system of nested expectations inductively based, but also makes a *claim* upon the conformative behavior of others. The objection, then, poses a dilemma: the expectations derived from the common knowledge about vow keeping either are not of the right kind, or, if they are, they are parasitic upon a promise keeping convention.

I could not, of course, agree more about the difference between expectations attending vows and those attending promises. But I want to claim that, far from being an objection, this is best explained by the present theory that derives promises from vows. The expectations that attend promising can best underscore the claim of the promisee on the promiser, because the former is entitled to them. And he is entitled to them because a right for him has been created. The normative claim-generating aspect is explained by the creation of his right, while the actual expectations are generated, not out of the creation of his right, but out of the general background belief

[21] This additional element of convention which I claim to be lacking is by no means derived from Lewis's theory. Cf. below, p. 136.

134

that people as a matter of fact do generally keep their vows. The burden of what I am saying is that promissory rights, together with prior regularities of behavior, are all that is needed to create the right kind of expectations. Moreover, I want to show now that it is these elements that are most likely to *generate* and sustain a convention, that regularities plus promissory rights are the *sine qua non* of convention.

To see this let us consider a theory that offers a rival account, whereby a convention is generated without the notion of entitlement to expect, without the notion of a contract and agreement. This is the celebrated theory of David Lewis (1969, pp. 39–42, 52–82). On his view, accordingly, a convention is a system of expectations (of the nested kind already discussed) which do produce conformative behavior, to which conformity there is at least one alternative, but which can be generated and sustained merely by the common *preference* to conform, i.e., the preference of each to conform, if others do. Under this conception, if you prefer to conform if others do, and *expect* others to, then, given ancillary premises about your *prudential* rationality, you *will* conform. Several things can get these expectations off the ground: promising can, of course, but need not. Statements of mere intent will serve as well; in fact, anything that leads people to expect a certain pattern of behavior (1969, pp. 32–6). Consider, for example, the simple case of lunching together. Suppose that you and I want to do this on a regular basis but we are indifferent to a range of time slots and restaurants (so long as we both, of course, eat at the *same* time and place). Whatever arrangement is settled upon and sustained on the basis of these mutual preferences and expectations is a convention in Lewis's sense.

But on Lewis's account a convention is not really normative on conformative behavior, although the system of expectations of which it consists may carry some measure of *entitlement* to such behavior, because those expectations are linked to the conditional preferences of oneself and others. In this respect Lewis's convention is only a shade stronger than the system of (epistemic) expectations that enshroud a mere regularity. To illustrate this in the lunching case, suppose that I no longer prefer to eat with you, but that that is not yet common knowledge. Then I still expect you to expect me to meet you, and hence your expectations may (I am not sure on Lewis's theory) import some entitlement; they may play a warranting role in my decision to continue to conform to them. But this is only because your continuing to expect the conformity rests upon the belief that I still have the requisite conditional preference. But when the change becomes common knowledge, the expectations dissolve and with them the convention.

The apparent weakness of this account is revealed by ostensible conventions closer to the kind germane to this chapter. Take, for example, Lewis's notion of linguistic conventions, viz., the convention of truthfulness in language $\mathscr{L}$.[22] This supposedly is a convention in Lewis's sense because it is regularity of behavior generated by a system of expectations and conditional preference to be truthful in $\mathscr{L}$ if others are. The nature of this conditional preference is a common interest in communication. We *want* others to understand us, and they us. But suppose that on a particular occasion it is in my interest to lie to you, and it is common knowledge that it is. Do you still *expect* me to tell the truth? Are you *entitled* to expect it in *this* instance? Are you entitled to expect it of me because you believe it to be an obligation? The answer to all of these seems to be yes, but that answer is unavailable on Lewis's conception.

He has a response to this though that is somewhat complicated. Typically he says, one has a preference to tell the truth (in language $\mathscr{L}$) if others do. That is what makes it a convention. But in the exceptional case in which the preference or interest is lacking, but in which there is still a preference to *hear* the truth (in $\mathscr{L}$) from others, then there is in addition an *obligation* for veracity.[23] This is because the regularity of truthfulness in $\mathscr{L}$ was *also* a *social contract* (and the exceptional case above just brought that to the fore). A social contract is characterized by a different structure of preferences which typically but not always converge on conventions. In a social contract the preference is only for the general conformity of others over general non-conformity.[24] In convention it is for conformity on the

---

[22] 'Truthfulness in Language $\mathscr{L}$,' as opposed to truthfulness in any language, is a convention, according to him, because the concept 'true-in-$\mathscr{L}$' is a conventional notion: a sign in language $\mathscr{L}$ is true in a particular instance 'only if that instance belongs to the truth conditions [conventionally] assigned to it by that language' (1969, p. 152).

[23] In other words, something much stronger than whatever entitlements may attach to conditional preferences.

[24] More precisely, general non-conformity is a state of nature, defined as the absence of this or any other alternative regularity, e.g., the absence of truthfulness in $\mathscr{L}$ or in $\mathscr{L}'$.

136

part of *oneself if* others conform also. There is no *point* in conforming unless others do,[25] for example, in the lunching case, or in the conformity to the practice of wearing ties when one *prefers* that there be no practice at all in this matter (1969, pp. 6, 45–6). The social contract differently involves the preference only for the general conformity of others, not necessarily of oneself (1969, pp. 88–96).

But granted this distinction, why is one obligated to tell the truth (in $\mathcal{L}$) just because, in the present circumstances, one prefers truthfulness in $\mathcal{L}$ (by others) to a state of nature? The answer, as far as I can tell, is that the obligation derives from a sense of *fairness* (i.e., the principle of fairness) (1969, pp. 93–4, 181–3). But we have already seen this to be fraught with serious difficulties (see above, pp. 128–30). The most viable alternative seems to be the principle of promise keeping.

The lesson in this, I think, is that the expectations predicated upon Lewis's conditional preferences, while they are perhaps normatively stronger than the epistemic ones connected with a mere regularity, are still too weak to *sustain* the broad range of practices (like truth telling) that we intuitively take to be conventional. For preferences are the kind of thing that are liable to change, perhaps frequent change (as when the normal preference for communication changes to that of deception). This is to erect a structure of social institutions on shifting sands. In fact it is the liability of men to change their minds that creates the need for conventions founded on something more bedrock. But this social milieu is precisely the same as what creates the need for promises. Both conventions and promises arise from the same sources in the human condition, and as promises explain how a system of expectations can achieve a normative, claim-making import, it appears the most likely candidate to serve in this sustaining function (see below, p. 139).

VII.   The assurance problem

There is still another objection to the 'conventionless' transition from vow keeping regularities to promise keeping expectations. The problem here derives from something already noted above in connection with conventions as systems of expectations: that the expectations typically surrounding promises really reflect a system

---

[25] This is because conventions are offered as solutions to coordination problems in game theory. See 1969, Ch. 1, pp. 5–35.

of *assurances* each of us have that others *will* keep their word. The new objection is that the transition from vowing regularities, plus the mutually recognized conferral of rights, cannot generate those assurances, because there is a much greater temptation to break a promise than a vow, especially in the prisoner's dilemma situation that is supposed to characterize a state of nature in which vows are possible. It is one thing to be bound to do something through our vows; it is another to be bound to *another person*, whose self-interest may turn out to be at odds with our own. Hence any expectations attaching to the regularity of vow keeping simply will not transfer over to promise keeping. If so, it seems impossible that even a mere regularity of promise keeping will get off the ground, let alone a *convention*. What is really needed is a system of extra-assurances that promises *will* be kept. We need, in other words, some kind of sanction against transgressors. Let it be either a social sanction or some quasi-legal enforcement mechanism. If it be a social sanction, that presupposes either a convention (which would imply that the regularity of promise keeping already exists) or a socially accepted rule, neither one of which can be explained out of the elements of vow keeping plus conferral of rights. And if it is an enforcement mechanism, that already presupposes some kind of legal structure, which implies social relations, social acts, which, again, could not be derived from the state of nature. Hobbes was not too far off the mark when he implied that without the sword, promises are but words (1958, Part I, pp. 115–19, 120).

This argument, however, is misconceived both in the premises and in the conclusion. The premise is wrong that there is more temptation to break promises than vows. On the contrary, there is more temptation to break a private vow (because it is not known about). There is even a sanction of sorts attached to breaking a publicly declared vow or decision: the man who often does so looks like a fool. The premise for the argument assumes, I think, that people are basically selfish, or at least devoid of a sense of fairness; it assumes that when it becomes clear to people that keeping promises goes against their self-interest (as in a prisoner's dilemma situation, typifying a state of nature), they will be strongly tempted not to keep it. Hence promising could not stabilize itself without the sanctions of some social or legal conventions.

I do not want to speculate on the degree of selfishness or fairness or benevolence that people generally have. All that is necessary is to show that if people *were* as self-interested as described therein, then they would manifest it even more so in their vows and decisions. For we defined both really as a commitment to do something even if it should later prove mistaken. 'Mistaken' was construed to mean something that goes against one's interest. So on this analysis a doggedly self-interested population would render unintelligible the concept of vows and decisions. The position being maintained when it is said that the vowing element is the key element in promising is that the motivation to keep promises is derived precisely from the motivation to keep vows. This means that given the expectations attached to vows, together with the recognized conferral of rights, there will evolve a regularity of promise keeping, which will evolve into a convention because the expectations of the promisee could play their putative role as a surrogate of strong entitlement. This in turn will allow the aversion to disappointing those expectations to be grounds for the social sanction. When this becomes common knowledge, the necessary psychology could develop and with it a stable social convention.

So much for the faulty premise. But suppose it be true that the temptation to break a promise is greater. How then would the requisite convention and the sanctions get established? One suggestion about the possibility of a convention, which generally is thought to work against everyone's interest and has no justification, is suggested by Lewis (1969, pp. 92–3, on the part about conventions that are not social contracts) and McNeilly (1972, pp. 72–3). This is a case in which people are motivated to conformative behavior, not out of preference, but to avoid public opprobrium. Examples offered by Lewis include the convention of wearing ties when everyone prefers no convention in this matter (a state of nature) and the convention prohibiting the declaration that the emperor has no clothes (1969, pp. 6, 45–6, 92). McNeilly, along these lines, suggests the possibility of a wise and dishonest high priest who tells people that promise breaking will be punished in the after-life. This is like a sovereign who threatens punishment for non-conformity (and for McNeilly illustrates the non-moral basis for motivation to keep promises (1972, pp. 72–6)). But these conventions are by nature unstable and thus fail to offer a convincing explanation of the requisite social sanctions.

The basic weakness of these explanations lies in this. If there is this temptation to break promises, then the same temptation forever haunts the very enforcement of them. Without an established convention of promise keeping, how can people have the assurance that the supposed enforcer *will* enforce the obligation to keep promises – especially when tempted to do otherwise? The same objection would prevent public opprobrium from carrying the main burden of enforcement, for, in the first place, that belies the supposition that the convention does not exist, and in the second place, public censure is susceptible to the same vices that can afflict the official enforcer. If we are to be assured against such miscarriages, then it looks as if the enforcement of promises is itself a kind of promise to enforce promises; and this will work only if we already have in hand some assurances about keeping promises in the first place.[26]

VIII. *Promising and utilitarianism*

The last difficulty, I think, indicates the general sort of problem with the utilitarian account of promising, an account which is so influential as to merit separate discussion. In this I follow the standard distinction of utilitarianism into the 'act' and 'rule' variety. In the former, the justification for keeping promises lies in their expectable utility, the utility consisting of the fact that the promisee will likely be expecting it. These likely expectations are distinguished from the utility of the thing promised (which might even be negative). It is, however, the former expectations that are the utilitarian source of the obligation to keep promises, which amount really to an obligation on the promiser not to disappoint the expectations of the promisee. So much of the rationale turns upon the real likelihood of there being expectations. But the addressee might also expect things on the part of the speaker which were not promised, but only stated as a current intention. The two related questions are: why is the expectation attending promises supposedly stronger, and why does it, as opposed to the other expectations, create a claim on the part of the hearer?

The nature of the difficulty is revealed by asking how promising

[26] The enforcement and assurance problem is one of the main puzzles (of the prisoner's dilemma) to which classical contractarianism is offered as a solution. Thus Hobbes's sovereign who holds absolute power (1958), and Locke's neutral third party judge (1927, II, pp. 123–4), can be read in this way, but they likewise seem to meet with the same vicious regress. But this is a complicated subject, which to some extent has been discussed elsewhere. See David Braybrooke, 1976.

can even get started in an act utilitarian society.[27] Because promising (as a practice) does not exist yet, the appropriate expectations, on this view, do not either, although there exist the ones that accompany statements of intent. In this respect the act utilitarians are in the position that I am, in that they have to generate promising without already presupposing the convention, but unlike the theory that I advocate, they cannot make the act parasitic upon the promiser's having already created a right on the part of the promisee. Instead the ordering between the right and the expectations is supposed to be reversed. The question, then, is how the promiser in this society of avowed act utilitarians, is to create the expectation of the right kind – the expectation that he *will* keep his promise even if he later discovers that the total weight of utilitarian reasons is against it. And the exclusionary intention to which these expectations refer could not even be had by a card carrying act utilitarian, because it is an intention to exclude precisely his credo of acting on the basis of optimific considerations. The exclusionary intention would thus be anathema, and since everybody in this society would know this *ex hypothesi*, they would never hold the matching expectations, and so never generate the practice or the obligation.[28] The problem here is analogous to the attempt to render enforcement of promises prior to their establishment. Accordingly, I suggest that the only way these expectations will get off the ground, and with them social sanctions, is by making them parasitic upon the more primitive idea of creating a right, etc.

Yet utilitarians have fashioned a plausible way out of this diffi-

[27] This is the line taken by D. H. Hodgson's refutation (1967, pp. 38–50), and in my article 'The primacy of promising' (1976b, pp. 323–7). The criticism I develop here and in the above article is cut from the same cloth as Hodgson's criticism.

[28] Many people have been of the opinion that the Hodgson type of argument invoked above has been refuted. The principal detractors are Singer, 1972, and Lewis, 1972. There is, however, a fatal assumption in both of their rejoinders: the assumption that promising is analogous to veracity – an analogy which Hodgson himself encourages (1967, pp. 39ff). That is why Singer and Lewis turn their guns on Hodgson on truth-telling, leaving the impression that the refutation on promising will take care of itself. But the two are not analogous. Consider, for example, one of Singer's most plausible arguments: that people lie in order to deceive, but that deception loses its point among act utilitarians. Does this apply to breaking promises? Hardly. One reason why breaking promises could occur (assuming that there would be a point to making them) would be lack of omniscience about whether the weight of reasons might later militate against keeping the promise – something that applies equally to act utilitarians. The only writer on Hodgson that deals squarely with promising of which I am aware is Mackie, 1977, but he concedes the point that the only kind of expectations that will arise in an act utilitarian society are those associated with mere statements of intent.

culty, by supplanting the act variety of utilitarianism with the ideal rule variety. The concept behind this maneuver is precisely the recognition of the utility of the rule of promise keeping (as expounded by Brandt, 1979, pp. 286–305, esp. 299–305), which rule necessitates giving up the act utilitarian justification. In starting from scratch (i.e., without the actual practice of promising), the rule exists only in ideal form. Thus in making the early promises, *people would not actually expect* them to be kept and could not actually rely on them. They do know, however, that under the idea rule they would rely on promises, and that this arrangement is justified as maximizing expectable utility. Our question is: why is one *obligated* to keep the early promises when it is common knowledge that no one is yet relying on them?

Brandt's answer is that you *are* obligated (now), because the ideal rule *would* obligate you, and this because people *would* expect it (1979, pp. 302–3). The standard objection to this (really to ideal rule utilitarianism in general) is proffered by the 'actual rule' utilitarians, viz., that only actual rules (i.e., actually practiced and/or accepted) give rise to obligations, not hypothetical (ideal) rules (see Diggs, 1970). Since the rule in question does not exist, they ask, how can the obligation? If keeping early promises is intended merely to contribute to bringing it about that the rule for promise keeping exists, then this is an act of supererogation, not an actual moral requirement. But it seems clear enough that the early promises obligate no less than later ones, so the obligation has yet to be explained.

This point is on the right track, but needs more development, lest it might degenerate into a verbal dispute as to what can be called an obligation (cf. Brandt's reply to Diggs, 1979, p. 302). The way I prefer to press the point is to grant that we are obligated to conform to ideal rules that are not actual and then ask if there is still any difference between an obligation required by an ideal rule, and one required by an ideal rule that is also actual, i.e., practiced and/or accepted. In the promising case, is there no difference for the utilitarian between the promissory obligation when the promisee is actually expecting and when he is not? It is hard to believe that there is not, and this all the more so for Brandt because, according to him, ideal rule utilitarians are not 'utopians' but 'incrementalists' (1979, pp. 290, 301). That means that people's actual beliefs, behavior, etc. cannot be totally disregarded. (That is why ideal rule utilitarians cannot, for example, be total pacifists (1979, pp. 297–8).) Now if

142

there is a difference, then the obligation attaching to the early promises cannot be quite as strong as it is now (or when the ideal rules get fairly established). And so the fact that one makes an early promise must carry even less weight in the scales of utility to offset the possible disutility of doing the thing promised. If so, then we seem to be in somewhat of a Hodgson predicament; we cannot get the practices started unless we justifiably act *as if* the rule *were* practiced; yet the fact that it *is not* practiced undermines the long-range expectable utility of doing precisely this! And thus it seems that promising will not get off the ground in a society of ideal rule utilitarians.

IX. *Promising as a speech act*

i. Illocutionary vs. perlocutionary intent As I see it, it is no accident that the expectation account of promising, be the expectations either actual or hypothetical, should prove a dead end. For we can see that they are nugatory in any role in the speech act of promising. I have already indicated how the expectations, if they occur, do not distinguish promising from other things. When a promise to one party is communicated to both him and another, and the other comes to expect it in the same degree as the promisee, his expectations do not create the slightest claim on the promiser.[29] Nor will it help if promises are marked off by saying that they are speech acts in which the perlocutionary intent is to create reliance, i.e., a reliance brought about either intentionally or knowingly.[30] For, once again, this fails to distinguish promising from advising, or distinguishing promises from stating an intention with the further intention that, given the circumstances, one can likely rely on the thing intended, but which falls short of promising (see Raz, 1972, 1977, p. 216; see also for discussion above in Chapter 1, pp. 8–9).

The main point of these distinctions is that a promise can be successful as a speech act without intentionally or knowingly inducing *any* reliance or expectation at all. In this respect it differs from threats whose purpose does require the perlocutionary intent to arouse expectations. Until recently, the received view was that promises and threats are formally identical (in perlocutionary intent), the only difference being in the content and in the fact that the promised act is

[29] As noted above, these examples as well as the following are cited in Raz, 1977, pp. 216–17.
[30] This is the strategy of MacCormick, 1972.

presumed to be welcomed by the promisee, but not so in the case of a threat.[31] Pall Árdal goes on to claim that since nobody has a prima facie obligation to carry out a threat, there is no prima facie obligation to keep a promise either, but that any overriding obligation must be traced to this difference, viz., that the promised act is desired by the promisee, and not the mere fact that it was promised (1968, pp. 232–3).

That a threat, however, does differ from a promise, in that only threats are necessarily connected with producing expectations, can be shown as follows. Observe that I can say without paradox 'I hereby promise, but I know that you do not expect me to carry it out (perhaps I have disappointed you too many times in the past),' whereas if I avowedly threaten you, but say, 'I know that you do not expect me to carry it out,' I have defeated – rendered pointless – the threat as a speech act. But what is the point of the promissory counterpart, it might be asked? The answer is that the point is illocutionary, not perlocutionary; it is to secure uptake of your understanding my creating a right for you and an obligation for me, but it is an illocutionary act wholly of the Gricean 'intention-constituted' kind. For the point is to bring about your understanding of my conditional exclusionary intention.

Some people have thought that the point must be the perlocutionary one of producing expectations because of the application of Moore's paradox: although I can promise but not intend to keep it, I cannot *say* 'I promise but I do not intend to keep it.' McNeilly makes the point by saying that if the promisee believes that the promiser does not intend, and the promiser knows this, then promising is as pointless as knowingly passing a bad check to someone who knows it to be bad (1972, pp. 73–5). But there is another explanation of the man who says, 'I promise, but do not intend to keep it,' which can distinguish it from the case in which he says, 'I promise, but I know that you do not believe that I intend to keep it.' Since the point of promising as a speech act is to intend to secure (illocutionary) uptake of the promiser's exclusionary intention, he is defeating that intention by saying he does not in effect have the exclusionary intention. But, in the second case, when the promiser intends to communicate that he has the exclusionary intention, he can secure uptake of *that* intention (the Gricean intention to communicate) while at the same

[31] Searle (1969, pp. 58–9) typifies this. See also Árdal, 1968 and 1981.

time knowing that the promisee does not believe that he has the exclusionary intention.[32] In other words, this account can explain why one can promise insincerely as a speech act (and even know that the promisee believes it to be insincere). The explanation is that one can still successfully communicate to another the understanding that one intends him to believe that one has the exclusionary intention, without believing it oneself.

ii.   Insincere promises These variety of promises have been thought to sound the death-knell for theories like the present one, i.e., for theories that derive the obligation essentially from the intention to bind oneself.[33] If promising is a matter of truly announcing an intention to bind oneself, etc., then it would seem that insincere promises are really not promises at all. Not only does this undercut the view just expressed, namely that insincere promises are promissory speech acts, but it also suggests that they are not obligatory.

This is a natural interpretation of my intention conception of promising, but it is mistaken. Not only are insincere promises bona fide promises, they are also best explained by an intention conception like the present one. Atiyah and others like him have erred in confusing the *concept* of an exclusionary intention with having that intention. This is because, as I see it, promising, being a speech or communicative act, is such that the *obligation* to keep it derives from the *concept* of an exclusionary intention getting mapped onto the Gricean intention to communicate it, secure uptake, etc. By that I mean that the exclusionary intention is semantically represented in

[32] Of course, if the promisee *knows* that the promiser does not have the exclusionary intention, and the promiser knows this, then the latter cannot successfully promise, and it does indeed become (deceptively) like the fraudulent check example. But that is not primarily because the supposedly essential perlocutionary object (of producing expectations) is defeated. It is because the promisee believes *truly* that the promiser does not *have* the exclusionary intention; and when the promiser knows this, then he cannot successfully intend to create in the promisee the *illocutionary understanding* that he intends to communicate that he *has* an exclusionary intention. For they both *know* that he has not. In other words, strengthening the promisee's belief to that of knowledge, and supposing the promiser's knowledge of this, blocks the bona fide intention to secure *illocutionary* uptake. The test, however, for the rival perlocutionary object view (to produce expectations) must be formulated with belief, not knowledge, since belief is all that is implied in successfully producing *expectations*.

[33] Patrick Atiyah, whose book, *Promises, Morals and the Law* (1981), was published after the present book was essentially written, makes this point repeatedly. This subsection is essentially an appendix to respond to what he considers to be one of his most powerful arguments.

the Gricean intention, and it is *that representation* in a communicative act that really generates the obligation. This allows for insincere promises because an exclusionary intention can, of course, be represented to an addressee without the speaker *having* that intention. But even though the promise can take effect without the speaker having the appropriate intention, it is still the concept of that intention that is so semantically represented and by means of which we come to understand what promising is in the first place. Those who try to interpret it without the concept of an exclusionary intention (e.g., the convention or expectation school) do so at their peril.

6

Autonomy and objectivity

In the last chapter I tried to sketch the way that promising precedes the emergence of conventions and their corresponding system of expectations. The position in that chapter is that if these conventions impose any obligation at all, it is because a promise was at work, its being able to carry so heavy a burden because of the way it builds upon the very structure of intentional action. This theory of social norms and convention reserves a central place for autonomy – at least in the moral, and perhaps the metaphysical, sense as well – in the idea that obligations thus considered are those which we placed upon ourselves; they are undertakings from our own intentional and voluntary activity.

Such a position, however, has disturbing implications for ethical theory – or at least objectivist ethics. For it needs to be asked whether any promise (no matter what its content) gives rise to an obligation of this kind, and whether this obligation is the only kind there is. If the answer to both questions be yes, then the central role of autonomy seems to be bought at the price of moral objectivity. For the concept of obligation would appear to be a matter of commitment and not much else. On the other side, if the obligation-generating capacity of promising is tempered by other kinds of obligations which may potentially conflict with it, then it becomes unclear the extent to which autonomy is a threat to objectivity. Not only would the boundaries of each kind of obligation become fuzzy in conflicting situations, but each kind of obligation would have disparate sources, the one autonomous, the other, if you will, 'heteronomous,' which do not readily cohere with one another within a single normative system.

Before attacking the problem head-on, it should be noticed that a certain amount of autonomy for creating the form of our moral world seems to be both a desideratum and a necessary datum for moral theory. Any ethical theory, it would seem, would have to account for the *special* obligations of a parent to his children, of one

147

friend to another, of an office-holder to his role-derived duties, and generally of any person who stands to others in some special relation. Although in this way people are intentionally shaping the form of at least a part of their moral world, their doing so does not pose a threat to objectivity. For what is underscored in such cases is exactly the objectivity of these prima facie obligations so undertaken; these are obligations which agents are under, not merely obligations which they think they are under.

Nevertheless, we must return to the possible clash, perhaps elsewhere, between autonomy and objectivity. There are, after all, promises and promises; some are trivial, others are immoral. If promissory obligations are restricted by some *ceteris paribus* clauses, then I owe an explanation as to the source of that restriction. For, as indicated, the idea that an important class of obligations arise from within our volition does not mesh well with there being restrictions from without. Our question must be this: how do other moral principles stand to the prima facie obligation to keep a promise? Is it a matter of all moral principles being relativized to what we have committed ourselves to, or is there some kind of objectively external constraint on those commitments?

I.   *The contractarian solution*

This is a perennial issue both to advocates of moral autonomy and to writers in the contractarian tradition in particular. The contractarians try to get around the difficulty by construing other moral or political obligations as arising out of some foundational, rational promise, which, because of the circumstances, is either very difficult to avoid making, or can be avoided only at our peril. Such a maneuver fashions objectivity out of autonomy by making the familiar panoply of moral or political obligations the content of our deepest commitments. And because it is understood to be grounded in commitment, the nature of obligation is a voluntary one. As for the analysis of the foundational promise, there are at this time two rival schools: one takes it to be a tacit promise à la classical contractarianism, while the other, the Rawlsian, construes it to be hypothetical. The 'tacit' school takes it to be a promise made in the course of our normal moral or political behavior; if it is to be evaded, it takes some special act of disavowal. The 'hypothetical' school takes it to be not an actual agreement (not even a tacit one), but one which every rational being *would* enter into if only he reflected on its nature, and on the bleak alternatives. Both solutions are fraught with notorious obstacles.[1]

II. The derived commitment solution

In this chapter I shall defend a position which relies in part on tacit promising – narrowly circumscribed – but which goes far beyond it and obviates the standard difficulties associated with the concept. Basically, my position is this: the familiar range of moral principles, for example, those listed by Ross as prima facie obligations, are not in my view in the content of either tacit or explicit promises, but they may be *implied* in various ways by such promises. The nub of the matter is that 'commitment,' and the claims and deontic judgments it warrants, is *closed under implication* (see above, Chapter 1, p. 15 n. 13); hence these implied moral principles can be *derived* from the commitments we undertake in a variety of tacit and explicit promises. In contrast, promising, like other propositional attitudes, is *open under implication*, which means that it does not entail that these derived commitments are themselves promises – not even tacit ones! Because of this disparity, we shall be able to avail ourselves of all of the advantages of tacit promises without being saddled with their notorious difficulties.

The matter can be put in this way. The main difficulty with tacit promises is the vagueness as to what kind of behavior, mental attitude, etc., counts as a promise, and a corresponding vagueness as to range and scope of such commitments. Given a specimen of behavior, it might be subject to rival interpretations along either or both of these dimensions. Since two agents might understand the behavior of each other differently, this disparity gives rise to the 'assurance problem,' the problem of whether and when one can take the other to be bound to some performance and whether he so conceives himself (see Rawls, 1971, p. 337). The difficulty might stem from this source; I cannot tacitly promise that p unless I am at least *aware* (or am presumed to be aware, given standing conventions) that I am committing myself to p. (The assurance problem registers the uncertainty of others knowing whether I am in the requisite mental state.) But given that commitment, as we have said, is closed

---

[1] For the standard criticism of tacit promises, see Hume, 1957, p. 30; Raphael, 1970, pp. 85–102; Rawls, 1971, p. 337; for criticisms of hypothetical contractarianism, see Brandt, 1979, pp. 234–45; and Melden, 1977, pp. 81–7.

under implication, I need not be aware in the slightest of any of the other commitments which can be *derived* from those commitments of which I am indisputably aware. Thus the assurance problem for derived commitment does not even arise.

Now if this move enjoys a measure of success, it resolves the tension between autonomy and objectivity in the spirit of contractarianism – insofar as the ensuing obligations are voluntary and the favored system of moral principles is erected upon the structure of intentional action. The main challenge, of course, is to show how the various moral principles are implied in our actual promises and undertakings. It should not be thought that there will be anything like a complete showing of that here, for that is the subject of another book. But I believe that I can sketch how one or perhaps two in the list of important principles can be so implied, and in so doing suggest some avenues of further research.

III. Tacit promising revisited

Since the derived commitments are to be derived from actual promises, it behooves us to study the latter, which are divided into the explicit and tacit variety. Explicit promises were studied in the previous chapter, so we are left with tacit promises and the controversies that surround them. I propose in this section to provide a rough, though serviceable, notion of tacit promising.

Historically, the doctrine of tacit promises arose in the literature as a way of binding descendants of the original contractors to the terms set out by their forebears. The main question which it addresses is this: how could people born into a political and social system, unfamiliar in many cases with alternatives, be said to have promised to support the government, obey the law, and live up to moral principles? If they did not promise expressly, did they do so tacitly? But 'tacitly' by doing or refraining from doing what? According to Hobbes, simple acquiescence in – not activity resisting – the laws of one's society constitutes acceptance (1958, Part II, Ch. 17, p. 143, Ch. 20, Sec. 3, p. 163), while Locke has said that availing oneself of the advantages and benefits of living in the society is a tacit promise to be so bound (1927, II, p. 177). The problem is compounded by whether one really has a choice in such matters. In countries, for example, where there is not even a legal right to emigrate or secede, it would be difficult to maintain that society is founded on a voluntary contract. Yet this is what Hobbes maintains (1958, Part I, Ch. 14, p. 117, also pp. 143, 163, 170). As Rawls sees it, a society based upon tacit consent is inherently unstable because of the assurance problem. He writes that if people are uncertain about whether one another is so bound to putative duties, 'the public conviction that all are tied to just arrangements would be less firm and a greater reliance on the coercive powers of the sovereign might be necessary to achieve stability' (1971, p. 337).

The other aspect of the assurance problem, the scope of the tacit promise, is unintentionally illustrated in Locke's *Second Treatise*. He says that merely traveling on the highway through a country (where one is not a citizen) is giving tacit consent to obey its laws, at least while so traveling (1927, II, p. 177). But why does traveling on the highways constitute tacit consent to obey all the laws instead of just traffic laws?

No doubt these are serious objections. But it would be a mistake to discard the notion wholesale. For one thing, there is a variety of situations in which, whatever one's theory, we could hardly get on without it. A man who is not a visitor from Mars, who orders food in a restaurant can safely be presumed tacitly to promise to pay for it. A person who accepts a position without an express contract tacitly promises to discharge its duties. Even *omissions* in certain clearly defined circumstances leave no ambiguity of presence of such a commitment. Take, for example, the Dean of a college who is responsible for the memoranda that his assistants send out on his stationery. If he reads a memorandum and offers no suggestions for changing it, does he not give tacit consent to its contents? Finally, consider the whole range of cases in which a person's past behavior entitles us morally, as opposed to epistemically, to expect its continuance (see above, p. 8, for a discussion of this distinction). According to David Hillel-Rubin, the difference seems best accounted for only by supposing that there was a tacit promise in the moral entitlement case, but not so in the epistemic entitlement case (1972, pp. 73–5). Thus, in his example, a man who in the past has regularly met us for cocktails at the same time and place, tacitly promises, in the absence of a clear disavowal, to continue to do so. But suppose that he also wears narrow ties with the same regularity. There can be no doubt that in the latter case we are only epistemically, not morally, entitled to expect him to continue doing so.

We find such cases clearly to exemplify tacit promises because they seem to be governed by conventions for such. It would make things tidy if we could limit our reliance on tacit promises to such cases. This would essentially put them, epistemically, on a par with express promises and defuse the assurance problem at the outset. But we know that tacit promises are like express promises in another way: neither is *merely* a matter of convention (if Chapter 5 is correct). First, there are instances in which, despite a clear convention, the circumstances and intentions indicate the contrary; and second, there are instances where the conventions, if they exist, are so weak and ambiguous that a reference to the agent's intentions is necessary to settle the matter. In either of these instances, I propose to limit tacit promises to cases where the agent is at least *aware* of *what* he is interpreted by others to be promising (which is not to say that he is aware that he is also promising or even taken to be promising). Thus a man who agrees to play a game whose rules have not been spelled out to him has not tacitly *promised* his opponents to abide by them. (A more interesting question, discussed below, is whether there can be a derived commitment to those rules in our sense of the term.) Nor, in the context of the principle of fairness, is a man to have promised to do his fair share when he voluntarily accepts a benefit from others but is unaware that that benefit is possible only by everyone's doing his fair share (see above, Chapter 5, pp. 130–2). Pursuant to my gloss on Nozick's example, a man who regularly turns the knob on his radio to a public radio station, but is unaware of the arrangements for financing it, is not, by the mere act of turning the knob, thereby making a tacit promise to send in his annual contribution. But I propose that even if there is awareness, it is only a necessary condition for tacit promising.

The sufficient and necessary conditions for tacit promising are derived from those set for promising proper: there will have to be (possibly a Gricean) intention to communicate to another the speaker's exclusionary intention to transfer to the other an exclusionary requirement upon the other's continuing assent. These conditions should assure us that tacit promises *are* promises, not degenerate ones. And so this is enough to rule out as tacit promises such dubious candidates as awareness coupled only with passive acquiescence or awareness coupled with an act of omission. What distinguishes tacit promises from express ones is the manner in

152

which the exclusionary intention is communicated. In a tacit promise, it is communicated by a form of non-verbal behavior; in an express promise it is through verbal behavior (although, of course, not necessarily by use of the word 'promise'). I think that in the evolutionary account provided in the last chapter the first promises were probably the tacit variety.

Because tacit promises do rely on non-verbal behavior, these specifications do not completely eliminate the assurance problem because of the residual cases where the final court of appeal is to the agent's mental state, his knowledge and intentions. But they do minimize it, first, by narrowing down the area in which such appeal is necessary, and second, by specifying the conditions that the intentions must satisfy. The clearer we are about those conditions the easier it will be to devise ways of communicating them unambiguously to others.

IV. *Some remarks on the logic of derived commitment*

We have said that we are relying in part on tacit promising because of the possibility of some important obligations being implied by the things we may have actually promised to do, tacitly or expressly. It is time now to look at the kind of implication involved and to some problems in its conceptualization and formalization. Recall that in contrasting derived commitment with promising (both tacit and express) we are contrasting the following two patterns of inference. The first is

(P) I promise to p
p entails q
_____

I promise to q.

This we have held to be invalid, largely because it would fail for any propositional attitude. In contrast we have adopted

(C) I am committed to p
p entails q
_____

I am committed to q.

We have gotten the commitment schema out of actual promising by assuming the principle for which we have argued in this book, namely

153

(Pr) (I promise to p) strictly implies (I am committed to p).[2]

The schema for derived commitment (C) presupposes the familiar deontic principle:

(D) if p entails q, then Op entails Oq

where 'is committed to' in (C) is substituted for the ought operator in (D) above, and where we are allowing the original promissory commitment as the first premise in (C) in order to detach by *modus ponens* the consequent of (D).

There is, however, a host of objections and puzzles associated with this principle (D). Some are paradoxes of deontic logic; others are controversies over the nature of practical reason. Some of these are rather technical, of limited bearing on the main argument of this chapter – appearances perhaps to the contrary notwithstanding – and some have convincing solutions readily available in the literature. For these reasons, I shall mention very briefly the tangential or resolved difficulties, saving the central controversial ones for the lion's share of the discussion.

i. *The Good-Samaritan paradox* One puzzle that can merely be noted is the so-called Good-Samaritan Paradox. That is the paradox in which the Good Samaritan has, say, an obligation to come to the aid of a victim of a crime. But being a victim of a crime entails that a crime was committed. Pursuant to (D), it therefore follows that the criminal was under an obligation to commit the crime! For the best

2 This last principle or something like it is what deontic logicians refer to as 'commitment.' Taking as an example that the act of promising implies the obligation to keep it, their main quarry is the formalization of this conditional obligation, whether it is represented as $O(p \supset q)$ or as $p \supset Oq$, or by some other connective than the horseshoe. My sense of 'commitment' in this book is somewhat narrower and different. I am not concerned with the form of conditional obligation as such but only with the connection between promising (and similar acts) and the obligation to keep it. I have been assuming here, if only for ease of exposition, that the 'ought' judgment is detachable from this conditional. Thus the first premise in the schema for derived commitment (C) is 'I am committed to p,' which has the force of a certain kind of ought operator on p. A truer if less perspicuous account would have to be formally more complex in light of the fact that the ought judgment is always prima facie, which on the one hand gives it the logical form of being relativized to the promise, and on the other hand, the logical form of an actual, detachable (though defeasible) moral *demand* which can be overridden by another moral demand. When the overriding occurs, however, it is at the cost of some compunction and perhaps some owed compensation to the holder of the promissory right. The *ceteris paribus* requirement is discussed in another connection, below, and these matters are set out at length in my paper, 'Practical inference, necessity, and defeasibility' (1983).

solution to this, and one which spawned a comprehensive theory of practical reasoning, the reader is referred to the work of Castaneda.[3]

ii.   The logic of satisfaction vs. satisfactoriness Somewhat less technical but no less complicated is Kenny's objection to (D) (see 1975, pp. 70–95). It is an attack on (D) as the logical form of the inference for deriving commitments, rather than an attack on the notion of derived commitment *per se*. Indeed Kenny appears to have his own counterpart to (D) for deriving commitments. For this reason my discussion of it will have to be somewhat briefer than the subject would otherwise warrant.[4]

Kenny claims that (D) is unsound even though it is, of course, the practical analogue of *modus ponens*. His main salvo against (D) is this. Suppose both that I think Op to be true, and, its being a deontic judgment, I intend to p. Suppose also that p is possible while q is not. Now, if I accept (D) I would be committed to intending, attempting the impossible, which violates the principle that 'ought' implies 'can.' Similar suspicions can be raised against other practical analogues of alethic assertoric logic. Suppose, for example, that I have the premises $O(p \cdot q)$ or $I(p \cdot q)$, where O is the ought operator and I is the intention operator. By the axioms of assertoric logic we can derive $Op \cdot Oq$, and from this detach Op. For Kenny, however, this commits the same mistake, since p may be futile without the performance of q. The reverse is true for the disjunction $O(p \lor q)$. In assertoric logic it is a fallacy to detach p from $p \lor q$, but this is precisely what we can do in practical logic, for if I have a reason to do either p or q then I can infer that I have a reason to do p.

These considerations lead Kenny to replace (D) with the practical principle

(~D) if p entails q, then Oq entails Op

which, of course, is the analogue, not to *modus ponens*, but to the

---

[3] See 1975, pp. 214–18. Castaneda proposes a modification of (D) in terms of a distinction between practitions – his term for the content or phrastics of intentions, imperatives, and other practical dicta – and propositions understood to be the content of assertoric mental attitudes. In his earlier work this was the distinction between actions prescriptively considered and actions that are mere circumstances within the deontic operator. Accordingly (D) is valid only if there is an entailment between practitions, p and q, rather than propositions.

[4] I have treated it more fully in my paper, 'Practical reasoning, commitment, and rational action' (1984).

Fallacy of Affirming the Consequent! But that is Kenny's point. Practical logic is the mirror image of alethic assertoric logic, so that what is a fallacy of affirming the consequent in the latter is a *modus ponens* inference principle in the former. Kenny, accordingly, characterizes practical logic as a logic of satisfactoriness, that is, a logic entailing conclusions enjoining the adoption of satisfactory (i.e., sufficient) means to our adopted ends ($\sim$D), instead of implicating us in the choosing of necessary means to our adopted ends (D).[5] Thus if Oq is true, and if, let us suppose, I also intend q, and further, if p is a satisfactory means to q (i.e., a sufficient condition), then I can derive Op. But there is a proviso to the effect that the derivation of Op is 'defeasible,' and can be defeated if Op turns out to be unsatisfactory in relation to an augmented set of promises containing some of one's *other* adopted ends (Kenny, 1975, pp. 92–6).

In what follows, I proffer a summary rejoinder[6] which relies on the views defended in the previous chapters. In this book we have been looking at practical reason as essentially the transmission of commitment (a transmission from the commitment in at least one of the premises to the commitment to the conclusion; this is analogous to the way that some have characterized practical reason as the transmission of intention). A concept that is complementary to the transmission of commitment is that of validity, for the latter pertains to the relation between the propositional contents or phrastics contained in different acts of commitment. Under this conception, if the inference from commitment in the premises to commitment in the conclusion is *valid*, and if for some reason we demure at embracing the conclusion, then we can avoid a *logical* mistake by simply backsliding on the original commitment in the premises. The test, accordingly, for a *valid* inference is to determine whether rejecting the conclusion in this fashion forces us, on pain of inconsistency, to backslide on the commitment to the premises. My critique of Kenny is simply that his principle ($\sim$D) appears non-valid under this procedure, because the relation of one thing's being a satisfactory means to something else is too weak a relation to transmit a commitment.

[5] If practical logic were built upon assertoric logic, it would perhaps be known as a logic of *satisfaction* (rather than satisfactoriness), because the satisfaction conditions of intentions, imperatives, and other practical dicta are the analogue of truth conditions of propositions, and because the rules for valid practical inference would be satisfaction-preserving in the same way as valid assertoric inference is truth-preserving.

[6] And which is fully expounded in my 'Practical reasoning,' (1983).

For suppose that I am committed to q, I know that p is satisfactory in relation to q, and yet I feel no inclination, no commitment in the slightest, to form the intention to try for p. Must such demurring indict me as inconsistent; must I escape the indictment only by back-sliding on my original commitment in the premises? I think not. Lurking in the background is always the possibility of alternative means, equally satisfactory, in relation to q but perhaps more efficient, or admitting of less disastrous side-effects in relation to r or s. To take Raz's example (1978, p. 11), suppose I want to kill a fly, and know that blowing up my house is satisfactory in relation to this. I fail to see how a commitment is transmitted – however relativized and defeasible – to the conclusion to blow up my house!

This leaves unanswered Kenny's objection to (P), namely when Op entails Oq but when q is impossible. Although this is not the place to develop it, the position has been assumed by many that background beliefs about possibility, like background beliefs about ability and opportunity, are presuppositions in the very forming of intentions and in the whole domain of the practical inferences that transmit the intentions. Accordingly, a showing that what we intend entails something impossible, also entails, by *modus tollens*, that the original intention is impossible, and hence violates a presupposition of the domain. This argument would show, I think, not that (C) is unsound, but that the first intention was not bona fide in the first place.

iii. *The alleged impotence of practical logic on action* The rejoinder above to Kenny's attack on (D) gives rise to an even more critical issue about (C). Recall that C was

I am committed to p
p entails q
―――――――――――――
I am committed to q.

The difficulty, persuasively expounded by Aune (1977, pp. 163–6), is that if I can escape the commitment in the conclusion by back-sliding on the commitment in the premises, then how are my derived commitments going to be commitments to *do* anything at all? Logic it is said, even practical logic, cannot force me to *do* anything; all that logic can do in a valid inference is make plain to me the *choice* between *either* committing myself to q *or* giving up the commitment to p. But if logic is indifferent to the choice, and if I am allowed to backslide on my original commitment, am I able to get out of my promises by later pointing out that they entail – unwittingly at the time – an unpalatable commitment? If so our derived commitments may turn out to be chimeras and the assurance problem, so endemic to tacit promising, breaks out all over again.

The objection, however, misfires. It is not logic alone that binds us to our derived commitments, but logic together with our commitment – the commitment which logic transmits – that binds us. It is indifferent to logic whether we backslide on our original exclusionary intention to p, but it cannot be indifferent to our exclusionary intention that we backslide, for the exclusionary intention was envisaging backsliding as the very thing to be excluded! In fact, even if the transmission of commitment is of the kind generated by a simple, non-exclusionary intention, we are still not so free to change our minds. For if Chapter 2 is right, then we are not allowed to backslide if it derives from *akrasia*, and that must include *akrasia* about adopting the conclusion of a practical syllogism as well as weakness in abiding by the original intention.

iv. *Ceteris paribus debilitations* To be sure, derived commitments are not absolute, but neither are ordinary promises: both are limited by the familiar *ceteris paribus* restrictions. In fact such clauses can be understood to qualify either the original commitment or only the derived one. In the first case they are transmitted, along with the original commitments, to any of the derived ones. In the second, they attach only to the derived ones. In either case, the commitment holds only if it is not overridden by another valid moral principle.[7] The second case presumably would be one in which an unacceptable conclusion – in the above sense – would be grounds for backsliding on the premises. But this concession may appear to blunt whatever advantage derived commitment was to enjoy over its 'tacit' counterpart. For is it not being conceded that the very process of the transmission of commitment is *not* perfectly closed or preserved across implication: that perhaps each new derived commitment carries with it the increased risk of running afoul of a basic overriding moral

---

[7] Discussions of 'detachment' of deontic conclusions also cite many other kinds of defeating conditions. But in my paper 'Practical inference, necessity, and defeasibility' (1983), I hold that these are best handled at a prior stage before one can even obtain a bona fide prima facie commitment or obligation.

principle? And if the commitment runs the risk of being weakened in the very process of transmission,[8] is not the doctrine ultimately open to something like the assurance problem?

I do not believe that it is. All that is being conceded is that *ceteris paribus* restrictions do allow an escape hatch from derived or original commitments, but only if they are demonstrably overridden by another moral principle. What is not conceded, however, is that the agent can backslide on a clear commitment in the premises on the ground that he did not *know* at the time that it entailed a commitment to a certain conclusion. It is the latter, not the former, that would constitute the assurance problem in the form germane to this issue (see above, p. 151). The assurance problem owes its source to the fact that promising, tacit or otherwise, is *open* under implication. In contrast, the weakening of the transmission of commitment owes its source to the fact that commitment is closed under implication, but only *ceteris paribus*. These are not the same thing. The distinction is that the *ceteris paribus* restrictions offer, we have said, an escape hatch from unwitting commitments to something perhaps horrendous, but not *because* they are unwitting. That is the point.

Nevertheless, if we are not to lose sight of the main issue of this chapter, viz. autonomy vs. objectivity, more must be said about the source of these *ceteris paribus* restrictions. The above account primarily makes them restrictions on our derived commitments, in order to avoid committing ourselves to horrendous consequences; yet it looked as though the strategy of this chapter was to reach this goal by making the concept of derived commitment the source of *ceteris paribus* restrictions on ordinary promises. Our position must be that the most *fundamental ceteris paribus* restrictions on low level, specific promises *are* derived commitments to elemental moral principles, e.g., respect for persons, truthfulness, etc. What is needed is an account, not only of how these *are* derived commitments, but also why *these* commitments (to truthfulness and respect, etc.) override the morally questionable ones. I postpone this until the next segment, for we are not quite finished with (D).

v. *The paradoxes of deontic material implication* Hoping that the battle scars it has sustained do not detract from its serviceability, we must now turn to the question, just what kind of entailment is meant in *p*

---

[8] I owe this way of putting the matter to Robert Audi.

159

entailing q, and again in Op entailing Oq? Suppose we try to formalize it in terms of the following material deontic implication:

(D$_1$) $(p \supset q) \supset (Op \supset Oq)$.

This, however, is supposed to be subject to the 'paradoxes' of deontic material implication, the main one of which is that an unfulfilled deontic judgment (or commitment in this case) implies the commitment to anything whatever. Thus suppose that our schema (C) is represented as

(C$_1$) $O{\sim}p$
$$\frac{{\sim}p \supset {\sim}q}{O{\sim}q}$$

and suppose further that p is the case. Then it follows from the mere conjunction of $O{\sim}p$ and p that

$O(p \supset q)$

for *any* q whatever. But what of it? There is nothing to worry about unless you can *detach* Oq. This, however, is exactly what some writers have tried to do (see e.g., Thomson, 1980, pp. 9–10), but only if you assume the dubious principle that

$[O(p \supset q) \& p] \supset Oq$ (Thomson, 1980, p. 10)

which would make $O(p \supset q)$ imply $p \supset Oq$! It should also be pointed out that since the 'paradox' arises out of the premises $O{\sim}p \& p$, and that the deontic judgment is derivative of commitment and intention, some writers have indicated that there is an inconsistency in endorsing both of those premises – an inconsistency from the agent's point of view.[9] On this view the paradox turns out to be merely the old chestnut that anything can be implied by a contradiction.

vi. The requirement connective As I see it, the difficulty with the horseshoe is that it is too weak to symbolize the actual entailments I have in mind, which are those of being a necessary condition (logically or causally) of what we intend. Recall that this was contrasted with Kenny's view that supposedly took the commitment to be transferred to sufficient conditions of what we intend – a view which

---

[9] See Aune, 1977, pp. 153–4. For another attempt to expound the anomaly in assigning a consistent set of truth values to $O{\sim}p \& p$, see Lenk, 1978, pp. 19–21.

we, likewise, held to be too weak. Now there are, then, two kinds of necessary conditions we want to formalize, the causal and the logical, the causal being the weaker of the two. Notice that if commitment is transmitted in the weaker case (is satisfaction-preserving, etc.) then it will certainly be transmitted in the stronger case, but not conversely. So we would be well advised to symbolize the weaker connection. This suggests a crude constraint on our formalization: we would want a connective that is somewhat intermediate between strict and material implication, one which would be implied by strict implication and in turn imply material implication, but not the other way around. This intermediate implication is roughly the suggestion of Aqvist in his $(p\ I\ q)$ (1963, p. 24), but it is left too inchoate. A more developed proposal was expounded by Stalnaker and Lewis, namely the conditional connective $p \rightarrow q$ (Lewis, 1973a and 1973b; Stalnaker, 1968; see also Lenk, 1978, pp. 22–6, on whom I am relying heavily). The semantic interpretation of this makes it weaker than strict implication because there is a possible world in which p is true and q is false, but such a world would be a greater departure from the actual world than one in which both the antecedent and the consequent are true. The connection meaningfully covers counterfactuals, and hence is rendered in the English equivalent, if p were true, then q would be true. But this connective is also too weak for our purposes because, although it is designed to signify lawful connections between p and q, it indiscriminately covers causal relations between them. But we should not think that our commitment is transmitted to the mere causal effects of what we intend, foreseeable or otherwise. In this vein we endorse the principle of double effect, although not in the form it is usually stated (see Harman, 1977, p. 58; Foot, 1967; and Anscombe, 1961). For you are committed only to what is *required* (logically or causally necessary) by what you intend. If the causal effects are not required, they are mere side-effects. The theory of derived commitment, in fact, bolsters the double-effect principle in this form, because it explains *why* and *when* an event is side-effect.[10]

---

[10] The mistake that is made in typically expounding double effect is to confuse the transmission of commitment with that of intention. For it is held that if we do A intentionally, and A requires B, then we do B intentionally or sometimes it is said that we 'aim' at B. But this mistake is of the same order as confounding derived commitment with tacit promises, really the mistake of thinking of propositional attitudes as closed under implication (as well as the mistake in getting tripped up on intensionality). In the intending case, I may intend to win a competitive game I am

For this reason it would be best to replace Lewis's connective with a requirement connective, $p \underset{r}{\rightarrow} q$. Although the semantics for this would have to be different from the conditional connective, it is a difference too subtle to be captured by the things so far mentioned. Both connectives would cover counterfactuals and in fact the contrapositive counterfactuals, and both would allow for a possible world in which p is true and q is false, etc., even though there is a lawful connection (although in the requirement case, not a causal connection) between them. And it should be added that, unlike both strict and material implication, both connectives do not admit of strengthening the antecedent.[11]

At any rate, since this is hardly the place to develop a formal semantics of requirement, we will have to make do with our intuitions, whereby requirement is separated from causation, and other counterfactuals. Tentatively, then, we may represent principle (D) as

$$(D_2) \ (p \underset{r}{\rightarrow} q) \supset (Op \underset{r}{\rightarrow} Oq).$$

V. Some moral principles as derived commitments

Let us now turn to some derived commitments that involve substantive moral principles. We shall consider only a few examples, postponing a full theory for another time. As previously noted, what we need to indicate is how these *are* derived commitments and why they are the kind that override the intuitively questionable ones – derived or otherwise – when the one kind is in conflict with the other. Beginning with the first question, we can consider some easy examples of derived commitments, which also operate as surrogates for commitments embraced in enlightened tacit promises. The surrogate takes over accordingly when the tacit promise is not enlightened or is careless.

---

playing with you; in fact I should intend to if I am really playing the game. Now my winning entails your losing; it is no mere side-effect. But to *intend* that you lose, far from being good sportsmanship, is unseemly! But I do not need not intend this ever; I am only committed to it.

Somewhat different puzzles would abound about 'legislative intent,' especially when the legislators have long been dead and the thing that they have 'intended' could not have even occurred to them!

[11] Strengthening the antecedent is the principle that if p entails q, then p and r entail q.

i. *Cheating* Consider, for example, the case of two people agreeing tacitly to play a game, which is defined by a system of constitutive rules. A careful person who tacitly promises to play the game therein tacitly promises to be bound to its rules (*ceteris paribus*, of course) and this because he is *aware* in part that playing the game entails abiding by its rules. And because he knows this, he is very careful not to commit himself to play the game until he finds out about its rules, and perhaps its strategies and other entailments as well. But suppose that John is just careless or impulsive about his tacit promises. And if because of this he is later advised that a certain move in a game is *cheating*, according to the rules, he chafes at the accusation, inclined perhaps to either persist in the illicit move anyway or just quit the game at that point. He justifies this behavior on the grounds that he did not, could not, have tacitly promised to conform to *that* rule, since he was not even aware of it! Now if the rule is entailed by playing the game – which would rule out cases of, say, regional variation – then John is committed derivatively at the time he promised, *whether he knew it or not!* In this fashion the assurance problem cannot arise for the *scope* of tacit promises – cannot arise, that is, as long as you are dealing with entailments.

ii. *Veracity* A more extended version of this argument involves the principle of veracity. Are we obligated to tell the truth, and whence did we effect such an obligation if we did? Again, a thoughtful, sensitive person – although this no doubt requires a good deal more thoughtfulness than in the game case – commits himself to veracity in a tacit promise, the kind of promise involved in adopting a natural language.[12] For such a person might consider when speaking a language that lying is like cheating at a game, or better, like pretending to play a game but not trying to win. .

It must first be established that truthfulness is entailed in this fashion in order to be convinced that the obligation to veracity is either an enlightened tacit promise or a derived commitment. There seem to be plenty of reasons, however, for doubting that it is, even if

[12] The question of tacitly promising to speak one's native, natural language is analogous, of course, to tacitly promising to obey the laws of one's native country. If the latter can be made intelligible, so can the former. Another alternative is to consider the commitment to the rules of language to be not a tacit promise, but a derived commitment from tacit promises for more specific things that do imply or require the use of that language. Assume for simplicity that it is a tacit promise.

the previous point about playing games is granted, i.e., that one cannot play a game without trying to win. It could be said that speaking a language is disanalogous exactly because language does not require conformity to truthfulness. Liars no less than honest men successfully speak and communicate *while* they are lying. Game throwers do not successfully play the game while they are throwing it. Moreover, if speaking a language did imply truthfulness, then it would be,contradictory or at least logically odd to assert '*p*' but not to believe it. But as Moore has shown, that is not where the contradiction or paradox lies. It is only in asserting '*p*' and *asserting* 'I don't believe *p*.' The contradiction, if there is one, is in *telling* your listener that you are lying about what you are telling him, not *in* lying about what you are telling him!

If this line of argument is correct, then why could not a clear-headed opportunist adopt as his maxim that he would lie to others when convenient and when he thinks it can go undetected. Such a person could concede without obvious inconsistency the now commonplace philosophical points – once thought more powerful than they are – that liars generally are parasitic upon truth tellers, that *he* rightly expects the truth when *he* is a listener, and that even half-universal lying would be self-stultifying. He can agree to all this without its being self-stultifying for *him* to lie when *he* is speaking.

I do not, however, think that this opportunist is so clear-headed and it is something of an irony that he would appeal to Moore's paradox to buttress his position. For that paradox (as well as perhaps the older liar paradox) will prove to be his undoing.

I propose to show this by looking at the paradoxical half of Moore's paradox and using this to shed light on the unparadoxical half. Now, the paradoxical part ('*p*, but I do not believe *p*') draws attention to some possible connection between speaking a language and conformity to truthfulness, for if there were no connection, then it would not even be paradoxical to assert '*p*' and to *assert* 'but I do not believe *p*.' This suggests that we must look at communicating as a goal-directed cooperative activity between a speaker and hearer which is such that the speaker's truthfulness is a presupposition necessary for the activity (of making assertions) to have any point. The *point* of asserting, we may say, is the perlocutionary one of getting the hearer to believe or to contribute to his believing what the speaker is saying. But the hearer cannot reasonably get from understanding to believing unless the activity whereby the hearer understands presupposes at least that the speaker believes what he is saying, believes that he has good evidence for it, and so on. When it becomes common knowledge that the truthfulness presupposition is false, then the activity of communication between a speaker and hearer ceases to have its point.[13]

Why, then, does asserting 'p' while not believing it not appear contradictory? For on the theory above it should, or at least should appear logically odd. The answer is that it's not appearing contradictory is only an illusion foisted on us by thinking of 'asserting,' 'speaking' and 'communicating' in a narrow degenerate sense, as being an activity whose principal goal is that of producing *understanding* in the hearer. Such a conception, however, cuts off communication from its social milieu in which the speaker uses language to produce beliefs, and to this end represents not only states of affairs but his beliefs about those states of affairs. That producing understanding is a truncated conception of communication is shown by the fact that if it were accurate, there would be nothing paradoxical about the first half of Moore's paradox, 'p, but I do not believe p.' Is not this paradoxical because it violates the assumption that asserting 'p' represents the speaker's belief that p? In fact, under the truncated conception, why should there be anything paradoxical about the older liar paradox, 'This statement is false,' if language and communication are cut off from the representation of truth via the speaker's beliefs about it.

But once we see that communication is a cooperative activity whose object is to contribute to producing beliefs in the hearer which match the beliefs represented by the speaker, then we can see that to assert 'p' but not to believe it, *is* self-stultifying – self-stultifying exactly in the way that playing a game but not trying to win is. For both involve the idea of engaging in a goal-directed, cooperative activity while secretly rejecting the very presuppostion that can give the activity its point.

Nevertheless, it should not be thought that these ruminations will blow away all the skeptics. They might remind us that vice can pay

---

13 By the act of communication ceasing to have its point, I mean that under the assumption above the speaker could not even *have* the perlocutionary intention to convince the hearer, much less realize it, in which case the illocutionary intention to produce understanding would lose its point too. At the same time, I do not mean to imply that all varieties of speech acts have this structure or that there might not even be varieties of degenerate cases. I mean only that this appears to be the structure of asserting. Cf. Holdcroft, 1977 and 1978.

tribute to virtue by the time-tested method of hypocrisy: by the liar's only *pretending* to satisfy the presupposition of truthfulness. This would amount to conceding that speaking a language in the standard sense *is* a goal-directed activity of this kind, but then asking why opportunists have to play the game in the ordinary way. Why cannot they play it their way? Because it will then be a different game, you may say? Very well, then call it a different game: ordinary speakers of language play a game called 'truespeak,' but liars play a new game called 'liespeak' which is exactly like truespeak except that when they are speaking and only when they are speaking, they need only pretend to be truthful! This argument is reminiscent of Nozick's reply to Williams when the latter argued that the distribution of health care should be on the basis of need rather than wealth because doctoring is an activity which has as its internal goal the curing of the sick. (Nozick, 1974, pp. 233–5, commenting on Williams, 1962). Nozick asks why conceding this bars a doctor from engaging in an activity called 'schmoctoring' which is just like doctoring except that its internal goal is to line the pockets of the doctor.

Now I do not think that I have given an answer here as to why one should not engage in either schmoctoring or liespeak (any more than I have shown why one should not play 'schams' instead of 'games' where the former are like the latter except they require only the pretence of winning). But it should be borne in mind, first, that this is a different question than the one which got this whole issue started. Our original query was whether speaking a language in the ordinary sense does carry with it the presupposition of truthfulness. And this, I believe, has been answered. The inveterate liar's communicative acts have been isolated as a different beast from the truth teller's – a degenerate variety (where 'degenerate' need only be understood in the descriptive sense in which it requires the pretence of accepting the presupposition that gives the ordinary variety its point). And so when the truth teller and would-be liar or dim-witted liar agree to speak language in the ordinary sense, they do commit themselves to the principle of veracity.

The second point is that this chapter, especially its last section, does imply a certain line of strategy for countering degenerate activities. It is that communication in the ordinary sense may itself be a derived commitment that converges upon a variety of other low level promises, namely, the kind of promises that may presuppose communication in the favored sense. But *how* is communication presupposed in the favored sense?

I suggest two answers. The one derives from the analysis of promises as such (and in this respect is like the derivation below of respect for persons), and the other fixes upon the kinds of things typically promised, which may be language-dependent in the favored sense.

Take the analysis of promising first. I have said, in Chapter 5, that the whole affair about transferring an exclusionary mandate does rely upon communication, verbal or non-verbal. Is this communication truespeak or liespeak? Notice that when the promiser is communicating to the promisee his conditional exclusionary intention, is it not assumed that he has that intention, that, in other words, he is not lying or pretending to have it? This dovetails with the point I made in the discussion of insincere promises: that the concept of an exclusionary intention, which is doing all the creative work, gets mapped onto his Gricean intention embedded in the act of communication. To emphasize again, this does not mean that he *has* the exclusionary intention, but only that the concept of it is mapped onto, or in other words, semantically represented in, the Gricean intention, in order that his act of promising be intelligible. This concept of mapping suggests that truespeak is represented in a promise, which is incompatible with representing liespeak.

This also seems to be true of my second answer which refers to the kinds of things that are promised. Typically, promising is involved in contracts and in cooperative schemes. Insofar as these invoke communication, either verbal or non-verbal, again it is communication in the sense that represents truespeak.

The upshot is that a large variety of human activities: contracts, cooperative schemes, small or large, permanent or temporary, and, of course, promises imply the representation of truespeak without which those activities would be impossible and unintelligible. Liespeak, of course, is possible where truespeak is represented, but it does not satisfy the truth conditions of all the underlying semantic representation; if it were so represented those activities would cease to have their point.

Let us now return to the actual agreement to speak language in the standard sense – the standard sense of 'asserting.' The next question is *how* the obligation to veracity falls upon such speakers. Is it an enlightened tacit promise or a surrogate for that? Now because – let us assume – that truthfulness is a logical presupposition of speaking one's natural language, we have said that a thoughtful person who shares this belief would take himself to have made a tacit promise to veracity upon adopting that language.[14] But suppose that the person is not as thoughtful as this about his tacit promise. Does this mean he is not, thereby, committed to tell the truth, and this on the grounds that he never considered the matter in that light? Again, the doctrine of derived commitment rescues veracity from such disavowals.

iii. Respect for persons Our last, but by no means least, principle, one which is a derived commitment but not a surrogate for an enlightened tacit promise, is the principle enjoining respect for persons. To put it mildly, this has been subject to a variety of interpretations in recent scholarship. My interpretation professes no exegetical originality, but goes back to Kant himself, who held that respect for persons is respect for their autonomy. In one current idiom this is respect for their choices. Our position with regard to autonomy has been that it and commitment are two sides of the same coin; we *express* our *own* autonomy by committing ourselves in various ways, including the forming of simple intentions. But respect for our own autonomy means honoring our commitments. For it would be hard to 'respect' our vows, plans, and promises if we thought we could change them at will. This idea of respect involves the old paradox, deprecated by Hume but which we have tried to dissolve, about the will obligating itself. The concept of autonomy here similarly is that of living under laws that we give to ourselves.

But what does that have to do with respect for the autonomy of others? I think that we have this respect when we accept the promises of others and hold them to account. The familiar Kantian–Rousseauian idea here is that even *enforcing* promises against the wishes of the would-be recalcitrant is a way of respecting *his/her* autonomy. And conversely, letting him/her off the hook when he/she has not been released shows a lack of respect. But this is only one

[14] Is it really a tacit promise or a vow? This is related somewhat to whether he commits himself to veracity in the language he is adopting or to veracity in any language. Lewis's theory of linguistic conventions may shed some light on this. For him semantic rules are conventions of truthfulness in language $\mathcal{L}$ as opposed to truthfulness in any language, which for him is not even a convention (see 1969, p. 152; see also 1975, pp. 27–32). Now it seems that this enlightened tacit commitment is only to truthfulness *in* the language we have adopted (truthfulness in $\mathcal{L}$). And since the language and therefore the truthfulness *in* it can be changed – but only by mutual consent – it seems also to be an enlightened tacit promise.

source of lack of respect for others; another is imposing obligations and the like on others which cannot – directly or indirectly – be traced to their own intentions. This seems to be the essence of slavery – or at least forced labor. This interpretation of respect for autonomy seems to put it squarely in the tradition of classical contractarianism with regard to that tradition's conception of a person and the source of his obligations.

Now this respect is also of the nature of a derived commitment *whenever* we recognize the vows or rely on the promises of another. The derivation, however, is somewhat oblique because the original commitment is another's, not ours (insofar as promising is one-sided). Our role comes into play when we recognize or accept that commitment, because we can do so only by recognizing that very power of autonomy which we implicitly recognize in the exercise of our own agency. We cannot, on this view, feel *entitled* to *rely* on the commitments of others without recognizing them as persons, who are to themselves the supreme lawgivers. The 'cannot' here, if it is not a kind of necessity involving strict implication, expresses perhaps the requisite degree of lawfulness in the requirement connective. For respect for autonomy becomes a necessary condition, not for a variety of things typically promised, but for the concept of promising itself.

iv. *Derived commitments as sources of* ceteris paribus *constraints* Finally, we must turn – but very briefly – to the question of how such derived commitments as veracity and respect for persons (in the above sense) function as *ceteris paribus* restrictions on our more immediate promises. The strategy, I believe, is to conceive of them as commitments we are all likely to be caught up in if we make any promises at all. I have indicated that respect for persons derives from accepting promises as such, and conformity to veracity in our adopted language is a commitment that derives from the myriad of commitments which, directly or indirectly, depend upon language, or even communication, broadly conceived. The strategy would conceptualize basic moral principles as analogous to primary goods in Rawls's theory of justice (1971, pp. 62, 90–5, 253–60, 346ff). For Rawls, himself a great supporter of autonomy, everybody is morally at liberty to adopt for himself a rational plan of life quite different from those of others. But although this generates in the short view a diversity in rational life plans, all of those plans imply residually a list of primary goods: a minimum amount of economic well-being, liberty, respect, and self-esteem. These are goods that anybody would want *if* he wants anything that is rational (1971, p. 93). We might then see moral principles as residual, foundational derived commitments of ourselves insofar as we make any actual commitments at all. Despite our diversity, we would thus conceive of ourselves living in a 'kingdom of ends,' of common principles, but principles that derive from our very own autonomy.

If such an idea can be brought to fruition, then we will indeed realize not only that we live under an objective moral order, but that it was fashioned out of our own will. The connection between these two is possible precisely because the mucilage of both autonomy and objectivity is the primitive concept of commitment. At the autonomy end, commitment is not a social construct of contractarianism, but the cement that holds together the elements of the most ordinary concept of intention, and without which intending to do something would be utterly unintelligible. On the other end, this very same commitment detaches itself from its subjective milieu because it is closed under implication. Living under an objective moral order then becomes possible essentially because it is the habiliment of our own agency.

References

Anscombe, G. E. M. (1961). War and murder. In *Nuclear Weapons: A Catholic Response*, ed. Walker Stein, pp. 45–62. New York: Merlin Press.

Anscombe, G. E. M. (1969). *Intention*. Ithaca, NY: Cornell University Press.

Aqvist, Lennart (1963). A note on commitment. *Philosophical Studies* **14**, 22–5.

Árdal, Páll S. (1968). And that's a promise. *Philosophical Quarterly* **18**, 225–37.

Árdal, Páll S. (1969). Reply to new. *Philosophical Quarterly* **19**, 260–2.

Árdal, Páll S. (1976). Promises and reliance. *Dialogue* (Canada) **15**, 54–61.

Árdal, Páll S. (1981). Promises and games. In *Afmaeliskvedja*, til Halldors Halldorssonar, pp. 219–43. Reykjavik, Islenska: Malfraedifelagid.

Armstrong, D. M. (1973). *Belief, Truth, and Knowledge*. Cambridge: Cambridge University Press.

Atiyah, Patrick (1981). *Promises, Morals, and the Law*. Oxford: Clarendon Press.

Audi, Robert (1973). Intending. *Journal of Philosophy* **70**, 387–402.

Audi, Robert (1979). Wants and intentions in the explanation of action. Journal of Social Behavior **9**, 227–49.

Aune, Bruce (1977). *Reason and Action*. Dordrecht: Reidel.

Austin, J. L. (1962). *Sense and Sensibilia*. Oxford: Oxford University Press.

Austin, J. L. (1965). *How to Do Things with Words*. Oxford: Oxford University Press.

Baier, Annette (1971). The search for basic actions. *American Philosophical Quarterly* **8**, 161–70.

Beardsley, R. W. (1978). Intending. In *Values and Morals*, ed. Alvin Goldman and Jaegwon Kim, pp. 163–84. Dordrecht: Reidel.

Beardsmore, R. W. (1969). *Moral Reasoning*. London: Routledge & Kegan Paul.

Bennett, Jonathan (1973). Shooting, killing, and dying. *Canadian Journal of Philosophy* **2**, 315–25.

Bennett, Jonathan (1976). *Linguistic Behaviour*. Cambridge: Cambridge University Press.

Berman, A. J. and Taub, E. (1968). Movement learning in the absence of sensory feedback. In *The Neuropsychology of Spatially Oriented Behavior*, ed. S. J. Freedman, pp. 173–92. Homewood, Ill.: Dorsey Press.

Brand, Myles (1979). The fundamental question in action theory. *Nous* **13**, 131–57.

Brand, Myles (forthcoming). Simultaneous causation. In *Time as Cause*, ed. Peter van Inwagen.

Brandt, Richard B. (1979). *Theory of the Good and the Right*. Oxford: Clarendon Press.

Bratman, Michael (1981). Intention and means-end reasoning. *Philosophical Review* **90**, 252–65.

Braybrooke, David (1976). The insoluble problem of the social contract. *Dialogue* (Canada) **15**, 3–37.

Cameron, J. R. (1972). The nature of institutional obligation. *Philosophical Quarterly* **22**, 318–32.

Carter, W. R. (1973). On promising the unwanted. *Analysis* **33**, 88–92.

Castaneda, Hector-Neri (1967). Indicators and quasi-indicators. *American Philosophical Quarterly* **4**, 85–100.

Castaneda, Hector-Neri (1968). On the logic of attributions of self-knowledge to others. *Journal of Philosophy* **65**, 439–56.

Castaneda, Hector-Neri (1975). *Thinking and Doing*. Dordrecht: Reidel.

Castaneda, Hector-Neri (1979). Intensionality and contingent identity in human action. *Nous* **13**, 235–60.

Chisholm, Roderick (1976a). *Person and Object*. LaSalle, Ill.: Open Court Publishing Co.

Chisholm, Roderick (1976b). The agent as cause. In *Action Theory*, ed. Myles Brand and Douglas Walton, pp. 199–211. Dordrecht: Reidel.

Chisholm, Roderick (1977). *Theory of Knowledge*. Englewood Cliffs, NJ: Prentice-Hall.

Chisholm, Roderick (1979). Transcendent evidence. Unpublished lecture presented to the University of Michigan, Ann Arbor, Michigan.

Corrado, Michael. Three problems with the causal theory of action. Unpublished paper.

Danto, Arthur (1963). On what we can do. *Journal of Philosophy* **60**, 435–45.

Danto, Arthur (1965). Basic actions. *American Philosophical Quarterly* **2**, 141–8.

Danto, Arthur (1973). *Analytical Philosophy of Action*. Cambridge: Cambridge University Press.

Davidson, Donald (1963). Actions, reasons and causes. *Journal of Philosophy* **60**, 685–700.

Davidson, Donald (1967). The logical form of action sentences. In *The Logic of Decision and Action*, ed. Nicholas Rescher, pp. 81–95. Pittsburgh, Penn.: University of Pittsburgh Press.

Davidson, Donald (1969a). On events and event descriptions. In *Fact and Existence*, ed. Joseph Margolis, pp. 74–84. Oxford: Clarendon Press.

Davidson, Donald (1969b). How is weakness of the will possible? In *Moral Concepts*, ed. Joel Feinberg, pp. 93–133. Oxford: Clarendon Press.

Davidson, Donald (1971). Agency. In *Agent, Action, and Reason*, ed. Robert Blinkley, Richard Bronaugh, and Ausomo Marras, pp. 3–25. Toronto: University of Toronto Press.

Davidson, Donald (1973). Freedom to act. In *Essays on Freedom of Action*, ed. Ted Honderich, pp. 132–56. London: Routledge & Kegan Paul.

Davidson, Donald (1975). Thought and talk. In *Mind and Language*, ed. Samuel Guttingham, pp. 7–24. Oxford: Oxford University Press.

Davidson, Donald (1976). Why animals can't think. Unpublished lecture presented at the University of Michigan, Ann Arbor, Michigan.

Davidson, Donald (1978). Intending. In his *Essays on Actions and Events*, ed. Ted Honderich, pp. 83–102. Oxford: Clarendon Press.

Davis, Lawrence (1979). *Theory of Action*. Englewood Cliffs, NJ: Prentice-Hall.

Davis, Lawrence (1980). Wayward causal chains. In *Action and Responsibility*, ed. Michael Bradie and Myles Brand, pp. 55–65. Bowling Green, Ohio: Philosophy Documentation Center.

Dennett, Daniel (1978). A cure for the common code. In his *Brainstorms*, pp. 90–108. Cambridge, Mass.: M.I.T. Press.

Diggs, B. J. (1970). A comment on some merits of one form of utilitarianism. In *Readings in Contemporary Ethical Theory*, ed. Kenneth Pahel and Marvin Schiller, pp. 307–17. Englewood Cliffs, NJ: Prentice-Hall.

Fain, Haskell (1978). Permissions, promises, and political communities. *Midwest Studies in Philosophy* **3**, 344–8.

Feinberg, Joel (1973). Review of *A Theory of Justice*. *Journal of Philosophy* **70**, 265–7.

Firth, Roderick (1978). Justified belief. Unpublished lecture presented at the University of Michigan, Ann Arbor, Michigan.

Foder, Jerry (1975). *The Language of Thought*. Cambridge, Mass.: Harvard University Press.

Foot, Phillippa (1967). The problem of abortion and the doctrine of double effect. In *Moral Problems*, ed. James Rachels, pp. 28–44. New York: Harper & Row.

Frankfurt, Harry (1978). The problem of action. *American Philosophical Quarterly* **15**, 157–62.

Gewirth, Alan (1978). *Reason and Morality*. Chicago: University of Chicago Press.

Goldman, Alvin (1970). *A Theory of Human Action*. Englewood Cliffs, NJ: Prentice-Hall.

Goldman, Alvin (1975). The volitional theory revisited. In *Action Theory*, ed. Myles Brand and Douglas Walton, pp. 67–84. Dordrecht: Reidel.

Goldman, Alvin (1979). What is justified belief? In *Justification and Knowledge*, ed. George S. Pappas, pp. 1–24. Dordrecht: Reidel.

Goldman, Alvin (1980). The internalist conception of justification. *Midwest Studies in Philosophy* **5**, 27–52.

Goldman, Alvin. The relation between epistemology and psychology. Unpublished paper.

Greenwald, Anthony (1970). Sensory feedback mechanisms in performance control: with reference to the ideo-motor mechanism. *Psychological Review* **77**, 73–101.

Grice, H. P. (1957). Meaning. *Philosophical Review* **66**, 377–88.

Grim, Robert (1977). Eventual change and action identity. *American Philosophical Quarterly* **14**, 221–30.

173

Hamlyn, D. W. (1962). The obligation to keep a promise. *Proceedings of the Aristotelian Society*, 179–94.

Hare, R. M. (1952). *The Language of Morals*. Oxford: Clarendon Press.

Hare, R. M. (1971). *Practical Inferences*. London: Macmillan.

Harman, Gilbert (1973). *Thought*. Princeton: Princeton University Press.

Harman, Gilbert (1976). Practical reasoning. *Review of Metaphysics* **29**, 431–63.

Harman, Gilbert (1977). *The Nature of Morality*. Oxford: Clarendon Press.

Harman, Gilbert (1980a). Reasoning and explanatory coherence. *American Philosophical Quarterly* **17**, 151–7.

Harman, Gilbert (1980b). Reasoning and evidence one does not possess. *Midwest Studies in Philosophy* **5**, 165–82. Also unpublished lecture in his National Endowment for the Humanities summer seminar, Princeton University, 1982.

Harman, Gilbert (forthcoming). Willing and intending. In a *Festschrift* in honor of H. P. Grice.

Hillel-Rubin, David (1972). Tacit promising. *Ethics* **83**, 71–9.

Hobbes, Thomas (1958). *Leviathan*, Parts I and II, ed. Herbert W. Schneider. Indianapolis: Bobbs-Merrill.

Hodgson, D. H. (1967). *Consequences of Utilitarianism*. Oxford: Clarendon Press.

Holdcroft, David (1977). Assertive acts, context, and evidence. Unpublished paper presented to the Working Group on Speech Acts, XIIth International Congress of Linguistics, University of Vienna.

Holdcroft, David (1978). *Words and Deeds*. Oxford: Clarendon Press.

Hume, David (1888). *A Treatise of Human Nature*, ed. L. A. Selby-Bigge. Oxford: Clarendon Press.

Hume, David (1957). *An Inquiry Concerning the Principles of Morals*. Indianapolis: Bobbs-Merrill.

Hume, David (1965). Of the original contract. In *Hume's Ethical Writings*, ed. Alasdair MacIntyre, pp. 255–74. London: Macmillan.

James, William (1890). *Principles of Psychology*, 2 vols., vol. 2. New York: Henry Holt.

Kenny, Anthony (1975). *Freedom, Will and Power*. Oxford: Basil Blackwell.

Keynes, John Maynard (1952). *A Treatise on Probability*. London: Macmillan.

Kim, Jaegwon (1979). Causality, identity, and supervenience in the mind–body problem. *Midwest Studies in Metaphysics* **4**, 31–50.

Lasley, K. S. (1917). The accuracy of movement in the absence of excitation from the moving organ. *American Journal of Physiology* **43**, 169–94.

Lenk, Hans (1978). Varieties of commitment. *Theory and Decision* **9**, 17–37.

Lewis, David (1969). *Convention: A Philosophical Study*. Cambridge, Mass.: Harvard University Press.

Lewis, David (1972). Utilitarianism and truthfulness. *Australasian Journal of Philosophy* **50**, 17–19.

Lewis, David (1973a). Causation. *Journal of Philosophy* **70**, 556–67.

Lewis, David (1973b). *Counterfactuals*. Oxford: Clarendon Press.

Lewis, David (1975). Language and languages. In *Minnesota Studies in the*

174

Philosophy of Science, vol. 7, *Language, Mind, and Knowledge*, ed. Keith Gunderson, pp. 3–35. Minneapolis: University of Minnesota Press.

Locke, Don (1974). Reasons, wants and causes. *American Philosophical Quarterly* **11**, 169–79.

Locke, John (1927). *Two Treatises of Civil Government* (II). London: Everyman.

Lyons, David (1965). *Forms and Limits of Utilitarianism.* Oxford: Clarendon Press.

Lyons, David (1974). The nature of the contract argument. *Cornell Law Review* **59**, 1064–76.

McCann, Hugh (1974). Volition and basic action. *Philosophical Review* **83**, 451–73.

MacCormick, Neil (1972). Voluntary obligations and normative powers. *Proceedings of the Aristotelian Society*, suppl. vol. **46**, 59–79.

Mackie, J. L. (1977). The disutility of act-utilitarianism. *Philosophical Quarterly* **23**, 289–300.

McNeilly, F. S. (1972). Promises de-moralized. *Philosophical Review* **81**, 63–81.

Martin, Jane (1972). Basic actions and simple actions. *American Philosophical Quarterly* **9**, 59–68.

Melden, A. I. (1977). *Rights and Persons.* Oxford: Basil Blackwell.

Nagel, Thomas (1970). *The Possibility of Altruism.* Oxford: Clarendon Press (1979), Princeton: Princeton University Press.

Narveson, Jan (1971). Promising, expecting, and utility. *Canadian Journal of Philosophy* **1**, 207–33.

Nozick, Robert (1974). *Anarchy, State, and Utopia.* New York: Basic Books.

O'Shaughnessey, Brian (1973). Trying (as the mental 'pineal gland'). *Journal of Philosophy* **22**, 365–86.

Pew, Richard W. (1974). Human perceptual motor performance. In *Human Information Processing: Tutorials in Performance & Cognition*, ed. B. Kantowitz, pp. 1–36. Hillsdale, NJ: Lawrence Erlbaum Associates.

Phillips, D. Z. and Mounce, H. O. (1969). *Moral Practices.* London: Routledge & Kegan Paul.

Prichard, H. A. (1928). The obligation to keep a promise. In his *Moral Obligation*, pp. 169–79. Oxford: Clarendon Press.

Prichard, H. A. (1940). Exchanging. In his *Moral Obligation*, pp. 180–1. Oxford: Clarendon Press.

Prichard, H. A. (1949). Acting, willing and desiring. In his *Moral Obligation*, pp. 89–98. Oxford: Clarendon Press.

Quine, W. V. (1960). *Word and Object.* Cambridge, Mass.: M.I.T. Press.

Quine, W. V. (1969). Speaking of objects. In his *Ontological Relativity and Other Essays.* New York: Columbia University Press, pp. 1–25.

Raphael, D. D. (1970). *Problems of Political Philosophy.* London: Macmillan.

Rawls, John (1955). Two concepts of rules. *Philosophical Review* **64**, 3–13.

Rawls, John (1963). The sense of justice. *Philosophical Review* **72**, 281–305.

Rawls, John (1971). *A Theory of Justice.* Cambridge, Mass.: Harvard University Press.

Rawls, John (1974). The independence of moral theory. Presidential address in *Proceedings of the American Philosophical Association* **68**, 5–22.

Raz, Joseph (1972). Reply to MacCormick on voluntary obligations and normative powers. *Proceedings of the Aristotelian Society*, suppl. vol. **46**, 80–103.

Raz, Joseph (1975a). Reasons for actions, decisions, and norms. *Mind* **84**, 481–99.

Raz, Joseph (1975b). *Practical Reason and Norms*. London: Hutchinson & Co.

Raz, Joseph (1977). Promises and obligations. In *Law, Morality and Society*, ed. Peter Hacker and Joseph Raz, pp. 210–28. Oxford: Clarendon Press.

Raz, Joseph, ed. (1978). *Practical Reasoning*. Oxford: Clarendon Press.

Rescher, Nicholas (1970). On the characterization of actions. In *The Nature of Human Action*, ed. Myles Brand, pp. 247–55. Glenview, Ill.: Scott Foresman.

Ripley, James (1974). A theory of volition. *American Philosophical Quarterly* **11**, 141–7.

Robins, Michael H. (1974). Hare's golden-rule argument: a reply to Silverstein. *Mind* **83**, 578–81.

Robins, Michael H. (1976a). Promissory obligations and Rawls's contractarianism. *Analysis* **36**, 190–8.

Robins, Michael H. (1976b). The primacy of promising. *Mind* **85**, 321–40.

Robins, Michael H. (1980a). On Prichard revisited: a reply to Davis on wayward causal chains. In *Action and Responsibility*, ed. Michael Bradie and Myles Brand, pp. 66–70. Bowling Green, Ohio: Philosophy Documentation Center.

Robins, Michael H. (1980b). Deviant causal chains. Delivered before the Seventy-Seventh Eastern Meeting of the American Philosophical Association, Boston.

Robins, Michael H. (1983). Practical inference, necessity, and defeasibility. *Indian Philosophical Quarterly* **10**, 405–23.

Robins, Michael H. (1984). Practical reasoning, commitment, and rational action. *American Philosophical Quarterly* **21**.

Robins, Michael H. (forthcoming). Deviant causal chains and non-basic action. *Australasian Journal of Philosophy*.

Rousseau, Jean Jacques (1968). *The Social Contract*. Baltimore: Penguin Classics.

Ryle, Gilbert (1949). *The Concept of Mind*. New York: Barnes and Nobel.

Samek, Robert (1965). Performative utterances and the concept of contract. *Australasian Journal of Philosophy* **43**, 196–210.

Schiffer, Stephen (1972). *Meaning*. Oxford: Clarendon Press.

Schwayder, D. S. (1965). *The Stratification of Behavior*. New York: Humanities Press.

Searle, John R. (1969). *Speech-Acts*. Cambridge: Cambridge University Press.

Searle, John R. (1979). *Expression and Meaning*. Cambridge: Cambridge University Press.

Sellars, Wilfred (1963). *Science, Perception, and Reality*. London: Routledge & Kegan Paul.

Sellars, Wilfred (1975). Volitions re-affirmed. In *Action Theory*, ed. Myles Brand and Douglas Walton, pp. 47–66. Dordrecht: Reidel.

Singer, Peter (1972). Is utilitarianism self-defeating? *Philosophical Review* **81**, 94–104.

Singer, Peter (1973). The triviality of the '"ought" "is"' debate and the definition of moral. *American Philosophical Quarterly* **10**, 51–6.

Stalnaker, R. C. (1968). A theory of conditionals. In *Studies in Logical Theory*, ed. Nicholas Rescher. Oxford: Clarendon Press. Also in *Causation and Conditionals* (1975), ed. Ernest Sosa, pp. 165–79. Oxford: Clarendon Press.

Strawson, P. F. (1964). Convention and intention in speech-acts. *Philosophical Review* **73**, 439–60.

Thalberg, Irving (1975). When do causes take effect? *Mind* **84**, 583–9.

Thalberg, Irving (1977). *Perception, Emotion, and Action*. New Haven: Yale University Press.

Thomson, Judith (1970). Individuating actions. *Journal of Philosophy* **67**, 774–81.

Thomson, Judith (1971). The time of a killing. *Journal of Philosophy* **68**, 115–32.

Thomson, Judith (1977). *Acts and Other Events*. Ithaca, New York: Cornell University Press.

Thompson, Judith (1980). Rights and compensation. *Nous* **14**, 3–15.

Vendler, Zeno (1972). *Res Cogitans*. Ithaca, New York: Cornell University Press.

Volrath, John (1975). When actions are causes. *Philosophical Studies* **27**, 330–6.

Warnock, G. J. (1971). *The Object of Morality*. London: Methuen & Co.

Williams, Bernard (1962). The idea of equality. In *Philosophy, Politics, and Society*, 2nd ser., ed. Peter Laslatt and R. G. Rincemen, pp. 110–31. Oxford: Clarendon Press.

Winch, Peter (1972). Nature and convention. In his *Ethics and Action*. London: Routledge & Kegan Paul.

Wittgenstein, Ludwig (1953). *Philosophical Investigations*. New York: Macmillan.

Wright, G. H. von (1963). *Norm and Action*. New York: Humanities Press.

Wright, G. H. von (1978). On so-called practical inference. In *Practical Reasoning*, ed. Joseph Raz, pp. 46–62. Oxford: Clarendon Press.

Index

O'Shaughnessey, Brian, 24–6

performatives, 17, 43 n. 24, *see also*
    speech acts
perlocutionary acts, *see* speech acts
permissions, 101–2, 115
pineal gland, 51
practical reasoning, 21–2, 115, 154–62;
    means-end reasoning, 33–8
preference, *see* desires
Prichard, H. A., 5, 9, 10–12, 97, 110–11,
    115–16, 128
primary goods, 169–70
private (non-social) acts, 3, 14, 16, 85–7,
    114
promises: hypothetical, 12, 106–7, 128,
    148; insincere, 145–6; as statements vs.
    performatives, 43 n. 24, *see also* speech
    acts; tacit, 2, 11, 15, 106,
    129–32, 149–53, 157–8, 163–9
propositional (or practitional) attitudes,
    see double effect, implication
psychokinesis, 51–2; *see also* causation

Quine, W. V., 17, 39, 45, 99, 128

rationality: espistemic rationality of
    exclusionary intentions, 90–2; of life
    plans, 169–70; practical rationality of
    exclusionary intentions, 92–4;
    prudential, 135
Rawls, John, 1, 4–5, 10–12, 22, 97,
    106–7, 111, 127–33, 148–9, 151–2,
    169–70
Raz, Joseph, 4, 7–9, 88–9, 102, 108–9,
    133, 143, 157
reasoning, *see* practical reasoning
reasons, exclusionary, 14 n. 12, 87–9
requirement(s): adverbial, 61–83;
    conative and cognitive, 61–83;
    requirement connective, 160–2;
    exclusionary, ch. 4, 96–8, 100–5,
    107–9, 110–25
respect for persons, 15, 109, 168–9
rights, *see* entitlement
Rousseau, Jean Jacques, 16, 168
rules: constitutive, 109–33, *see also* level-
    generation; in the expectation sense,
    13–46; rule utilitarianism, 9 n. 5, 40,
    141–3; *see also* convention

satisfaction vs. satisfactoriness, logic of,
    155–7
Schwayder, D. S., 14
Searle, John, 9–10, 12, 17–18, 42–4,
    108–11, 124–8, 144
second-level intentions or reasons, *see*
    intention
similitude between intention and action,
    ch. 3, esp. 60–3; *see also* causation
    (causal theory of action)
social acts, 13–14, 16–18, 85–7, 96–105,
    107–9, 111–24
speech acts: illocutionary, 125, 143–6;
    perlocutionary, 143–6
state of nature theory, 15–16, 116–17,
    123, 136–43

tacit promises, 2, 11, 15, 106, 129–32,
    149–53, 157–8, 163–9, *see also*
    promises
transcendental argument, 38–9
transferring (in an act of promising), 14,
    103–4, 111, 115–24
truthfulness, *see* veracity, principle of; in
    $\mathcal{L}$, 135–7, 168
trying, 22, 24–6; *see also* volition

utilitarianism: rule utilitarianism, 9 n. 5,
    40, 141–3; theory of promising, 7–9,
    140–3; *see also* expectable utility

validity, 156–7
veracity, principle of, 12, 15, 98, 141,
    145–6, 163–8
VIPs and MIPs, 52–7; *see also* movement,
    volition
volition, 12, 19, 22, 24–6, 28, 30, 44–59;
    causal relation between it and
    movement, 52–5, 58; ideo-motor
    thory of, 51–9; non-causal relation
    between it and intention, 12, 19–20,
    30, 44, 46–7; VIPs and MIPs, 52–5, 58
vows, 2, 13–14, ch. 4, 96–100, 102–4,
    107–24, 133, 137–41, 143–4

weakness of the will, *see* akrasia
willing, ix, 15; willing an obligation, *see*
    obligation (voluntary); *see also*
    volition
Winch, Peter, 96
Wittgenstein, Ludwig, 17